■ The Nebraska State Constitution

The Oxford Commentaries on the State Constitutions of the United States
G. Alan Tarr, Series Editor

Professor G. Alan Tarr, Director of the Center on State Constitutional Studies at Rutgers University, serves as General Editor for this important new series which in its entirety will cover each of the 50 states. Each volume of The Oxford Commentaries on the State Constitutions of the United States contains a historical overview of the state's constitutional development, plus a section-by-section analysis of the state's current constitution. Other features included in the volumes are the text of the state's constitution, a bibliographic essay, table of cases, and index. This series provides essential reference tools for those investigating state constitutional development and constitutional law.

The Nebraska State Constitution

Robert D. Miewald
and
Peter J. Longo

Foreword by Robert M. Spire

THE OXFORD COMMENTARIES ON THE STATE CONSTITUTIONS OF THE UNITED STATES
G. Alan Tarr, Series Editor

OXFORD
UNIVERSITY PRESS

OXFORD
UNIVERSITY PRESS

Oxford University Press, Inc., publishes works that further Oxford University's objective of excellence in research, scholarship, and education.

Oxford New York
Auckland Cape Town Dar es Salaam Hong Kong Karachi Kuala Lumpur Madrid Melbourne Mexico City Nairobi New Delhi Shanghai Taipei Toronto

With offices in
Argentina Austria Brazil Chile Czech Republic France Greece Guatemala Hungary Italy Japan Poland Portugal Singapore South Korea Switzerland Thailand Turkey Ukraine Vietnam

Previously published in 1993 by Greenwood Press

Published by Oxford University Press, Inc.
198 Madison Avenue, New York, New York 10016

Library of Congress Cataloging-in-Publication Data

Miewald, Robert D.
The Nebraska State Constitution / Robert D. Miewald and Peter J. Longo ; foreword by Robert M. Spire.
p. cm. — (The Oxford commentaries on the state constitutions of the United States)
Includes bibliographical references and index.
ISBN 978-0-19-977931-4 (hardback)
1. Constitutions—Nebraska. 2. Constitutional law—Nebraska.
3. Constitutional history—Nebraska. I. Longo, Peter Joseph.
II. Nebraska. Constitution (1875) III. Title.
KFN4011875.A6 M538 2011
342.78202—dc22 2011003229

Note to Readers
This publication is designed to provide accurate and authoritative information in regard to the subject matter covered. It is based upon sources believed to be accurate and reliable and is intended to be current as of the time it was written. It is sold with the understanding that the publisher is not engaged in rendering legal, accounting, or other professional services. If legal advice or other expert assistance is required, the services of a competent professional person should be sought. Also, to confirm that the information has not been affected or changed by recent developments, traditional legal research techniques should be used, including checking primary sources where appropriate.

(Based on the Declaration of Principles jointly adopted by a Committee of the American Bar Association and a Committee of Publishers and Associations.)

CONTENTS

SERIES FOREWORD

In 1776, following the declaration of independence from England, the former colonies began to draft their own constitutions. Their handiwork attracted widespread interest, and draft constitutions circulated up and down the Atlantic seaboard, as constitution-makers sought to benefit from the insights of their counterparts in sister states. In Europe, the new constitutions found a ready audience seeking enlightenment from the American experiments in self-government. ven the delegates to the Constitutional Convention of 1787, despite their reservations about the course of political developments in the states during the decade after independence, found much that was useful in the newly adopted constitutions. And when James Madison, fulfilling a pledge given during the ratification debates, drafted the federal Bill of Rights, he found his model in the famous Declaration of Rights of the Virginia Constitution.

By the 1900s, however, few people would have looked to state constitutions for enlightenment. Instead, a familiar litany of complaints was heard whenever state constitutions were mentioned. State constitutions were too long and too detailed, combining basic principles with policy prescriptions and prohibitions that had no place in the fundamental law of a state. By including such provisions, it was argued, state constitutions deprived state governments of the flexibility they needed to respond effectively to changing circumstances. This—among other factors—encouraged political reformers to look to the federal government, which was not plagued by such constitutional constraints, thereby shifting the locus of political initiative away from the states. Meanwhile, civil libertarians concluded that state bills of rights, at least as interpreted by state courts, did not adequately protect rights and therefore looked to the federal courts and the federal Bill of Rights for redress. As power and responsibility shifted from the states to Washington, so too did the attention of scholars, the legal community, and the general public.

During the early 1970s, however, state constitutions were "rediscovered." The immediate impetus for this rediscovery was former President Richard Nixon's appointment of Warren Burger to succeed Earl Warren as Chief Justice of the United States Supreme Court. To civil libertarians, this appointment seemed to signal a decisive shift in the Supreme Court's jurisprudence, because Burger was expected to lead the Court away from the liberal activism that had characterized the Warren Court. They therefore sought ways to safeguard the gains they had achieved for defendants, racial minorities, and the poor during Warren's tenure from erosion by the Burger Court. In particular, they began to look to state bills of rights to secure the rights of defendants and to support other civilliberties claims that they advanced in state courts.

The "new judicial federalism," as it came to be called, quite quickly advanced beyond its initial concern to evade the mandates of the Burger Court. Indeed, less than two decades after it originated, it has become a nationwide phenomenon. For when judges and scholars turned their attention to state constitutions, they discovered an unsuspected richness. They found not only provisions that paralleled the federal Bill of Rights but also constitutional guarantees of the right to privacy and of gender equality, for example, that had no analogue in the U.S. Constitution. Careful examination of the text and history of state guarantees revealed important differences between even those provisions that most resembled federal guarantees and their federal counterparts. Looking beyond state declarations of rights, jurists and scholars discovered affirmative constitutional mandates to state governments to address such important policy concerns as education and housing. Taken altogether, these discoveries underlined the importance for the legal community of developing a better understanding of state constitutions.

Yet the renewed interest in state constitutions has not been limited to judges and lawyers. State constitutional reformers have renewed their efforts with notable success: since 1960, ten states have adopted new constitutions and several others have undertaken major constitutional revisions. These changes have usually resulted in more streamlined constitutions and more effective state governments. Also, in recent years political activists on both the left and the right have pursued their goals through state constitutional amendments, often enacted through the initiative process, under which policy proposals can be placed directly on the ballot for voters to endorse or reject. Scholars too have begun to rediscover how state constitutional history can illuminate changes in political thought and practice, providing a basis for theories about the dynamics of political change in America.

Miewald and Longo's excellent study of the Nebraska Constitution is the thirteenth volume in the series, The Oxford Commentaries on the State Constitutions of the United States, which reflects this renewed interest in state constitutions and will contribute to our knowledge about them. Because the constitutional tradition of each state is distinctive, the volume begins with the history and development of the Nebraska Constitution. It then provides the complete text of Nebraska's current constitution, with each section accompanied by commentary that explains the provision and traces its origins and its interpretation by the courts and by other governmental bodies. For readers with a particular interest in a specific aspect of Nebraska's constitutional experience, the book offers a bibliography of the most important sources dealing with the constitutional history and constitutional law of the state. Finally, the book concludes with a table of cases cited in the history and the constitutional commentary, as well as a subject index.

G. Alan Tarr

■ FOREWORD

"He is most powerful who has power over himself." This thoughtful counsel of Seneca nineteen centuries ago underscores our practical need to control ourselves, both individually and collectively, if we are to live together in harmony. We achieve collective control over ourselves through the institution of constitutional government. The result is a political and social environment that makes possible for each of us our search for personal fulfillment. Viewed in this context, our federal and state constitutions serve as truly living documents, absolutely vital to our everyday needs and aspirations.

In this engaging study, Professors Miewald and Longo describe in fascinating detail the development, historical significance, and very real present day meaning of the Nebraska constitution. The professors make it clear that the Nebraska constitution is no museum piece collecting dust, but rather an exciting reflection of, and legal basis for, the ambitions and dreams of Nebraskans today.

What special characteristics does the Nebraska constitution contain? What does it say about Nebraskans? What lessons does it provide as we seek answers to the complexities and challenges of contemporary life? Pertinent insights and answers to these questions appear throughout this well-researched, clearly written, and informative work. Professors Miewald and Longo describe many instances in which the Nebraska constitution sheds light upon these questions.

I suggest that three separate and unrelated Nebraska constitutional provisions are particularly instructive.

1. the initiative and referendum procedures that reserve to individual citizens profound direct legislative power, and prevent legislators from ever forgetting that they are servants, not masters
2. The establishment of a unicameral legislature, which requires a high degree of accessibility by legislators to their constituents and, at least to some extent, holds down the size of government
3. the imposition of substantial restrictions upon corporate ownership of farms and ranches

These seemingly disparate constitutional edicts, when examined both individually and together, tell us many things.

1. Nebraskans like to think for themselves. They want to direct their own lives, not be smothered by an omnipresent or overreaching government.
2. Government must be genuinely accessible to citizens. It must recognize that those citizens do in fact have highly independent views and are not guided by a "pack mentality."

3. Nebraskans value a fundamental relationship between the family as a unit and the farm as a means of livelihood. This presupposes that traditional Nebraskan rural lifestyles and values should not be lost in our increasingly impersonal and urban age of high technology and giant institutions.
4. Government functions best which understands that fierce individual independence and sincere group cooperation are complementary, not adversarial concepts. There is a time and a place for each, as Nebraskans demonstrate through constitutional precepts that stress both individual independence and collective cooperation.

State constitutions today are assuming more influence upon our lives. Many issues that have recently been decided by federal courts interpreting the U.S. constitution are now being adjudicated in state courts on the basis of state constitutions. Thus, this timely work of Professors Miewald and Longo reminds us of the wisdom of Cicero' s admonition: "It is not by muscle, speech or physical dexterity that great things are achieved, but by reflection, force of character and judgment."

As we plan for the future, we must exercise this "reflection, force of character and judgment" as we ask: Will Nebraskans independent and individualistic views meet the necessary cooperative challenges of the future—better education for all, effective economic development, cures for the ravages of poverty? The sound analysis of Professors Miewald and Longo demonstrates that the Nebraska constitution is broad enough, and can be reasonably amended, to provide a flexible legal base for the future. In short, the Nebraska constitution creates present stability with the means for the necessary future changes that are inevitable as society evolves. This is all that can be asked of a constitution.

As citizens we have the obligation to responsibly use and build upon our Nebraska constitution. Professors Miewald and Longo have competently provided us with the background and knowledge we must have for this task. The rest is up to us. As Shakespeare wrote in *Julius Caesar*, Act I, Scene II: "Men at some time are master of their fates. The fault, dear Brutus, is not in our stars, but in ourselves."

Robert M. Spire

PART ONE

The History of the Nebraska Constitution

In a strict sense, the Nebraska Constitution is that document written and approved in 1875. As such, only seventeen states have older basic laws. The authors and voters of 117 years ago, however, might not recognize their work since, from its adoption on October 12, 1875 through May 1992, it has been amended 194 times. The creation of the unicameral legislature was only the most notable of these many changes.

The durability of the 1875 Constitution cannot be attributed to its elegant construction or its deathless prose. As state constitutions go, it is certainly not a masterpiece of elegant construction. Yet Nebraskans seem comfortable with it, and there have been few demands in the past decade for any great revisions. The major interests in the state apparently regard it as a level playing field for their political games. It works, Nebraskans feel, or at least at each election, this or that side has an adequate opportunity to try for amendments.

In 1875, given the history of the previous efforts at constitution making, one might not have predicted a long life for the document. Indeed, some Nebraskans, disillusioned by the hard life on the Great Plains, probably did not see much hope for the state itself. Nebraska survived and prospered, and the 1875 Constitution continues to shape the political life of the state.

LURCHING TOWARD STATEHOOD[1]

It was a long time before a political community was established in Nebraska within which a viable constitution could take root. The territory that was to become the state moved from one jurisdiction to another for more than fifty years. As the state began to take form, it was usually shaped by national considerations such as slavery or Manifest Destiny. And the politicians who wrote the first constitution may have been more concerned with their careers than with the public interest.

The few non-Indian trappers and other adventurers who wandered across what is now Nebraska before 1803 were governed, if at all, by a succession of French and Spanish colonial administrators located in New Orleans. After the Louisiana Purchase, Nebraska was part of the Indiana Territory from 1804 to 1805, the Louisiana Territory from 1805 to 1812, and finally part of the Missouri Territory from 1812 until Missouri became a state in 1821. The Nebraska area, after 1821, was included in a vaguely defined region called the "Indian country." All these formal changes were probably irrelevant since Nebraska had no non-Indian inhabitants and little in the way of organized government.

The situation came into clearer focus with the passage of the Indian Country Act in 1834.[2] The legislation was a short-lived effort by the federal government to solve the "Indian question" by prohibiting further settlement west of the Mississippi. The pressure of westward expansion soon made a mockery of the law, as trappers, traders, farmers, religious groups, gold seekers, and assorted pilgrims began their quests for something and somewhere new.

Nebraska has always been the most convenient place to get from here to there and back again. Regardless of the reason driving people to the west, Nebraska just seemed to be in the way. Although some early explorers tried to depict the land between the Missouri River and the Rockies as the Great American Desert, the climate, soil, topography, flora, and fauna do not make it the most forbidding real estate in the country. Some of the transients gave up their dreams of wealth or freedom in California, Oregon, or Utah and stopped just on the other side of the Missouri.

Some pioneers, that is, saw potential, even if they could not say for sure what it was, in the vast tract stretching toward the west. They were encouraged by policy makers in Washington and elsewhere who realized this land bridge was critical to the development of the nation. The future of the area immediately

---

[1] The general outline of Nebraska's constitutional history is derived largely from the following sources: Albert Watkins, rev. and ed. *Official Report of the Debates and Proceedings in the Nebraska Constitutional Convention,* 3 vols. (Lincoln: Nebraska State Historical Publications, 1913); Addison E. Sheldon, *Nebraska: The Land and the People,* vol. I (Chicago: Lewis Publishing, 1931); and James C. Olson, *History of Nebraska,* 2nd ed. (Lincoln: University of Nebraska Press, 1966).

[2] 4 Statutes 729 (1834).

became tied to the foreign and domestic controversies of the time. "Nebraska was born of the Oregon controversy with England" when Secretary of War William Wilkins in 1844 suggested the organization of a territory to protect the immigrants to the Pacific Northwest.[3]

A more powerful impulse behind the "idea of Nebraska" was the competition between the North and the South for a railroad route to the Pacific and, ultimately, for the destiny of the unsettled regions of the nation. Opponents of a southern route had a masterful advocate in Stephen Douglas of Illinois, as a Representative and as a Senator. Major impediments to the northern route included the Indian Country Act of 1834 as well as all the high drama of the impending crisis over the issue of slavery. The solution of Congress to both obstacles was the KansasNebraska Act of 1854.

Bills to organize a Nebraska Territory were introduced in 1844, 1848, and 1853. With one eye on a Chicago-Pacific railroad and the other on the presidency, Douglas was instrumental in all the actions. The Senator from Illinois was finally successful when he backed a measure which effectively nullified the Missouri Compromise of 1820. The earlier law had, for Northerners, guaranteed that most of the old Louisiana Purchase territory would be admitted as free states. The Kansas-Nebraska Act opted for the more ambiguous concept of "popular sovereignty." The act provided that when Nebraska achieved statehood, it "shall be received into the Union with or without slavery as [its] constitution may prescribe."[4] The Missouri Compromise was specifically repealed when Congress stated that "the true intent and meaning of this act [is] not to legislate slavery into any Territory or State, nor to exclude it therefrom, but to leave the people thereof perfectly free to form and regulate their domestic institutions in their own way, subject only to the Constitution of the United States."[5]

"The people thereof" in the newly created Nebraska Territory were few and far between. It was a vast area, including land that is now part of the states of Colorado, Wyoming, Montana, North Dakota, and South Dakota. The first census of November 1854, which may have included several Kansans, counted only 2,732 whites of whom 929 were males over the age of twenty-one. The Kansas-Nebraska Act provided the most rudimentary form of government. A governor was appointed for four years and a secretary for five years by the President. The judicial power was vested in a supreme court of three members who were also to serve as district court judges. The legislature was the legislative assembly, composed of a thirteen-member council and a twenty-six-member house of representatives, elected by white males over the age of twenty-one.

[3] Sheldon, *Nebraska*, 230.

[4] 10 Statutes 277 (1854).

[5] 10 Statutes 283 (1854).

This bare framework of government for a handful of eligible participants was enough to keep the political pot boiling for several years. The state's agricultural wealth was yet to be realized and, although wild hopes abounded, there were few mineral resources to exploit. In the first years, the most reliable sources of income in Nebraska were real estate speculation and government. The two fields of endeavor were often intertwined. As James Olson notes of those territorial heroes, "early pioneers seem to have come to Nebraska in significant numbers for the express purpose of carving political careers for themselves in the new territory; others to use politics as one means of financial gain."[6] The creation of a model political commonwealth may not have had a high priority with the men who drove Nebraska toward statehood.

Instead, many of the state's founders were keen watchers of the main chance. Government positions were a stable source of income and were available if one backed the right political faction. Wildcat banking was lucrative, especially since undersubscribed banks could easily obtain a charter from the legislature. Land speculation was another option and the "boomers," some honest and some out for a quick profit, soon covered the map of the prairie with imaginary cities. If any of the would-be cities had a chance, it would require the location of some facility, so government offices became a great prize, second only to winning a railroad. The grandest prize of all was the territorial capital. Omaha had managed to seize that jewel, but other communities were always ready to tear it away. In fact, the location of the state capital was not finally resolved until well into the nineteenth century, and the desire to keep it in Lincoln, or to remove it, colored future constitutional developments.

While town fought town for any advantage, a larger sectional question emerged around which territorial politics was organized. The Platte River, noted for being too wet to plough and too muddy to drink, posed a formidable geographical barrier to territorial unity. It was too shallow to ferry, its bottom was too soft to ford, and its wide expanse made bridge building prohibitively expensive. The North Platters and the South Platters developed a sense of antagonism toward each other and were suspicious of any government initiative which might benefit the other's territory. So disgruntled were the South Platters that at one time they sought annexation to Kansas. This sectional split was to influence Nebraska politics even after statehood.

In its first official census in 1860, the Nebraska Territory contained 28,841 people. The first serious effort at achieving statehood also took place in that year, a move largely promoted by South Platters who saw statehood as an opportunity to reopen the question of the location of the state capital and, perhaps, to wrest it away from Omaha.[7] Whatever the reasons, the legislature passed a measure

---

[6] Olson, *History of Nebraska*, 116.

[7] Watkins, *Official Reports*, III, 474.

calling for an election on March 5, 1860 on the question of statehood. Fifty-two delegates to a constitutional convention were also to be elected to serve in the event that the voters opted for statehood.

But the winds were blowing in many strange directions, and the territorial politicians were uncertain about which tack to take. Democrats had become accustomed to their patronage positions, but it was unclear that the national party would win the election of 1860. The new Republican Party was growing in numbers at the local level, although its long-term prospects were still in doubt. The change from territory to state posed too many uncertainties for all sides.

On a more substantial level, the sentiment in favor of statehood was subdued. The population of Nebraska was still small, and the people had not yet discovered a reliable source of wealth. Some argued that it was better that Washington continue to provide financial support for their government. Statehood, for many, seemed an unnecessary extravagance. Those supporting statehood contended that the status would attract people and capital. Nebraska was also putting in jeopardy possible land grants from the federal government by delaying entry into the union.

The voters rejected statehood, 2,732 to 2,094. Republicans won a large majority of the delegates to the constitutional convention that was never to be. The turnout of voters was relatively light, reflecting considerable ambivalence about the issue. The outcome was probably decided largely by sectional considerations, as Addison Sheldon notes: "Its most cordial support came from the counties south of the Platte, but Douglas [Omaha] and Sarpy counties went strongly against it, doubtless because the people there thought that under a state organization some other place than Omaha might be selected as capital."[8] Nebraska's first attempt at constitution making was stillborn.

The attention of Nebraska and the nation was diverted by the Civil War, but by 1864 both territorial and national leaders revived the question of statehood. Republicans in Washington were dominant, and they saw a state of Nebraska as a sure source of further help in Congress and in presidential elections. Territorial Republicans were eager to have a try at federal and state offices. On a vote marked by sharp partisan differences, the territorial legislature petitioned Congress for admission to the union.

By the Enabling Act, passed April 19, 1864, Nebraskans were "authorized to form for themselves a constitution and state government."[9] The act set down some explicit requirements, the most important of which gave the citizens the power "to vote for and choose representatives to form a convention, under such rules and regulations as the governor of said territory may prescribe, and also to vote upon the acceptance or rejection of such constitution as may be formed by

[8] Sheldon, *Nebraska,* 300.

[9] 13 Statutes 47 (1864).

said convention, under such rules and regulations as said convention may prescribe."[10] Once the constitution had been approved by the voters, the President of the United States was to proclaim that Nebraska had become a state. The specific question of whether or not to become a state was not directly posed to the voters. In the rather bizarre campaign that followed, the issue became the membership of the convention.

Territorial Governor Alvin Saunders called an election for June 6, 1864 to elect fifty-two members to a constitutional convention. At once, the opponents of statehood endorsed a slate of candidates who pledged to move for an immediate and permanent adjournment of the convention. Some voters were still not convinced that statehood was more than an expensive luxury; they dreaded the higher taxes associated with supporting a new government. The Democrats were generally reluctant to aid and abet the national Republicans, especially since they were unlikely to receive any plums from a Republican administration. Thus, after the convention had organized itself in Omaha on July 4, 1864, the first motion made was as follows: "Resolved that this convention adjourn, sine die, without forming a constitution."[11] The motion carried, 37 to 7, and the second attempt at writing a constitution for Nebraska ended abruptly.

By now, the friends of statehood apparently had enough of the idea of "open covenants openly arrived at." In 1866, the Republicans in the territorial legislature, with the assistance of a few Democrats, decided on another tactic. The legislature itself would produce a constitution, a move that Governor Saunders and other Republicans saw as a way to steal a march on the now relaxed opponents of statehood. A constitution was prepared for presentation to the voters at the most propitious moment. Even contemporary observers were uncertain about the exact membership of the committee that met to put together the document. Albert Watkins says "the constitution was prepared by a self-appointed committee of lawyers which met for the purpose in Experience Estabrook's office in Omaha, and it based its legitimacy upon the enabling act of 1864 and acknowledged acceptance of its terms, notwithstanding that the act specifically directed that the constitution should be formed by a convention to be organized according to its specific prescription."[12]

When the "boys in the backroom" had written their constitution, they persuaded a friendly Democrat to introduce it to the legislature. Perhaps "railroaded" is not the appropriate term, but the train was clearly on the track. As Olson comments, "under pressure from Governor Saunders and other federal officials, the issue was made a party matter and the constitution was pushed through the legislature in a way that would have been unusual for even the most

[10] 13 Statutes 48 (1864).

[11] Watkins, *Official Reports*, III, 486.

[12] Ibid., 494.

minor, noncontroversial measure."[13] In four days, the constitution had been approved by the legislature in a most irregular manner. Members had no printed version of the document and amendments were not permitted.

Since we are unsure as to their identity, it is hard to evaluate the motives of the "founders" of Nebraska. One thing is clear: they were not going to be beaten again by those frugal voters who feared the expense of state government. In a tradition that carries down to the present day, the watchword of Nebraska government became "cheap." Sheldon quotes the bitter words of one opponent of the constitution: "A respectable state government would, they argued, frighten the people and they would reject the constitution. A cheap government of cheap men answered the purpose designed."[14] The salaries, even by the standards of the 1860s, were minimal. The governor was to earn $1,000 per year, and other elected officials would receive a proportionally reduced amount. State legislators were to be given $3.00 per day, with a limit of forty days per session. Members of the supreme court would earn $2,000 per year.

Although Nebraska's existence had been determined by the slavery issue, the framers of the first constitution were not decisive in resolving all the issue's ramifications. To be sure, they prohibited slavery, but at the end of the Civil War this was hardly a courageous action. It is more difficult to explain their position on the question of race. Nebraska had become, within a few years, a staunchly Republican state. Moreover, while some Nebraskans may have been sympathetic to the Confederate cause and to Southern ideals, there were hardly enough blacks in the state to make race an urgent matter. The framers deliberately included a constitutional provision which restricted the franchise to "white citizens of the United States" or "white persons of foreign birth who shall have declared their intentions to become citizens."[15] The restriction was probably added to win the support of Democratic voters. J. Sterling Morton, for decades the leader of the Democratic Party, was adamantly opposed to black enfranchisement.

In general, it can be said that the authors exhibited little inventiveness in their final product. The structure of government was derived directly from the territorial model of the Kansas-Nebraska Act. The executive officers—governor, secretary of state, auditor, and treasurer— were the same. The judicial system remained the three members serving both as district judges and as a supreme court. The legislature was a thirteen-member senate and a thirty-nine-member house of representatives. It appears that the general strategy was to convince the voters that the change to statehood would involve no great dislocation. However, as officials and citizens would learn, so primitive a constitution was hardly workable.

---

[13] Olson, *History of Nebraska*, 124.

[14] Sheldon, *Nebraska*, 339.

[15] Nebraska Constitution (1866), Art. II, Sec. 1.

The legislature had authorized an election on the proposed constitution, as well as the election for officials of the new state, for June 2, 1866. The voters approved the constitution, and thus statehood, by a vote of 3,938 to 3,838. Both parties immediately launched charges of voting irregularities, but the Republicans and pro-statehood forces had taken the precaution of rigging the canvassing board; the constitution along with most of the Republican ticket were counted in. The Democrats continued to grumble in vain that the election was crooked.

Congress was informed that Nebraska had met the conditions set by the Enabling Act of 1864, and that body, apparently distracted by the fury of post-Civil War politics, did not inquire into the origins of the constitution. What did attract the interest of the Republican leadership was the restriction on the right to vote. The Democrats were also unenthusiastic about the admission of a solidly Republican state. However, the bill admitting Nebraska as a state passed both houses of Congress in the waning days of the session. President Andrew Johnson, fighting his congressional enemies on a number of fronts, felt he did not need to reinforce them and so he applied a pocket veto to the bill. Nebraska would not become a state in 1866.

When Congress met again in December 1866, the restriction on the rights of blacks became a critical issue. A heavily revised bill was introduced, including a provision that "this act shall not take effect except under the fundamental condition, that within the State of Nebraska there shall be no denial of the elective franchise, or of any other right to any other persons, by reason of race or color, excepting Indians not taxed, and upon the further fundamental condition, that the Legislature of said state, by a solemn public act, shall declare the assent of said state to these fundamental conditions, and shall transmit to the President of the United States an authentic copy of said act, upon receipt whereof the President, by proclamation, shall forthwith announce the fact, whereupon said fundamental conditions shall be held as part of the organic law of the state, and thereupon without any further proceeding on the part of Congress, the admission of said state into the Union shall be considered as complete."[16] President Johnson applied a second veto, which Congress quickly overrode. It was now up to Nebraskans to deal with the provisions of the act.

Territorial Governor Saunders called a meeting of the legislature for February 20, 1867 to consider the question. There was some resistance to accepting the fundamental conditions posed by the act but eventually, by a largely partisan vote, the measure was approved. The President was notified of Nebraska's acceptance of the conditions and Johnson issued the proclamation of statehood on March 1, 1867. The Constitution of 1866 was not in effect.

Olson maintains that "Nebraska's transition from territorial status to statehood, because of the wrangle in Congress over its constitution, was more complicated

---

[16] 14 Statutes 392 (1867).

than that of any other Louisiana Purchase state."[17] The national government was content with what it had done, but in Nebraska doubts continued to be raised about the way in which the Constitution of 1866 had been written, approved, and amended. The matter was resolved in the 1873 case of *Brittle v. The People.*[18] Chief Justice Oliver P. Mason and Associate Justice Lorenzo Crounse, both men having been present at the creation in 1866, gave differing interpretations of the confusion surrounding the constitution.

The case concerned the citizenship of blacks in Nebraska. Brittle was found guilty of burglary in Douglas County and in his appeal, he claimed that Howard W. Crossley, a black, had been included in the jury in violation of state law. Since jury duty was not a basic right, it was not included as one of those "other rights" protected by the "fundamental condition." Mason agreed and went on to argue that the amendment to the Nebraska constitution and the promise by the legislature that the state would not deny to blacks the right to vote "or any other right" had been illegally coerced by Congress. "Could Congress," he asked, "change the constitution which the people had adopted, and admit the State into the Union with its fundamental law so changed, without the consent of the people?"[19] He concluded that the action of Congress in imposing the fundamental condition was void and so he dissented from the opinion of the court.

The majority upheld Brittie's conviction. In his opinion, Justice Lorenzo Crounse cautioned that it was not prudent to inquire too closely into the origins of the Constitution of 1866. There was little evidence that the document was the result of a conscious decision by a sovereign people. It "was originally drafted in a lawyer's office by a few self-appointed individuals."[20] That the draft was later approved by the legislature was irrelevant since, according to the Enabling Act, "there was no more authority in the Territorial legislature to direct the people to vote upon the constitution than might be possessed by a religious conference, a teacher's institute, or a woman's rights convention."[21] And what of the voters who approved it? Crounse described the irregularities "which might easily overcome,the declared majority of a hundred."[22]

A judicial inquiry into the legitimacy of the 1866 Constitution posed all manner of dangers, including the question whether a court created by an illegitimate constitution had any power to rule on its legality. The admission of states into the union was a purely political question and "[i]t is an act of Congress that gives vitality to the action of the people."[23] Furthermore, "to say that the

---

[17] Olson, *History of Nebraska*, 144.

[18] 2 Neb 198.

[19] Ibid., 228.

[20] Ibid., 211.

[21] Ibid., 212.

[22] Ibid., 214.

[23] Ibid., 216.

people of a Territory must frame—that is, write out—their constitution in the first instance, is not correct. The document might be imported from Japan, or fall from the clouds; and if, by any subsequent action, it becomes the constitution of the State, we are bound by it, and cannot question where it came from."[24]

The "subsequent action" in this instance was the behavior of Nebraskans. Voters had voted, governors had governed, legislators legislated, and judges judged as if the constitution were valid. The state, through its legislature, had accepted the offer of statehood by Congress with all the conditions. It was an offer, in fact, that was "the first of all the proceedings had up to this time which had the semblance of regularity."[25] The Constitution of 1866, in all its particulars, had to be regarded by the courts as completely legitimate, despite its dubious pedigree.

REMAKING THE CONSTITUTION: 1867–1875

The Republicans and the South Platters won the first statewide election, and the capital as well as the University of Nebraska were located in the rude village that was to become Lincoln. Because of poor planning, inferior materials, and shoddy workmanship, the new state capitol and the first building at the university began to disintegrate almost as soon as they were put to use. Much the same could be said of the Constitution of 1866.

The political climate remained unsettled as towns continued to compete with each other for advantages dispensed by government and the hostility between North and South Platte endured. Substantive issues were also clouded by the character of many of the state's early political leaders. Olson summarizes the first years: "the years in which Nebraska's state government was being established was characterized by gross public immorality in financial matters and an all-too-general practice of using public funds for private gain."[26] Charges and countercharges were hurled by intensely partisan antagonists and almost every politician was accused of some sort of corruption. The biggest scandal surrounded the actions of Governor David Butler in his handling of public funds. In 1871 he was impeached, convicted, and removed from office. Over a century later and with an education in the rhetoric of Watergate, one could make the argument that Butler was the victim of the "new morality," that he as no more larcenous than many of his fellow statesmen. But the incident was deeply disturbing to a new generation of Nebraskans who were now streaming into the state. The old idea that government was just one more exploitable resource was slowly being replaced by a sterner concept of public morality.

---

[24] Ibid.

[25] Ibid., 219.

[26] Olson, *History of Nebraska*, 143.

The newer settlers may have been misled by claims about Nebraska's natural bounty, but they were not inclined to believe they would become rich overnight. They were in it for the long haul and were interested in establishing some degree of stability in their communities. That stability was not guaranteed by the 1866 Constitution nor by the type of politicians who had led Nebraska since statehood.

The new settlers were concerned that the Constitution of 1866, first of all, was an ineffective check on the rascals then dominating the state's political scene. There was also a feeling that state government could be adapted as a more positive instrument for promoting the common good. Indeed, the harsh, unpredictable conditions of frontier Nebraska demanded collective action; one could not be expected to survive drought, blizzards, grasshoppers, tornados, floods, and lord knows what else all alone. By the turn of the century, the settlers of the 1870s and 1880s had developed their ideas of public policy into the platforms of the Populists and Progressives. In the first years of statehood, they were still trying to articulate their notions about proper public activity.

The new mix of attitudes posed an interesting paradox for any constitutional authors. Government obviously was an alluring target for scoundrels and so steps had to be taken to limit their opportunities for criminality. At the same time, this government was to engage in a variety of activities designed to promote the welfare of everyone. Added to this was the lingering feeling that taxes were an unnecessary evil. To this day, despite their conservative reputation, Nebraskans exhibit progressive attitudes on a number of issues and are willing to endorse noble causes, just as long as it does not cost much. These ambiguous attitudes about government still shape constitutional considerations.

The Constitution of 1866 from the outset was under attack from every quarter. Most politicians wanted a modification of the miserly salary schedule. Lawyers were interested in a more efficient court system. Legislators felt that longer sessions were necessary. Lincolnites wanted to insure their city's status as the capital was given constitutional protection. Among ordinary citizens, there were the first rumblings of the discontent that was to come to full force in the Populist Party. An increasing distrust of corporations, especially railroads, led to the demand for greater government regulation. The question of woman suffrage was another cause for passionate debate. These factors, coupled with the continuing revelation of corruption, made constitutional change inevitable.

According to Article IX, the only means for changing the constitution was by a convention approved by the voters after the issue was put by the legislature. The fifth session of the legislature, in 1869, called for such an election to be held on October 11, 1870. The convention was approved by a vote of 3,968 to 979. Perhaps indicative of the agendas being pursued by various interests, the question was approved by Lincoln voters, 523 to 2. At a subsequent election, fifty-two members of the convention were chosen to meet in Lincoln on June 13, 1871.

Before it adjourned on August 19, the convention had considered in detail every aspect of state and government, great and small; the debates filled 1,600 pages when the shorthand transcription was eventually published in 1904. As a model for their work, the Nebraskans took the Illinois Constitution of 1870. This so-called "Granger Constitution" proved to be a popular pattern in the new western states.[27] Whether it was a constitution for the ages is debatable. Samuel W. Witwer, president of the 1970 Illinois Constitutional Convention, concluded that it was "deliberately fashioned so as to shackle the hands of those entrusted with the executive, legislative, and judicial departments of government. It was weighed down with detail and provisions customarily found in statutes and ordinances." In short, Witwer argued, it was marked by all sorts of checks and balances and written for the needs of rural society.[28] At the time, however, it impressed Nebraskans as a solid basis for reform.

The writers made few innovations in the traditional tripartite division of government; their main contribution here was to make possible higher salaries for all state officials. The greatest changes came in the area of substantive, rather than procedural, matters. The convention followed the lead of Illinois by empowering state government to regulate the railroads. In two other areas, their efforts backfired since the provisions caused the greatest resistance to ratification. A particularly deadly clause exempted church property up to the value of $5,000 from taxation. This provision was urged by poor Protestant congregations, particularly Methodist, and alienated the wealthier Catholic and Episcopalian churches in Omaha. Another issue attempted to govern the disposal of unused railroad rights-of-way, a proposal that did not sit well with the promoters of speculative rail projects—and the citizens in the many communities who hoped to benefit from the projects.

The convention could not come to total agreement on a number of questions and so submitted five proposals separately. These propositions included such subjects as the liability of stockholders in banks, a prohibition against local government aid to corporations, compulsory education for all children between eight and sixteen years of age, and the first attempt to introduce the prohibition of alcohol.

A final issue involved the extension of the right of suffrage. The members of the convention debated for days about the question of woman suffrage and the result was a rather ambiguous compromise. The article provided that "the legislature may extend by law the right of suffrage to persons herein not enumerated, but no such law shall be in force until the same shall have been submitted to a

[27] Janet Cornelius, *Constitution Making in Illinois*, 1818–1970. (Urbana: University of Illinois, Institute of Government and Public Affairs, 1972), 85.

[28] Ibid., xii.

vote of the people at a general election, and approved by a majority of all the votes cast on the question at such election."

This was not the first attempt at extending the franchise to women. The territorial legislature came close to approving such an expansion in 1856. In 1871, a measure to permit women to vote on calling a constitutional convention was defeated by a tie vote. Efforts at woman suffrage would continue throughout the rest of the nineteenth century.[29]

For all their months of work, the members of the convention proved only that loquacity does not equal political perspicacity. The delegates were apparently out of touch with popular opinion, and the entire constitution was rejected by a vote of 8,627 to 7,986. All the specific proposals did even more poorly, with woman suffrage defeated, 12,496 to 3,502.

The legislature played with the idea of reconvening the convention in order to remove the more objectionable elements of the constitution. The attention of the lawmakers, however, was soon diverted by their participation in some scenes from the theater of the absurd. Acting Governor James, who had replaced Butler, declared the legislature adjourned but a handful of members remained in Lincoln in order to, among other things, impeach James. The governor responded by cutting off the coal supply to the capitol, hoping to freeze out the defiant legislators. And things soon degenerated after that.

Government in Nebraska had become a bit of a mess, with Democrats fighting Republicans when the members of each party were not feuding among themselves. Taxes were delinquent and local governments continued their dangerous practice of issuing bonds for railroad construction, thus courting bankruptcy. The new settlers felt that their views were not being adequately represented at the state level. In addition, none of the issues which had lead to the Convention of 1871 had been resolved.

Political ferment was stimulated by "panic, hard times, political jobbery and popular discontent."[30] New political parties and other forms of political action were taking shape, with a People's Independent and Prohibition Party formed to contest the election of 1874. But most unsettling of all was the invasion of grasshoppers in the years between 1874 and 1877. As always, farming in Nebraska depended on good fortune, and the plague of grasshoppers was a definite sign that the luck of the pioneers had finally run out. It was as if nature were determined to show the settlers that they really did not know what hard times were all about.

The Census of 1870 found 122,993 Nebraskans. The population continued to push westward, up to the Colorado border. The new communities soon learned

---

[29] See Ann Wilhite, "Sixty-Five Years till Victory: A History of Woman Suffrage in Nebraska," *Nebraska History* 49 (1968): 149.

[30] Sheldon, *Nebraska*, 479.

that they lacked representation in state government, and the westerners concluded that they were being dominated by the voters in the eastern counties. Under intense pressure, the legislature submitted another proposal for a constitutional convention. At the election in October 1874, the voters overwhelmingly approved the proposition by a vote of 18,067 to 3,880. Delegates were chosen in April 1875, and the sixty-nine members began their deliberations in Lincoln on May 11, 1875.

It was a somber group which met and frugality was their driving motivation. The members cut back on their own expenses, including the elimination of a verbatim shorthand transcript of the proceedings. Therefore, our knowledge of this meeting is not as complete as the convention of 1871. That the members were fed up with the shenanigans of the recent past is indicated by the adoption of a motion that the convention "so revise the subject matter of the new constitution that nothing but pure, unadulterated English language shall be employed in its wording."[31]

The convention again relied upon the Illinois Constitution of 1870. However, they were astute enough to remove the provisions that were generally thought to have led to the defeat in 1871, namely, the taxation of church property and the disposal of railroad rights-of-way. The major issues revolved around the modernization of state government. The expansion of the legislature was easily resolved; a house of representatives of eighty-four members and a senate of thirty were quickly approved. Unfortunately, the legislative districts were described in the constitution, making future reapportionment almost impossible.

The expansion of the executive branch was a more controversial question. The offices of lieutenant governor, superintendent of public instruction, attorney general, and commissioner of public lands and buildings were added, despite the strenuous objections of those dedicated to greater economy in government. As a concession to the economizers, the attorney general and superintendent of public instruction were forbidden from hiring any clerks (Art. III, Sec. 24). Of greater importance to the future of the state was Article III, Section 26, which said, "No other executive state office shall be continued or created, and the duties now devolving upon officers not provided for by this constitution shall be performed by the officers herein created." This provision made it impossible for the state to set up the machinery to enforce one of the centerpieces of the new constitution—the regulation of the railroads.

The primitive judicial system of 1866, a relic inherited from the Kansas Nebraska Act, was thoroughly reformed. Instead of three district judges doubling, en banc, as the supreme court, a separate and enlarged district court system was approved. The office of county judge was also created.

In economic matters, the Constitution of 1875 retained the provisions of 1871 giving the legislature the power to "pass laws to correct abuses and prevent

[31] Watkins, *Official Reports*, III, 535.

unjust discrimination and extortion in all charges of express, telegraph and railroad companies in this state" (Art. XI, Sec. 7). This brave language, however, did little to curtail the real or imagined power of the railroads, and the later Populists rode the issue to political power. Municipalities were restricted in their financial affairs, an outcome of their abuses of the power to tax and to borrow in the 1870s. Even the state government was limited to an indebtedness of $100,000, a restriction still in effect.

The convention submitted two separate proposals for consideration by the voters. The first would allow voters to express a preference for U.S. Senator. Even though it passed, the provision had little effect on future senatorial selections since serious candidates continued to pursue other avenues to election by the legislature. The second measure protected Lincoln as the state capital. It also passed, but as late as 11911, efforts were made to locate the capital elsewhere.

At the election held on October 12, 1875, Nebraskans showed their enthusiasm, if not for this particular document at least for some sort of change from the past, by approving it 30,322 to 5,474. The foundation of the present Nebraska constitution had been laid.

CHANGING THE CONSTITUTION: 1875–1920

With the Constitution of 1875, Nebraska achieved some degree of political maturity and was ready to enter the mainstream of American politics; indeed, for one brief, improbable moment under William Jennings Bryan, it was the mainstream. The politics of the last quarter of the nineteenth century was distinguished by the rise of the People's Independent Party—the Populist movement.

Populism forms the most exciting chapter in Nebraska's political history, and on a superficial level it appears to have left an important legacy. Today, any moderately unusual event or personality is likely to be characterized by journalists as a resurgence of the old prairie populism. Yet one can search the current political landscape without finding very many significant monuments left by those angry reformers. The radicalism of the movement had remarkably little effect on the way Nebraskans practice their politics then and now. Populism came and went, and the state government in 1910 looked much as it did in 1875.

Part of this stability can be attributed to the fact that the radicalism of Nebraska was more apparent than real. Populism was a spasm of agrarian discontent which, at least in Nebraska, did not lead to any enduring solutions. As Stanley Parsons said of the Populist animus, "the farmers' ideology was so weak that one good crop year sent them scurrying back to the major parties. This is hardly an example of indigenous American radicalism. It is, instead, the temporary desperation of a frustrated pragmatic capitalist."[32] Moreover, it was a

[32] Stanley P. Parsons, *The Populist Context: Rural versus Urban Power on a Great Plains Frontier* (Westport, Conn.: Greenwood Press, 1973), 147.

frustration that the opportunistic politicians of the day were delighted to exploit, leading to "the deluge of aspiring village editors, lawyers, politicians, and businessmen into the Populist ranks."[33] If Lawrence Goodwyn is correct, Nebraska may have been the worst thing that happened to the Populist movement, as ideological purity became contaminated within the state's concoction of moralism and individualism. In his view, Nebraska Populism was a "shadow movement" without purpose. Sincere Populists offered "little more than a quest for honorable men who would pledge themselves to forsake corrupt practices."[34] The heart of the movement was abandoned by political careerists whose major concern was winning the next election.

But one must also acknowledge that if there was any momentum for drastic change, it may have been diverted by one immutable fact: the Constitution of 1875 was almost impossible to amend. Article XV allowed the legislature, by a three-fifths vote of each house, to propose amendments for submission to the voters at the next scheduled election of senators and representatives. The amendment had to be approved by "a majority of the electors at such election."

The Nebraska Supreme Court interpreted that phrase to require a majority of the highest number of votes case at a general election. In its final word on the matter, the court declared that "our conclusion is that to secure the adoption of an amendment to our constitution it is necessary that the favorable votes be in excess of one-half of the highest aggregate number of votes cast at said election, whether such highest number be for the selection of an officer or upon the adoption of a proposition."[35] Judge Norval, dissenting, agreed with this interpretation but he lamented that "taking the past as a criterion by which to foretell the future, it would seem, under the construction adopted, it will be almost, if not quite, impossible to change the present constitution, however meritorious may be the amendment proposed."[36]

Thus while the legislature was willing to submit amendments to the voters, between 1882 and 1904 only one out of twenty-three proposals was approved in a way that met the court's standard. The one amendment, in 1886, raised some suspicions since it increased the pay of state legislators and it succeeded only after the legislature undertook its own recount of the votes, an investigation which some cynics felt may have been based on the use of excessively creative mathematics. Of the remaining twenty-two proposals, all but four of them received a majority of the votes cast on the proposal itself. They failed because

---

[33] Ibid., 84.

[34] Lawrence Goodwyn, *Democratic Promise: The Populist Movement in America* (New York: Oxford University Press, 1976), 400.

[35] Tecumseh National Bank v. Saunders, 51 Neb 805.

[36] Ibid., 816.

citizens who voted for other officers and neglected to make a choice on the amendments were counted, in effect, as negative votes.

Ways of getting around the restrictions on amendments were sought. In 1896, the Republican-dominated legislature suggested twelve amendments, the major ones concerning the number and salaries of judges and executive branch officials. A separate ballot box was provided for the amendments and the votes were to be counted separately. However, the year marked the zenith of power for the Democratic-Populist fusion and the Republicans suffered their worst defeat ever. Although the amendments were approved by the people, the recount process in the legislature degenerated into a partisan brawl and all were eventually held to be rejected.

A solution was found in 1901 when the legislature passed a bill permitting party conventions to take a position on proposed amendments. The so-called "party circle law" allowed canvassers to count all straight tickets ballots in favor of the amendment if the party had indicated its approval. Each ballot informed the voters that "If you wish to vote a straight ticket, make a mark in the circle at the top of the ballot to the right of the name of your party, and your ballot will then be counted for every candidate, and as approval of party action on any constitutional amendment, of that party on your ballot." By this device, according to Victor Rosewater, "the negligent, easier-way voter would be transferred from the 'against' column to the 'for' column though he might have had no intention of supporting the amendment."[37]

The system was not applied until the election of 1906 when both Democrats and Republicans endorsed an amendment creating a Board of Railway Commissioners; the amendment was overwhelmingly approved. In 1907, the legislature replaced party conventions with direct primaries as nominating methods and included in the law a provision permitting voters at primaries to give a party's blessing to amendments. The parties could no longer avoid taking a stand for or against changes in the constitution.

In 1907, the Nebraska Supreme Court sanctioned the party circle law, after the Ohio Supreme Court had upheld a similar law in that state.[38] In rejecting the argument that the law prevented voters from making separate decisions on each proposal, the court responded that the voter still had the choice of whether or not to vote a straight ticket ballot. Further, the court declared:

> It is not the duty of the court to suggest methods of submitting constitutional amendments to the vote of the people. The duty of devising and applying such methods is devolved upon the legislature and, unless the method adopted by the legislature is manifestly a violation of the constitution, and unless it clearly appears that the

---

[37] Victor Rosewater, "A Curious Chapter in Constitution-Changing," *Political Science Quarterly* 36 (1921): 413.

[38] State v. Laylin, 69 Ohio 1.

> method adopted by the legislature will not make it practicable for the voters to express their judgment as to each amendment proposed, the courts are not at liberty to disregard the will of the legislature.[39]

Between 1906 and 1918, sixteen amendments were proposed. Ten were approved with the help of the party-circle law. The measures so approved included municipal home rule and the creation of a Board of Commissioners for State Institutions. The most dramatic change, however, was the institution of the popular initiative and referendum. By that amendment in 1912, "the people reserve to themselves power to propose laws and amendments to the constitution, and to enact or reject the same at the polls independent of the legislature." The provision, as amended in 1920, continues to be a critical element in the constitutional system of Nebraska.

Even with the possibility of amending the constitution, there was a feeling among some leaders that the document of 1875 needed a more extensive overhaul. For many others, caution seemed to be called for since there were new interests in the state promoting what some saw as radical ideas—for example, prohibitionists and suffragettes—so that conservatives were fearful of unleashing a chain of events they could not control. The Nonpartisan League, following its success in North Dakota, had moved into Nebraska and its program for economic reform terrified established business interests. The real reform impulse, however, was no longer represented by agrarian radicals, and Populism was less influential. By 1910, the progressive wing of the Republican Party was pressing for change, and its agenda differed from that of the Populists.

As Robert Cherny described the difference, "populists advocated a reordering of social values and a redistribution of wealth and economic power. Republican progressives favored no such radical change, proposing regulation but never redistribution."[40] The Progressives, best represented by George W. Norris, were in the tradition of "good government" reformers of the early twentieth century. Tinkering with the machinery of government would provide economy and efficiency, as well as inspire civic virtue among the people.

In 1914, the Nebraska Popular Government League was formed to promote the idea of a constitutional convention. In one of the League's publications, Judge Arthur Wray developed a theme to be repeated often: "It is true, at nearly every election, we are amending, or attempting to amend our constitution. At best, it is an old garment, patched up, with many misfits. What we need, and should have in Nebraska, is a constitutional convention to revise, make modern, and bring up to date our fundamental law."[41] Among the features of the progressive

---

[39] State v. ex rel. Thompson V. Winnett, 78 Neb 391.

[40] Robert W. Cherny, *Populism, Progressivism and the Transformation of Nebraska Politics*, 1885–1915 (Lincoln: University of Nebraska Press, 1981), 160.

[41] Arthur G. Wray, "A Constitutional Convention: Next Logical Step," *The Nebraska Popular Government Bulletin* 1 (June 1914): 2.

platform which most excited the Nebraska reformers were "the short ballot, installation of merit systems, a unicameral legislature, a modern method of taxation, and new and better judicial procedures."[42]

Other forces in Nebraska politics were able to restrain their enthusiasm for a convention, and the efforts to call one languished in the legislature. The League than announced a long-term strategy. Through the initiative, they would amend the constitution so that a convention would be called in October 1919 with only minimal involvement by the legislature. The threat worked and the legislature called an election on the question of a convention at the November 1918 election. The voters approved it by the wide margin of 121,830 to 44,491.

But by 1918, the political stew in Nebraska had become even spicier. World War I left some ugly scars in the state, as the large German population felt they had been abused by the nativist hysteria caused by the war effort. So strong was the anti-German sentiment that the legislature passed a law prohibiting the teaching of foreign languages, an action that the U.S. Supreme Court was to find in violation of the Fourteenth Amendment in the leading case of *Meyer v. Nebraska*.[43] The conservatives were alarmed by various groups of reformers, such as the Popular Government League or the Non-Partisan League, and hastened to point out that many of their members were foreign-born. Most Nebraskans, like other Americans, were weary of years of political turmoil and yearned for the "return to normalcy."

In November 1919, the 100 delegates to the convention were elected. A coalition of reform-minded groups called the "Progressive League" was opposed by a conservative group, the "New Nebraska Federation." The Federation fought what it saw as the socialist, bolshevist, and generally un-American tendencies of the other side. But for all the fury of the rhetoric of the campaign, most Nebraskans appeared indifferent and the election was marked by a very low turnout.

Professor John Senning and A. E. Sheldon, both stalwart Progressives, were disappointed by the convention and concluded that it had been dominated by the conservatives.[44] The judgment may be unfair. To be sure, the progressive, "good government" agenda was not approved. Several attempts at a short ballot for state government, including some elements of a commission form of executive, were voted down. The proposal for a unicameral legislature, sponsored by John Norton, died on a tie vote. However, even the conservatives in the convention could agree that there were some serious defects in the 1875 document that

[42] A. B. Winter, "Constitutional Revision in Nebraska: A Brief History and Commentary," *Nebraska Law Review* 40 (1961): 585.

[43] 262 US 390 (1923).

[44] John P. Senning, "The Nebraska Constitutional Convention," *National Municipal Review* 9 (1920): 421–26; A. E. Sheldon, "The Nebraska Constitutional Convention, 1919–1920," *American Political Science Review* 15 (1921): 391–97.

needed to be remedied, and while they avoided a wholesale revision, they were able to solve some of the more serious problems of state government. At least they seem to have agreed that the state constitution should be brought into line with what had become the practice in state government. The party circle law was only one of the constitutional subterfuges that was rectified.

The most pressing need for effective twentieth-century government was in the executive branch. The economizers of 1875 thought they had put a definite limit to the expansion of government, but they could not have foreseen the demands that citizens were now placing on the state. Among the little ruses that allowed Nebraska to function was a determination by the supreme court that stenographers were not those awful "clerks" whose employment was specifically prohibited.

Much more serious was the proscription against any further state officers. As functions were added to state government, they had to be assigned to one of the existing constitutional offices, a procedure that made real control of the executive branch almost impossible. The constitutional restrictions were the root cause of an issue in Nebraska which, for the modern student, is almost inexplicable. Republican Governor Samuel McKelvie, in anticipation of approval by the convention of greater executive flexibility, advocated in 1918 the creation of a civil administrative code. The code would have brought under more logical departments the various government functions which had been hidden here, there, and everywhere to get around the letter of the constitution. The Democrats, now led by the younger Bryan brother, Charles, turned the code into a controversial issue that was to shape campaigns for the next decade. Repeal of the code became the Democrat's raison d'être and, in 1922, "Brother Charlie" was able to parlay it into the governorship.

A major amendment proposed by the convention permitted the legislature to create other executive offices. The delegates also reaffirmed that the governor holds the "supreme executive power," but it did not go as far as the Progressives wished in making that power a reality. The governor was still in competition with other elected state officials, and the references to an executive budget were rudimentary at best. Since there are few constitutional restrictions, the legislature has up to the present felt free to insulate specific government officials and programs from effective gubernatorial control.

As for the legislature, while unicameralism was deferred, some adjustments were made, especially in terms of salaries and length of terms. The court system was also revised significantly by the convention; among the innovations here was a requirement for a extraordinary majority of the supreme court to rule a legislative act unconstitutional. In matters involving elections, the members lowered the requirements for the use of the initiative and referendum. The election by districts to various boards and commissions was also approved.

In substantive matters, the members of the convention appear to have been rather liberal in that they gave to the legislature the power to set up a commission on industrial relations to oversee labor disputes in the state, to set a minimum wage, and to regulate the employment conditions of women and children. The state government was also granted permission to modernize its revenue system with a provision that allowed the use of alternatives to the property tax. Finally, the Convention added four important provisions relating to water resources.

The nativism inspired by the war was evident in some propositions. English was now to be the official language of the state and the only medium for instruction in the public schools, a moved aimed at those communities in which German was the common language of the people. The status of non-citizens was changed by the provision that "the rights of aliens in respect to the acquisition, enjoyment and descent of property may be regulated by law."

In a final important change, the convention clarified the method for amending the constitution. A simple majority of voters voting on a specific proposal was sufficient, if the affirmative vote was equal to at least 35 percent of the total vote cast in the election. The party circle law was now obsolete.

At the special election held on September 21, 1920, a very light turnout approved all of the forty-one amendments submitted by the convention. Although the suffrage question was still not resolved, the convention provided for separate ballot boxes for males and females. Only one measure was rejected by the men but carried when the women's vote was added to the total; it dealt with the size of the state senate.

Professor Senning complained that the convention was very conservative and, moreover, its "changes in the structure of both legislative and administrative systems ignore entirely modern scientific principles of government."[45] But Nebraskans were not in a mood to be lectured about the "principles" of good government. They were satisfied that the convention had gone far enough. Any further changes would occur in an erratic and highly unscientific manner.

1920 TO THE PRESENT

The delegates to the 1919–20 convention apparently did an excellent job in meeting the demands of Nebraskans for constitutional change. Not only did all forty-one amendments pass, but in the remainder of the decade only two more questions were submitted to the voters, both of which were rejected. In the 1930s, thirteen proposals were put to the citizens and six were accepted. The most notable change was the switch to a non-partisan, unicameral legislature. Professor Senning, a leader of the unicameral movement, at last had some version of good scientific government.

The political folklore of the state says that unicameralism was on the same ballot as amendments for the repeal of prohibition and the authorization of

[45] Senning, "The Nebraska Constitutional Convention," 426.

parimutuel betting; unicameralism rode in on the votes of drinkers and gamblers who voted for everything to make sure they got their favorite vices. The reasons behind this dramatic reform, however, are more substantial. The idea had been popular in Nebraska for some time and when Senator Norris put his considerable energy and prestige behind the idea, it gathered momentum. The bicameral legislature, elected in 1932, contained many freshmen and its performance was judged to be poor. And of course, as a reason for unicameralism, one should not overlook a critical selling point for Cornhuskers—one house would obviously be cheaper than two.

The 1940s was a slow decade for constitutional change, with only two out of seven proposals being accepted by the voters. But the pace picked up in the 1950s. Voters considered twenty-nine proposed amendments and rejected only ten of them. A proposal in 1952 clarified the number of delegates and the method of selection for future constitutional conventions, but no such convention was called. In the 1960s, it appeared to some that the amending process was getting out of hand. In that decade, fifty-eight propositions were submitted to the people, of which thirty-four were approved.

The election of 1966 was particularly sobering for students of direct democracy. Nebraska was one of the last states to conclude that the property tax was not an efficient means for financing state government and, reluctantly, Governor Norbert Tiemann and the legislature hammered out a bill instituting an income tax system. Irate citizens hit the streets armed with petitions to call a referendum on the measure. At the same time, another petition was circulated calling for a constitutional amendment to abolish the state's real property tax. When the election was over, Nebraskans said, in effect, "No taxation, with or without representation" since both measures passed. The state was faced with the possibility that it would not be able to raise any money. The crisis was averted when the legislature agreed on a combined sales and income tax system, but some political leaders were concerned about the viability of their system of government.

The legislature, in 1969, approved LB 244 which established a Nebraska Constitutional Revision Commission. This twelve-member body was charged with the responsibility of making "a complete study of the Constitution of Nebraska to determine what changes, if any, should be made therein. The commission shall place special emphasis on simplifying and condensing the Constitution for the purpose of giving the Legislature broad powers, rather than numerous individual amendments."[46] The commission was to submit its recommendations to the Executive Board of the Legislative Council and thence to the whole legislature which would determine which proposals to put before the people. The Commission presented its report on September 24, 1970.

---

[46] LB 244, Legislative Bills, 80th Session, 1969.

Concluding that the "current Constitution is too good a document to be discarded," the Commission sought out places for improvement, "consistent with the philosophy of government that Nebraska has always had."[47] The Commission worked for more than a year and submitted to the legislature over one hundred suggestions. From the list, the legislature eventually submitted forty-nine proposals to the voters at three consecutive elections: the general election of 1970, the primary election of 1972, and the general election of 1972. Citizens were in a particularly positive mood at the 1972 election since all sixteen amendments were accepted. Over the two-year period, thirty-eight changes were made in the constitution.

While the voters seem to have trusted the wisdom of the Commission and the legislature, it is interesting to note that six of the rejected proposals dealt with legislative compensation and procedures. The rejection rate, as well as the controversy might have been greater if the legislature had passed on to the voters all the Commission's proposals. While many of the changes concerned the removal of obsolete language and other minor details, some of the recommendations were more innovative. No doubt reflecting the concern over the fiscal fight of 1966, the Commission had recommended that revenue and appropriations matters be declared off-limits for the initiative and referendum process: "Only the Legislature, through its process of deliberation and debate, should be permitted to legislate in these areas."[48] In the executive branch, the Commission wanted to remove the auditor and treasurer as elected officials. The Commission also advocated the streamlining of the amending process, including the establishment of a decennial constitutional convention. None of these proposals made it past the legislature.

AMENDING THE CONSTITUTION

Since 1972, the legislature has continued to modify the constitution in a piecemeal fashion, but none of the amendments has changed the document in a significant way. The Constitution of 1875, heavily amended, has no serious enemies at the present and there is no agitation for a complete revision. For the various parts of the Nebraska political equation, the document provides adequate scope for their maneuvering. Part of the durability of the constitution may be the apparent ease with which significant interests can bring an amendment for consideration by the voters.

Presently, the constitution can be amended in three ways. The most common method is by legislative action. If three-fifths of the forty-nine-member unicameral legislature approves, a proposal can be submitted at the next election for

[47] *Report of the Nebraska Constitutional Revision Commission* (Lincoln, 1970), September 24, 1970, viii.

[48] Ibid., 29.

members of the legislature. If four-fifths of the legislature feels it necessary, a special election can be called. The proposal must appear on a ballot separate from that of the candidates. The amendment is approved if a majority of the voters on the specific issue are in favor, and if the majority represents at least 35 percent of the total number of votes cast at the election.

Secondly, three-fifths of the legislature can recommend to the voters that a convention be called to revise, amend, or change the constitution. If the voters approve, the legislature, at its next session shall provide by law for such a meeting. Again, a majority representing at least 35 percent of the total vote is needed to approve the calling of a convention. The convention shall consist of no more than 100 members who are to be nominated and elected by district. Any proposals coming from the convention must be approved by the voters. Nebraska has had no state constitutional convention since 1919–20.

Finally, the citizens can amend the Nebraska Constitution through the use of the initiative. A petition signed by ten percent of the voters will put the matter on the ballot, provided that the signatures are distributed in such a way to include five percent of the voters in each of two-fifths of the state's ninety-three counties. If the signatures are valid, the secretary of state must put the question to the voters at the next general election. The same measure cannot be submitted to the voters more than once every three years. If conflicting measures are approved at the same election, the one with the highest number of "yes" votes will be governing.

In a more innocent era, most Nebraskans would have agreed that the initiative was a method for constitutional change which "represents the utmost in popular sovereignty and has been proven a desirable and successful supplemental method of amending the constitution."[49] Therefore, it came as a shock to Nebraskans (or to that part of them who pay attention to such matters) that this one legacy of Populism, this defiant answer to the question, "Shall the people rule?", could be compromised. In 1986, three state senators, the most powerful lobbyist in the state, and several other people were charged with improprieties in the circulation of petitions to get on the ballot a measure dealing with a state lottery. Immediately, visions of being Californicated were raised; the instruments of direct democracy were being sullied by paid petition circulators, high-powered public relations firms, and powerful interest groups who could buy their amendments to the constitution. "Eternal watchfulness in the citizens," as an inscription on the state capitol enjoins, "is the salvation of the state." The moralists in Nebraska politics are on guard, but the purity of the old system has been lost.

Since 1875, through legislative recommendations, proposals from the convention, and through citizen initiatives, Nebraskans have had 290 opportunities

---

[49] Betty Peterson, "Procedures of Amending the Nebraska Constitution," *Nebraska Law Review* 22 (1943): 44.

Table 1

Years	Submitted		Approved		Rejected		% Approved
1882–1890	8		1		7		12.5
1892–1900	14		0		14		0
1902–1910	5		3		2		60.0
1912–1920	12	(3)	7	(1)	5	(2)	58.3
Convention	41		41		0		100.0
1922–1930	4	(1)	1		3	(1)	25.0
1932–1940	13	(3)	6	(2)	7	(1)	46.2
1942–1950	6	(3)	1	(1)	5	(2)	16.7
1952–1960	37	(3)	27	(1)	10	(2)	73.0
1962–1970	66	(3)	49	(1)	17	(2)	74.2
1972–1980	59		40		19		67.8
1982–1990*	25	(4)	18	(2)	7	(2)	72.0
TOTAL	290	(20)	194	(8)	96	(12)	66.9

* Including primary election of 1992
(0) indicates amendments proposed by citizen initiative
Source: Nebraska Blue Book, 1990–91.

to change their constitution. They have approved 194 amendments and have rejected ninety-six for an approval rate of 66.9 percent. Table 1 indicates that the rate of change has varied over the decades, with the largest number of amendments coming between 1962 and 1980.

What subjects have occupied the attention of the keepers of the constitution? Proposals dealing with budgets, taxation, assessment, and other revenue matters have been the most popular—or better said, because of their unpopularity have been most often discussed. A number of changes in the three branches of government have also been presented to the voters.

The proposals rejected since 1920 are also indicative of the interests of Nebraskans. By far, the most distasteful proposals for Nebraskans were those dealing with legislative compensation. One can admire the persistence of the legislature or the consistency of the voters, but thirteen plans for increasing legislative pay were rejected, thus continuing a tradition of stinginess begun in territorial days. Issues related to taxation and assessment have also been unpopular.

Of the 290 propositions put to the voters, twenty were initiated by the citizens themselves. Eight have been approved and twelve rejected. The eight citizeninitiated amendments have included some important questions. The unicameral legislature, the abolition of closed shops (the "right to work" amendment) and, most recently, the right to bear arms all started with the petition. Overall, the initiative route to constitutional change has been taken most often by those interested in what we might call "lifestyle" issues. If we could find some oldtimer who had signed every petition in the last sixty years, he or she could be a family farmer who owns a gun, hates any form of taxation, and likes to play the ponies, slot machines, bingo, and the lotteries. Such a person is not participating in the process as a disinterested student of the science of government.

CONCLUSION

The Constitution of 1875 is alive and well as a brief summary of events in a single year will indicate. In 1991, the Nebraska Supreme Court found that the state's personal property tax was unconstitutional, thus beginning the worst fiscal crisis since 1966. One state senator was forced to resign his position with a state college, while at least three others faced the choice of service in either the legislative or executive branch since the supreme court said they cannot do both. A man sat on Death Row awaiting a final decision about the legality of the constitution's system for dispensing clemency. The governor tested the meaning of the constitutional phrase "for cause" in an effort to dismiss three members of the Board of Pardons. The Democratic governor was also engaged in a running feud with the Republican attorney general over who gets to decide when the state goes to court. The state's lawyers and educators were anxiously awaiting the first decisions by the court of appeals and the post-secondary education coordinating commission, both created in the election of 1990. The final chapters appeared to have been written by the courts in two of the state's most controversial issues over the last decade: the limits on corporate farming and the reimbursement of depositors in a failed savings and loan company.

All that is the purpose of a constitution. It functions, as in Nebraska, as an arena within which some issues can be raised while some issues can finally be resolved. In that sense, the Constitution of 1875 is a success.

PART TWO
The Nebraska Constitution and Commentary

The following is a section-by-section commentary on the Nebraska Constitution, including remarks on the historical background of significant provisions and the interpretation of the sections by the Nebraska Supreme Court. Comparisons will be made with the Constitution of 1866 and with the rejected Constitution of 1871. The 1871 document is emphasized because the published proceedings of the convention give us the best introduction to the issues dominating the 1870s.

The Nebraska Constitution of 1875 is an unwieldy document and although its 20,000 words do not qualify it as one of the longest state constitutions, it is, in places, unnecessarily involved. As we indicated in our historical analysis, Nebraskans are not quite sure about their government (or their governors) and they have chosen to erect numerous restraints. Moreover, as Professor A. B. Winter observed, politicians have chosen to add, often after a campaign by special interests, powers that the state already had.[1] We do not intend to give equal attention in our commentary to every word or every section or to spend too much time on subjects only of intense interest to specialists. Rather, our intention here is to illuminate the salient features of the state's basic law and how Nebraskans have chosen to govern themselves.

---

[1] A. B. Winter, "The State Constitution," in Robert D. Miewald, ed., *Nebraska Government and Politics* (Lincoln: University of Nebraska Press, 1984), 13–14.

The text discussed below is that found in *Constitution of the State of Nebraska*, 1991 edition, prepared by the office of the Secretary of State. The text of the 1992 amendments is found in Legislative Resolution 291CA (1992). The headings for each section are taken from the version of the Nebraska Constitution in Volume 2 of the *Nebraska Revised Statutes, Reissue of* 1988.

PREAMBLE

> We, the people, grateful to Almighty God for our freedom, do ordain and establish the following declaration of rights and frame of government, as the Constitution of the State of Nebraska.

The first ten words of the Preamble are identical to those of the 1866 Constitution, but the earlier version then went off in a paraphrase of the U.S. Constitution. The Preamble of 1871, copied from the Illinois Constitution of 1870, was as much a prayer as it was a statement of political principles.

For more than a century, the Preamble was regarded as a nice rhetorical flourish which emphasized the idea that political power was grounded in "the people." In 1986, a more formidable function for the words was suggested. The plaintiffs in *Omaha National Bank v. Spire* argued that the Preamble was a remarkable threshing machine which could separate the wheat from the chaff of constitutional amendments. In their view, the Constitution was confined by the Preamble to describing only declarations of rights or the frame of government. An amendment approved in 1982 limiting the ability of corporations to own farmland (see Art. XII, Sec. 8, below) was neither and must therefore be considered a statute which could be changed or eliminated by ordinary legislative action.

The Nebraska Supreme Court disagreed, saying:

> First, the Preamble is not a part of the Constitution, but only a general statement of purpose. . . . Secondly, even if the Preamble were to be considered to be an operative part of our Constitution, it could be amended in any way that any other part of the Constitution may be amended. No part of the Constitution, including the Preamble, is inviolable. To hold to the contrary would give absolute finality to a portion of the Constitution and would thwart the express will of the people when they retained the right to amend their Constitution.

In other words, the Preamble merely acts as a cover page for the following constitutional text and the real content of the Constitution is defined by the actual words, the relevant case law, and the custom and usage which have shaped the Constitution of 1875.

Article I

Bill of Rights

The Bill of Rights, like its counterpart in the U.S. Constitution, defines basic personal liberties, identifies the elements of the criminal justice system, and establishes safeguards for personal property. The Nebraska version also provides for access to the courts to protect these rights. Although state courts are able to interpret the protection provided by their constitutions more liberally than the U.S. Supreme Court, most follow the leads indicated by the federal judiciary. Nebraska is no exception here. For example, in matters of criminal justice, Barry Latzer found that Nebraska was one of the states least likely to deviate from U.S. Supreme Court guidelines.[2]

The Bill of Rights of the 1866 Constitution did not break much new ground but instead followed the pattern set by the U.S. Constitution. The authors borrowed from the Virginia Declaration of Rights the words: "The blessing of a free government can only be maintained by a firm adherence to justice, moderation, temperance, frugality, and virtue, and by frequent recurrence to fundamental principles." The writers of 1871 modified this little lecture to read "A frequent recurrence to the fundamental principles of civil government is absolutely necessary to preserve the blessings of liberty" (Art. I, Sec. 24). How those statements could be implemented is not clear.

---

[2] Barry Latzer, *State Constitutions and Criminal Justice* (Westport, Conn.: Greenwood Press, 1991), 160–61.

The current Constitution retains most of the points covered in the two earlier documents. The text of 1875 has remained largely unchanged, with one section of the article added in 1920 and one section repealed in 1990. Six other amendments to the Bill of Rights have been approved.

In interpreting the Bill of Rights, the Nebraska Supreme Court "will consider its history, the development of the evil sought to be restrained by its provisions, the established laws, usages and customs of the country at the time of its adoption and the scope of the remedy its terms imply" (First Trust Co. of Lincoln v. Smith, 1938).

SECTION 1. STATEMENT OF RIGHTS

All persons are by nature free and independent, and have certain inherent and inalienable rights; among these are life, liberty, the pursuit of happiness, and the right to keep and bear arms for security or defense of self, family, home, and others, and for all lawful common defense, hunting, recreational use, and all other lawful purposes, and such rights shall not be denied or infringed by the state or any subdivision thereof. To secure these rights, and the protection of property, governments are instituted among people, deriving their just powers from the consent of the governed.

The stately Jeffersonian prose is certainly familiar, but Nebraskans, on a couple of occasions, have seen fit to elaborate on the nature of those fundamental natural rights. The writers of 1871 followed Illinois by inserting the words "and the protection of property" and they were retained in the 1875 Constitution. A more discordant note was added by the 1988 amendment which suggests that, among other things, skeet shooting is one of those inherent and inalienable rights of all people. The clause beginning, "and the right to keep and bear arms . . . " was approved by the voters after a petition campaign orchestrated by the National Rifle Association succeeded in getting it on the ballot. The NRA and other opponents of gun control felt the change was necessary in light of the U.S. Supreme Court's refusal to extend the protection of the Second Amendment to state government.

The passage of the "right to bear arms" amendment caused some concern that the state's gun regulations were obsolete, but the supreme court eventually ruled that little had changed. The possession of certain types of firearms was still illegal since the state could exercise its police power to determine what are "lawful purposes" (State v. Comeau, 1989). In *State v. LaChapelle* (1990), the court concluded that a law banning the possession of machine guns, short rifles, or short shotguns was valid especially since it was directed at weapons which are "used almost exclusively for a criminal purpose." Laws preventing felons from possessing firearms are also acceptable (State v. Harrington, 1990). In approving the

1988 amendment, Nebraskans did not inadvertently repeal the death penalty through a reaffirmation of the idea that there is an "inherent and inalienable" right to life (Anderson v. Gunter, 1990).

The "right to bear arms" amendment, it seems safe to say, has had little impact on the power of the state to regulate firearms. The 1991 session of the legislature spent much time debating a waiting period for the purchase of handguns. That the final product was watered down to the point of meaninglessness was a function of political and not of constitutional considerations.

Finally, concerning Section 1, it should be noted that the authors of 1875 did change "all men" to "all persons," indicating some degree of sensitivity to questions of gender equality.

SECTION 2. SLAVERY PROHIBITED

There shall be neither slavery nor involuntary servitude in this state, otherwise than for punishment of crime, whereof the party shall have been duly convicted.

Although they did not allow blacks the right to vote or to serve in the legislature, the framers of 1866 showed their dedication to Republican principles by giving the anti-slavery provision a prominent position in the Bill of Rights. The language of the section was unchanged in the 1871 and the 1875 Constitutions.

The Nebraska Supreme Court agrees with the meaning of "involuntary servitude" stated by the U.S. Supreme Court as limited to the use or threat of physical force or legal coercion to extract labor from an unwilling worker. There is nothing in Section 2 "which requires different treatment than does the Constitution of our nation" (Abbott v. Gould, Inc., 1989).

SECTION 3. DUE PROCESS OF LAW

No person shall be deprived of life, liberty, or property, without due process of law.

The Constitution of 1866 did not include a general "due process" clause. The language here, from Illinois, was used in 1871 and carried over into the 1875 Constitution. The words are identical to the clause of the Fourteenth Amendment to the U.S. Constitution. Unlike that amendment, this section does not concern itself with "equal protection of the laws." Article III, Section 18, dealing with special legislation, insures Nebraskans that similar persons will be treated similarly by the state (Porter v. Jensen, 1986). In some instances, the supreme court has regarded equal protection as synonymous with Article III, Section 18 and has even referred to "the equal protection clauses of the U.S. and Nebraska Constitutions" (State v. Kubik, 1990).

The requirements of due process do prevent the legislature from passing laws that are vague or overbroad (State v. Sinica, 1985). Vagueness and overbreadth are conceptually distinct "constitutional vices." In the court's words, "an overbroad statute need lack neither clarity nor precision, and a vague statute need not reach constitutionally protected activity" (State v. Copple, 1987). A statute is overbroad if it "prohibits the exercise of constitutionally protected conduct, such as the exercise of First Amendment rights" (State v. Frey, 1984).

In *State v. Sailors* (1984), the court spelled out the test for vagueness:

> The test for determining whether a statute is vague is whether it forbids or requires the doing of an act in terms so vague that men of common intelligence must necessarily guess at its meaning and differ as to its application. . . . A statute will not be deemed vague if it uses ordinary terms which find adequate interpretation in common usage and understanding. . . . In determining whether a statute is vague and therefore does not give a defendant adequate notice that his conduct is proscribed, the statute must be examined in light of the conduct with which the defendant is charged. . . . The prohibition against vagueness does not invalidate a statute simply because it could have been drafted with greater precision. The test is whether the defendant could reasonably understand that his conduct was proscribed by the statute.

In *State v. Adkins* (1976), the supreme court declared unconstitutional the Controlled Substances Act which had made it a felony for a person to be in a place where he or she knew illegal substances were being used. The law was too vague since in application it left to conjecture the line between what is lawful and unlawful. As the court noted in *Markham v. Brainard* (1965), a law that makes criminal an act which the utmost care and circumspection would not enable one to avoid is invalid. The question to be decided is not poor draftsmanship of the law but instead whether the words give sufficient warning to people of reasonable intelligence that certain actions are forbidden (State v. Robinson, 1979).

Violations of due process are noted most often in the procedures established by the legislature or the courts. When an individual's case is being adjudicated, due process requires, at a minimum, that the person must be given a meaningful opportunity to be heard (Carroll v. Moore, 1988). If a law threatens to place a financial burden on property owners, there must be notice and an opportunity to give evidence before a unit of government is empowered to impose that burden (Schutte v. Schmitt, 1956). This stricture applies only when liberty or property is the subject and does not protect privileges, such as the authority to operate a motor vehicle (Hadden v. Aitken, 1952). The proceedings must be appropriate for a particular subject matter and must affect all with an identifiable class (State ex rel. Nebraska State Bar Assn. v. Jensen, 1960). Due process does not require any specific form or method of state procedures so long as the essence of the procedures protect the right to notification, hearing, and defense (Hroch v. City of Omaha, 1987).

That essence is the right of affected parties to be heard. This includes notice to a person whose right is affected by a proceeding, a reasonable opportunity to refute or defend against a charge or accusation, a reasonable opportunity to confront and cross-examine adverse witnesses and present evidence on the charge or accusation, representation by counsel, and a hearing before an impartial decision maker (In re Interest of L.V., 1992).

The aforementioned requirements of notice and hearing are applicable only in governmental decisions adjudicative in nature; "legislative action is exempt from the constitutional protection of procedural due process" (State ex rel. Spire v. Northwestern Bell Tel. Co., 1989). The legislature still has to exercise some care in the substance of its enactments. The courts, for example, can review legislatively set utility rates, such as those for cable TV subscribers, to determine whether "they are so arbitrary and unreasonable as to be confiscatory" and thus an unconstitutional taking of property (Bard v. Cox Cable of Omaha, Inc., 1987).

The courts must pay special attention to those instances where the legislature's exercise of its police power interacts with the citizen's right to the use of personal property. In 1970, the Nebraska Supreme Court was asked to determine if a statute which restricted liquor wholesalers from giving discounts to some retailers violated Section 3. Finding that the liquor industry was one "susceptible to regulation" for the public good, the court held that the statute was not arbitrary, capricious, or unreasonable even though it did restrain trade (Central Markets West, Inc. v. State, 1970). A few years later, the court ruled that a similar statute regulating the liquor industry created a monopoly and was a trade barrier; the statute was an unreasonable invasion of the property rights of individuals since the law bore no real or substantial relationship to furthering the public health, safety or welfare (Louis Finocchiaro, Inc. v. Nebraska Liquor Control Comm., 1984). It would seem that, currently, the legislature must make a clear case that its regulations are not an unreasonable burden on the enjoyment of property if a statue is not to be found in violation of the due process of law.

SECTION 4. RELIGIOUS FREEDOM

All persons have a natural and indefeasible right to worship Almighty God according to the dictates of their own consciences. No person shall be compelled to attend, erect or support any place of worship against his consent, and no preference shall be given by law to any religious society, nor shall any interference with the rights of conscience be permitted. No religious test shall be required as a qualification for office, nor shall any person be incompetent to be a witness on account of his religious beliefs; but nothing herein shall be construed to dispense with oaths and affirmations. Religion, morality, and knowledge, however, being essential to good government, it shall be the duty of the Legislature to pass suitable laws to protect every religious denomination in the peaceable enjoyment of its own mode of public worship, and to encourage schools and the means of instruction.

Section 4 guarantees the free exercise of religion and prevents the state from giving preferential treatment to any particular religion. The language in this section is almost identical to that of the 1866 Constitution. The 1871 Convention took a more negative stance, stressing the limitations on the practice of religion. Following Illinois, it said that "liberty of conscience" could not be used "to dispense with oaths or affirmations, excuse acts of licentiousness, or justify practices inconsistent with the peace and safety of the state."

By 1875, Nebraska contained a number of mutually antagonistic denominations so the framers were anxious not to permit the state to assume a role in sectarian activities, particularly education. Article VII, Section 11, below, requires that "All public schools shall be free of sectarian instruction," thus allowing Nebraska to avoid many controversies, such as school prayers, that have concerned the federal courts (Gaffney v. State Department of Education, 1974).

There has nonetheless been considerable tension between the state and religious groups over the question of sectarian education. The issue of religious freedom was brought to a head in the 1980s with the rise of fundamentalist congregations which demanded the right to operate "Christian schools" free from any sort of state oversight or regulation.

The struggle represented a classic confrontation of immovable object and irresistible force. On the one hand, the teaching profession was represented by the Nebraska Education Association, widely regarded in the early 1980s as the most potent lobbying force in the state. On the other were the fundamentalists who insisted that the public schools were hotbeds of sin and secular humanism. Moreover, they argued that the teaching of their children was an integral part of their religious practice and could not be controlled by the state. The Faith Baptist Church in Louisville, led by Reverend Everett Sileven, created its own school and proceeded to teach children in disregard of the rules of the Department of Education and particularly those concerning the credentials of teachers. In 1981, the court concluded that the state had a "compelling interest in the quality and ability of those who are to teach its young people" (State ex rel. Douglas v. Faith Baptist Church of Louisville). The teachers in the Christian schools had to demonstrate the same proficiency as those in the public schools.

The decision did not resolve the matter. Sileven and his congregation continued to defy the authorities, leading to the padlocking of the church school, the citing of Sileven for contempt of court, and the arrest of some parents. National attention focused on the little church in a small town in Nebraska. Even moderate politicians were dissatisfied with the court's dismissal of the claims of the church and were troubled by the argument of fundamentalist leaders that the question was not "teaching," that is, the idea that only those credentialed by the education establishment were capable of teaching others; rather, the issue was "learning"—did children in non-conventional programs learn as much as other students. A commission appointed in 1983 by Governor Robert Kerrey concluded that parents should be able to choose alternative curricula and teachers if test scores of their children were equal to the average of scores of students in the state. As Professor Richard Shugrue summarized the situation, "The underlying theory of the Commission's conclusion was that the state's interest is, in truth, in the result of education and not of the process by which the result is obtained."[3]

The commission recommendations were too much for the NSEA and its members. The profession was loathe to permit the power of certification to slip from its hands. Meanwhile, the tension continued and eventually the legislature realized it had to finesse some solution. In 1984, it approved a bill which, through a series of compromises, enabled non-conforming schools to continue while giving the appearance, at least, of ultimate control by the State Board of Education and the Department of Education. As Shugrue concluded, "The Nebraska experience demonstrates that a compromise, if not wholly satisfactory, can never the-less be hammered out. It can be refined without the continuous resort to litigation which marshalled the adversaries against one another."[4]

SECTION 5. FREEDOM OF SPEECH AND PRESS

> Every person may freely speak, write and publish on all subjects, being responsible for the abuse of the liberty and in all trials for libel, both civil and criminal, the truth when published with good motives, and for justifiable ends, shall be a sufficient defense.

The 1866 version of this section contained more detail about libel trials, which is not surprising since the writers were familiar with a brand of journalism that prized vituperation rather than objectivity. The current language was taken from the Illinois Constitution by way of the Constitution of 1871. The truth is not an absolute defense in a libel action. The truth must have been published "with good motives, and for justifiable ends."

It cannot be claimed that the Nebraska Supreme Court has added much to the jurisprudence of free expression. Its most recent decisions have dealt with the argument that certain statutes are overbroad by impinging on the rights protected by Section 5. The supreme court has rejected such arguments in a case

---

[3] Richard E. Shugrue, "An Approach to Mutual Respect: The Christian Schools Controversy," *Creighton Law Review* 18 (1984–85): 256.

[4] Ibid.

upholding the constitutionality of a law prohibiting false statements on an initiative petition (State v. Fellman, 1991). Another statute prohibiting obscene phone calls was found constitutional in *State v. Kipf* (1990). The court stated that the "portions of the statute before us are not impermissibly vague—they give fair notice of exactly what is forbidden in terms which are understandable to persons of ordinary intelligence." Furthermore, "We have held that Article I, Section 5, providing that every person 'may freely speak. . . being responsible for the abuse of that liberty' does not provide any greater protection regarding the overbreadth of the statutes than does the 1st Amendment to the U.S. Constitution." As to whether the law involves a legitimate state interest, the court said, yes. "The statute thus concerns itself with sexual speech which intrudes upon the privacy of innocent citizens, not for the purpose of communicating any thoughts, but for the purpose of causing mental discomfort by conjuring up repugnant sexual images. It therefore regulates in an area in which the state has a compelling interest."

In recent years, the supreme court has been called upon to evaluate statutes restricting the use of menacing words and actions by one person to another. Socalled "fighting words" or expressions deliberately intended to elicit a reaction from another are not protected by Section 5 (State v. Groves, 1985), nor are menacing threats of crime against another person (State v. Bourke, 1991). The same statutory prohibition against menacing action was upheld in *In re Interest of Siebert* (1986); in that case, a simulated karate kick was a form of expression not protected by the U.S. or Nebraska Constitutions.

SECTION 6. TRIAL BY JURY

> The right of trial by jury shall remain inviolate, but the Legislature may authorize trial by jury of a less number than twelve in courts inferior to the District Court, and may by general law authorize a verdict in civil cases in any court by not less than five-sixths of the jury.

The essence of this section—that a jury may consist of fewer than twelve members—was contained in all three versions of the Constitution. The amendment permitting a five-sixths decision in civil trials was added in 1920. The court said that Section 6 does not create a new right but only preserves one that existed under common law and statutes at the time the Constitution was adopted; thus, for example, one is not entitled to a jury trial for a charge of drunk driving under a municipal ordinance in the absence of statute (State v. Hauser, 1939).

The legislature has authorized five-sixths verdicts in civil cases (Neb Rev State 25-1125) and six-person juries in county court cases (Neb Rev State 25-2705). The legislature may also provide that the trial of petty offenses in violation of city or village ordinances can be tried without a jury (State v. Johnson, 1974).

SECTION 7. SEARCH AND SEIZURE

The right of the people to be secure in their persons, houses, papers, and effects against unreasonable searches and seizures shall not be violated; and no warrant shall issue but upon probable cause, supported by oath or affirmation, and particularly describing the place to be searched, and the person or thing to be seized.

The language in this section was taken directly from the Fourth Amendment and restated in nearly the same manner in the 1866, 1871, and 1875 Constitutions. The Nebraska court has suggested that its definition of unreasonable searches and seizures could be more stringent than that of federal constitutional law; in practice, the court has taken a fairly conservative interpretation (see State v. Havlat, 1986). Citizens may waive their rights under this section (State v. Juhl, 1989; State v. Prahin, 1990). However, the waiver must be voluntary and not a result of duress or coercion (State v. Walmsley, 1984).

Section 7 applies only to officers of the state. How far does it go in restricting searches of a residence by a private person? The supreme court has upheld the conviction of someone using illegal drugs after the evidence was uncovered by an off-duty police officer who was also the landlord of the residence searched (State v. Walker, 1990). The court also approved the search conducted by a private person who, although he had been contacted by the police beforehand was not "regarded as having acted as an instrument or agent of the State" (State v. Sardeson, 1989).

The Nebraska Supreme Court has not used this and other sections of the Bill of Rights to construct, as its federal counterpart, a right to privacy. In fact, in a case which the Hawaiian Supreme Court criticized as the "spectre of judicial self-emasculation" (Fergerstrom v. Hawaiian Ocean View Estates, 1958), the Nebraska court declared that "if such a right is deemed necessary or desirable, such right should be provided for by action of our Legislature and not by judicial legislation on the part of our courts" (Branson v. Ranks Army Store, 1955). One commentator did feel that there is some protection for privacy in the constitutional requirement that the truth alone is not a defense against libel.[5] The legislature has enacted statutory protection for the right to privacy (Neb Rev Stat 20-201 through 20-211).

SECTION 8. HABEAS CORPUS

The privilege of the writ of habeas corpus shall not be suspended, unless, in case of rebellion or invasion, the public safety requires it, and then only in such manner as shall be prescribed by law.

[5] Mary T. Powers, "The Right to Privacy in Nebraska," *Creighton Law Review* 13 (1980): 935–53.

Section 8 of the Constitution of 1866 contained the habeas corpus provision as well as other elements of criminal justice which were separated into Sections 8, 9, 10, and 12 of the 1875 Constitution. The writ of habeas corpus provides a method for a person being detained by the government official to have the court assess the lawfulness of that detention. It is an ancient right and, in a case asserting the power of the supreme court to review the denial of habeas corpus by a district court, Judge Chappell wrote that "the writ of habeas corpus is the precious safeguard of personal liberty and there is no higher duty imposed upon courts and legislative bodies than to maintain it unimpaired" (In re Application of Tail, Tail v. Olson, 1944).

"The availability of habeas corpus in Nebraska is restricted . . . ;" those seeking relief under this provision must prove that the sentence they received was absolutely void (Rust v. Gunter, 1988). Post-conviction relief is available only when a constitutional right has been infringed or violated (State v. Jackson, 1987). Those persons lawfully convicted of a crime do not have access to the writ (Kerns v. Grammer, 1987).

Habeas corpus is available in cases other than those involving a prisoner's incarceration. A mental patient may request review of his or her hospitalization (Almarez v. Hartmann, 1982); it may be invoked in child custody disputes (Green v. Green, 1965); and it can be applied in a review of relinquishment in adoption proceedings (D.S. v. United Catholic Social Services of Archdiocese of Omaha, 1988).

SECTION 9. BAIL; FINES; IMPRISONMENT; CRUEL AND UNUSUAL PUNISHMENT

All persons shall be bailable by sufficient sureties, except for treason, sexual offenses involving penetration by force or against the will of the victim, and murder, where the proof is evident or the presumption great. Excessive bail shall not be required, nor excessive fines imposed, nor cruel and unusual punishment inflicted.

Through bail, one accused of a crime can be released from custody pending trial after posting a suitable amount of money or other collateral with the court. The words "sexual offenses involving penetration by force or against the will of the victim" were added by an amendment approved in 1978. The court has held that the remaining words of the sentence apply to the addition. In order for one charged with a sexual offense to be ineligible for bail, it must appear to the trial court that either the proof of the charge is evident or the presumption is great (Parker v. Roth, 1979).

Excessive bail refers not to a specific dollar amount but instead to whether the amount is unreasonable and disproportionate to the crime charged in the indictment (In re Scott, 1893).

Although the state has not executed anyone since the mass murderer, Charles Starkweather, in 1959, the death penalty exists and several convicts are now on Death Row. The court believes that the legislature is empowered to select such punishment it considers most effective in deterring crime, provided that the penalty is not grossly disproportionate (State v. Ruzicka, 1984). The court found that the death penalty may deter offenders, is not always disproportionate to the crime of murder, and is not *per se* cruel and unusual punishment (State v. Simants, 1983). At the other extreme of crime and punishment, the court concluded that the loss of a driver's license as a punishment for drunk driving was not cruel or unusual (State v. Michalski, 1985).

According to the supreme court, the word "fine" has a distinct meaning: "it is a pecuniary punishment imposed by a lawful tribunal upon a person convicted of crime or misdemeanor" (Sinner v. State, 1935). Not all pecuniary penalties, however, are fines. A parental liability statute which imposes a liability only for the actual damage caused by children is not covered by Section 9, while a system of punitive, vindictive, or exemplary damages might violate the Constitution (Distinctive Printing and Packaging Co. v. Cox, 1989).

SECTION 10. PRESENTMENT OR INDICTMENT BY GRAND JURY; INFORMATION

No person shall be held to answer for a criminal offense, except in cases in which the punishment is by fine, or imprisonment otherwise than in the penitentiary, in case of impeachment, and in cases arising in the army and navy, or in the militia when in actual service in time of war or public danger, unless on a presentment or indictment of a grand jury; *Provided,* That the Legislature may by law provide for holding persons to answer for criminal offenses on information of a public prosecutor; and may by law, abolish, limit, change, amend, or otherwise regulate the grand jury system.

This section describes the way in which formal charges are brought against a person to set the stage for a criminal trial. It permits the traditional grand jury system, but it also allows the legislature to provide for the filing of information by the local prosecutor.

Among the specific provisions in the Bill of Rights, few were debated with greater intensity by the members of the 1871 Convention than the right to indictment by a grand jury. The defenders of the grand jury contended it was the foundation of republican government. Mr. J. Myers orated that, "It is true we have crushed kingly power in the United States, and this is the only power in the world which had done so; but there are other powers as insidious and powerful as a monarchy which require to be removed. There are individuals who will crush out individual rights of the citizen, and therefore I want this bulwark of liberty, this foundation stone of our early fathers, who contended for that right before King John, preserved; I want that we should continue this custom in our State, notwithstanding that a few grown States have undermined it." Former Chief Justice Oliver Mason rejected the idea of leaving it to the legislature to decide, since "Pray, what did the people send us here for, if it was not to stand up as barriers to the Legislature and other departments? Why, sir, if these things were safe, you need no Constitutional convention."

The opponents argued that "the system of grand juries grew up in the dark ages, and it is the work of barbarism. The time for the use of this kind of machinery in our courts, has passed, and the system should be done away with." Moreover, several speakers suggested, grand juries were too expensive and time-consuming; the presentment by a public prosecutor was cheaper. And from the high ideals expressed, the debaters drifted into a denunciation of the other side's mechanism: grand juries were likely to be made up of nasty neighbors who, in secret session, use their "little dirty hate and spite" to ruin innocent citizens. The prosecutor, said the defenders, "is generally some little pettifogging jackleg of a lawyer."[6]

The 1871 Constitution did not grant the legislature the power to modify grand juries, but the 1875 Convention settled on the current compromise language: the grand jury is provided, except when the legislature decides otherwise, which the Nebraska legislature has largely done, with the original legislation passed in 1885 (Neb Rev Stat 29-1601).

Indictment by a grand jury is not required by the Constitution (State v. Lehman, 1979), nor is it part of the due process guaranteed by the U.S. Constitution (Jackson v. Olson, 1946). Even charges of murder can be prosecuted through an information (Hawkins v. State, 1900).

SECTION 11. RIGHTS OF ACCUSED

In all criminal prosecutions the accused shall have the right to appear and defend in person or by counsel, to demand the nature and cause of accusation, and to have a copy thereof; to meet the witnesses against him face to face; to have process to compel the attendance of witnesses in his behalf; and a speedy public trial by an impartial jury of the county or district in which the offense is alleged to have been committed.

This section indicates the fundamental elements in one's "day in court" when charged with a criminal offense and thus contains many of the features also found in the Sixth Amendment of the U.S. Constitution. The rights of the

[6] *Official Report of Debates and Proceedings in the Nebraska Constitutional Convention,* vol. I (Lincoln: Nebraska State Historical Society, 1906), 224–46.

accused remained very nearly the same in all three constitutions. The present language was taken almost verbatim from the Illinois Constitution.

The court has refined the several elements of this section although it has had to remind convicted plaintiffs that they are not guaranteed a "perfect trial" (State v. Nearhood, 1989). In terms of the nature and cause of the accusation, the court has said that "the Nebraska constitutional provision requires that an information must inform the accused with reasonable certainty of the charge against him so that he may prepare his defense thereto and be enabled to plead the judgement therein as a bar to a later prosecution for the same offense" (State v. Harig, 1974). It is sufficient, however, for the charge to describe the crime in the language of the statute (State v. Jarrett, 1964).

The accused person is guaranteed the right to appear and defend in person (State v. Beasley, 1969). The right "to meet the witnesses against him face to face" is more specific than the guarantee in the Sixth Amendment "to be confronted with the witnesses against him." A limitation on the right to confrontation can be necessitated by a showing of the compelling public interest; in a case involving the testimony of child witness through closed-circuit television, the refusal to allow confrontation did not indicate a compelling need for protection of the witness (State v. Warford, 1986).

In criminal proceedings, the accused is entitled to a speedy public trial (State v. Brans, 1966). The statute implementing this section calls for a trial within six months of the filing of information or indictment (Neb Rev Stat 29-1207). However, the statutory and constitutional concepts of speedy trial must be considered independently, and so the courts can review any unreasonable delay prior to filing of an information (State v. Gingrich, 1982). Nevertheless, the right to a speedy trial is relative and depends upon the circumstances of the case; it is not denied if the delay can be satisfactorily explained by government and if the accused is brought to trial as soon as is reasonably possible (State v. McNitt, 1984). The courts must use a balancing test in each case to determine whether a speedy trial has been denied. That test involves the length of delay, the reason for the delay, the defendant's assertion of the right, and the prejudice of the delay to the defendant (State v. Trammel, 1992).

In civil cases, such as parental termination proceedings, a speedy trial is not constitutionally mandatory under this section (In re Interest of C.P., 1990).

A central element of a fair trial is the composition of the jury. Nebraska passed a law allowing prosecutors to exclude persons who are opposed to the imposition of the death penalty, that is, to create a "death-qualified" jury. When a convicted murderer claimed this law resulted in a jury which was not representative of a fair cross-section of the community and one which was predisposed to convict, the Nebraska Supreme Court upheld the practice. The jury is expected to apply the law and find the facts; the statute in question "serves to ensure that the petit jury is in fact impartial" (State v. Burchett, 1986). Jurors are apt to have opinions, but those opinions must not lead to a predisposition or partiality for or against the accused.

The accused has the right to effective counsel and the opportunity to make proper preparations for trial (Stagemeyer v. State, 1937). If the record does not show the accused had the opportunity for counsel, it may not be presumed that the right guaranteed by Section 11 was respected (State v. Ellis, 1984). The court has also set a standard by which to evaluate the defense of "ineffective counsel." In *State v. Carter* (1990), it was held that defendants must demonstrate deficient representation and that the deficient performance prejudiced the defense, "that is, a demonstration of reasonable probability that, but for counsel's deficient performance, the result of the proceeding would have been different." It is a high standard and one very similar to that established by the U.S. Supreme Court.

SECTION 12. EVIDENCE AGAINST SELF; DOUBLE JEOPARDY

No person shall be compelled, in any criminal case, to give evidence against himself, or be twice put in jeopardy for the same offense.

This language was taken from the 1866 Constitution which, in turn, followed the Fifth Amendment. The court has held that the protection against self-incrimination applies only in criminal cases (State v. Burrow, 1986) and that it does not apply in contempt of court proceedings (State ex rel. Wright v. Barlow, 1937).

In terms of double jeopardy, Nebraska does not recognize any standard higher than that articulated by the U.S. Supreme Court (State v. Munn, 1982). A retrial for the same crime after a hung jury does not violate this section (Shaffer v. State, 1932). The section does not prevent the successive prosecution of an individual by the U.S. and state governments (State v. Pope, 1971).

SECTION 13. JUSTICE ADMINISTERED WITHOUT DELAY

All courts shall be open, and every person, for any injury done him in his lands, goods, person or reputation, shall have a remedy by due course of law, and justice administered without denial or delay.

This section was retained from the two previous constitutions and is intended to ensure the prompt consideration of civil cases by the courts. The supreme court has ruled that this "provision of the Constitution does not create any new rights but is merely a declaration of a general fundamental principle. It is a primary duty of the courts to safeguard this declaration of right and remedy but where no right of action is given or remedy exists, under either the common law or some statute, this constitutional provision creates none" (Muller v. Nebraska Methodist Hospital, 1955).

Under the court's interpretation of this section, methods of conflict resolution which do not include the judiciary are highly suspect in Nebraska. "Arbitration agreements entered into before a dispute arises which purport to deny the parties the right to resort to the courts" are particularly offensive (Babb v. United Foods & Commercial Workers Local 271, 1989). In a doctrine going back to the 1880s and refined by Roscoe Pound when that noted legal authority served as a supreme court commissioner, contracts between parties which require arbitration are unenforceable since such a stipulation would "oust the courts of their legitimate jurisdiction" (German-American Ins. Co. v. Etherton, 1889). The submission of a future controversy to arbitration cannot be enforced since citizens cannot barter away their constitutional rights (Hartford Fire Ins. Co. v. Hon, 1902). In a more recent application of this doctrine, the Nebraska Supreme Court threw out a statute authorizing binding arbitration in labor disputes; contracts containing such provisions for handling a dispute before it arises "oust the courts of jurisdiction and are thus against public policy and therefore void and unenforceable" (State v. Nebraska Assn. of Public Employees, 1991). A statute setting up a system of referees for handling domestic disputes was also in violation of this section since the courts must be open to citizens at all levels of adjudication and not only on appeal (Drennen v. Drennen, 1988).

SECTION 14. TREASON

Treason against the state shall consist only in levying war against the state, or in adhering to its enemies, giving them aid and comfort. No person shall be convicted of treason unless on the testimony of two witnesses to the same overt act, or on confessions in open court.

Section 14 defines the crime of treason and describes the special evidence needed for conviction of the offense against the state. The provision is similar to that of other states and the U.S. Constitution. No cases involving treason have ever come before the Nebraska Supreme Court.

SECTION 15. PENALTIES; CORRUPTION OF BLOOD; TRANSPORTING OUT OF STATE PROHIBITED

All penalties shall be proportioned to the nature of the offense, and no conviction shall work corruption of blood or forfeiture of estate; nor shall any person be transported out of the state for any offense committed within the state.

This section is virtually identical to the language of 1871, except the earlier version contained the "cruel and unusual" clause. The present language is taken directly from the Illinois Constitution. The ban on transporting criminals refers to the old British practice of shipping convicts to penal colonies. The section applies to those convicted of crimes within Nebraska and is not the same as the interstate extradition of refugees from justice in other states as permitted by the U.S. Constitution. A penalty is not out of proportion unless it is so excessive as to shock the sense of mankind (McMahon v. State, 1904). The application of reasonable rules and regulation for the proper administration of a prison, even if some of the prisoner's rights are limited thereby, does not result in a disproportionate punishment (Meis v. Grammer, 1987).

The ancient doctrine of "corruption of blood" says that one convicted of certain crimes can be marked for life, even after release from prison. The "corrupted" person could never inherit property or transmit it to an heir, nor could he enjoy other basic rights. In a 1927 case upholding the right of a person once convicted of a felony to bring a civil suit, the court said the meaning of Section 15 was that "Civil death, as known to the common law, is without place in our jurisprudence" (Bosteder v. Duling, 1927).

SECTION 16. BILL OF ATTAINDER; RETROACTIVE LAWS; CONTRACTS; SPECIAL PRIVILEGES

No bill of attainder, ex post facto law, or law impairing the obligation of contracts, or making any irrevocable grant of special privileges or immunities shall be passed.

This section attempts to put restrictions on the power of the legislature, a question of considerable concern in the 1870s. The 1875 Constitution retrieved from the 1866 version the prohibition against bills of attainder, or legislative acts that establish the guilt of individuals or groups without benefit of judicial action. An ex post facto law is "one which applies to events occurring prior to enactment of the law and which disadvantages the offender affected by it" (State v. Peiffer, 1982). The prohibition applies only to penal or criminal matters (In re Estate of Rogers, 1946).

Contracts are written with reference to existing law and the law affecting a contract is read into it and is understood as a part of it. By changing the law, the legislature may not also impair the contractual rights implied by the old law (Pfeifer v. Ableidinger, 1958).

The Nebraska Supreme Court has taken a more limited view of the obligation of contract than its federal counterpart. In declaring unconstitutional a state law establishing a moratorium on making mortgage payments during the Great Depression, the court denied that the legislature had the emergency power to impair contractual agreements. The invalidated law probably would have survived scrutiny by the U.S. Supreme Court under the federal contracts clause (First Trust Co. of Lincoln v. Smith, 1938).

As an indication of the wariness with which Nebraskans of the 1870s regarded their legislators, the words forbidding "any irrevocable grant of special privilege" were created in 1871 and retained in 1875. The prohibition apparently was effective in stopping the granting of charters for banks and other dubious enterprises. Today, the words are read in the same way as the ban on special legislation in Article III, Section 18. Special classes can be created if there is a real and substantial difference among classes (State v. Edmunds, 1982; Colton v. Dewey, 1982).

The Nebraska Supreme Court has not made much use of the concept of "substantive due process," but at least on one occasion it staked out a position more stringent than that of the U.S. Supreme Court. The federal court upheld a Nebraska statute which limited the amount of the fee to be charged by private employment agencies; the law did not violate the Fourteenth Amendment (Olsen v. Nebraska, 1940). The case was remanded to the state court and there the law was held to be repugnant to the due process requirements of Section 3 (Boomer v. Olsen, 1943).

SECTION 17. MILITARY SUBORDINATE

The military shall be in strict subordination to the civil power.

According to Article IV, Section 14, the governor shall be the commander-in-chief of the military and naval forces of Nebraska. This section has never been litigated.

SECTION 18. SOLDIER'S QUARTERS

No soldier shall in time of peace be quartered in any house without the consent of the owner; nor in time of war except in the manner prescribed by law.

The two sections dealing with the military were written in 1866 and retained in the two later versions. They were obviously influenced by the U.S. Constitution and were not indicative of any problems, then or now, with civil-military relations within the state. No cases have come before the court involving these sections.

SECTION 19. RIGHT OF PEACEABLE ASSEMBLY AND TO PETITION GOVERNMENT

The right of the people peaceably to assemble to consult for the common good, and to petition the government, or any department thereof, shall never be abridged.

The right of petition and peaceful assembly is similar to the guarantees in the First Amendment. The authors of 1871 adopted the Illinois language which included the right "to make known their opinions to their representatives." The 1875 Constitution reverted to the language of 1866.

The people may petition their legislature; they may also contact the governor concerning proposed legislation (Weis v. Ashley, 1899). A political meeting or convention is the sort of assemblage protected by this section and, short of libel or slander, the members of such a body may speak and write about candidates for office, including those running for judicial or educational offices (State ex rel. Ragan v. Junkin, 1909). Statutes making it a crime to swear falsely on an initiative petition do not violate Section 19(State v. Fellman, 1991).

SECTION 20. IMPRISONMENT FOR DEBT PROHIBITED; EXCEPTION

No person shall be imprisoned for debt in any civil action on mesne or final process, unless in cases of fraud.

Despite the Convention of 1875's resolution to write a constitution in plain, unadorned English, the delegates went back to the obscure language of 1866 in this section. The archaic phrasing simply means that one cannot go to jail in either an intermediate or final judgment of indebtedness. People looking to avoid the payment of some legal obligation have seen this section as the solution to their problems, but clearly such reasoning cannot be afforded much judicial support. Specifically, one can be imprisoned for failure to meet a court order for child support since the obligation is not a debt (Doak v. Milbauer, 1984). The same principle applies to failure to meet alimony payments (Jensen v. Jensen, 1930). Also, the law making bad check writing a criminal offense does not violate this section since elements of fraud are involved (White v. State, 1938).

SECTION 21. PRIVATE PROPERTY COMPENSATED FOR

The property of no person shall be taken or damaged for public use without just compensation therefor.

The 1866 Constitution makes no mention of eminent domain, but within five years, the taking of private property by the state, especially in the interests of the railroads, had become a major issue. The delegates to the 1871 Convention prepared a very detailed section, including the statement, taken from the Illinois Constitution, that "The fee of land taken by railroad tracks, without the consent of the owners thereof, shall remain in such owners, subject to the use for which it was taken." This sentence became very controversial in the election as the railroad promoters and local communities felt it would cause great economic hardship. Commentators point to it as a major reason for the rejection of the document by the voters. The authors of 1875 included the much simpler version in effect today.

But simpler is not always clearer, and the court has heard an enormous number of cases challenging the power of government to take property. The major questions, most of which hinge on minute details, include what constitutes property, for example, does an unexercised option to purchase real estate constitute property (Phillips Petroleum v. Omaha, 1960)? While it is established that eminent domain cannot be used to take private property for a private use (Burger v. City of Beatrice, 1967), what is a public use or public improvement? And perhaps most controversially, exactly what is "just compensation?" In general, the term refers only to the market value at the time taken and does not have to acknowledge any peculiar value for special reasons to its owner (Wiles v. Department of Public Works, 1931).

The authors of 1875 also caused a quantum leap in the workload of the courts by going beyond the language of the Fifth Amendment prohibiting the taking of property by adding "or damaged." The words include all damages arising from the exercise of eminent domain which cause a diminution in the value of private property (Omaha v. Kramer, 1889). This is a right which did not exist prior to the approval of this section (Omaha & Republican Valley Railroad Co. v. Standen, 1887), and it is self-executing in that legislative action is not necessary to make it available to the individual (Kula v. Prososki, 1985).

SECTION 22. ELECTIONS TO BE FREE

All elections shall be free; and there shall be no hindrance or impediment to the right of a qualified voter to exercise the elective franchise.

This language was written for the Constitution of 1871; the 1866 Constitution did not recognize this right. However, the right to vote assumes the existence of a system that makes the vote meaningful. The court has generally given the legislature a great deal of leeway in constructing electoral machinery even if, in some instances, specific elements of the system may appear to limit the right. For example, laws regulating nominations and prescribing the ways in which new parties can be formed are constitutional as long as elections are left free and open to all electors (State ex rel. Nelson v. Marsh, 1932). A statute limiting the role of government employees in political conventions has also been upheld (State ex rel. Baldwin v. Strain, 1950).

SECTION 23. CASES IN FELONY; RIGHT OF APPEAL TO SUPREME COURT; OPERATE AS A SUPERSEDEAS

In all capital cases, appeal directly to the Supreme Court shall be as a matter of right and shall operate as a supersedeas to stay the execution of the sentence of death until further order of the Supreme Court. In all other cases, criminal or civil, an aggrieved party shall be entitled to one appeal to the appellate court created pursuant to Article V, section 1, of this Constitution or to the Supreme Court as may be provided by law.

Only those convicted of a capital crime have the right to appeal directly to the Nebraska Supreme Court, and the execution cannot be carried out until approved by the court. Before 1990, there was greater opportunity for felons to appeal their convictions to the highest court. The original language of 1866, retained in 1871 and 1875, was "The writ of error shall be a writ of right in all cases of felony." A 1972 amendment changed the wording to "In all cases of felony the defendant shall have the right of appeal to the Supreme Court." The latest changes, approved in 1990, include the creation of an appellate court (see Art. V, Sec. 1) and the limitation of an automatic appeal to the Supreme Court to capital cases, although the language of Article V, Section 2, also approved in 1990, says "The judges of the Supreme Court, sitting without division, shall hear and determine all cases involving the constitutionality of a statute and all appeals involving capital cases." The legislature now has the power to determine how all other cases may be appealed to which courts.

In a case in which a convicted felon appealed his incarceration for pre-sentencing evaluation, the supreme court held that an appeal was not permissible since a final order in the case, that is, the sentence, had not been imposed. An evaluation period did not qualify as a final order (Kaba v. Fox, 1983).

SECTION 24. REPEALED, 1990.

This section, first adopted in 1875, said, "The right to be heard in all civil cases in the court of last resort, by appeal, error, or otherwise, shall not be denied." It had the effect of permitting every lawsuit, however unimportant, to make its way to the state's highest court, although the court did recognize the legitimacy of "reasonable rules and regulations" (Nebraska State Bank v. Dudley, 1979). Even with such rules, the supreme court had found itself overwhelmed by appeals and by the late 1980s had a considerable backlog. The repeal of this section and the creation of another appellate court was the solution approved by the voters in 1990.

SECTION 25. RIGHTS OF PROPERTY; NO DISCRIMINATION; ALIENS

There shall be no discrimination between citizens of the United States in respect to the acquisition, ownership, possession, enjoyment or descent of property. The right of aliens in respect to the acquisition, enjoyment and descent of property may be regulated by law.

The sentence about the right of aliens was added to the original words of the 1866 and 1875 Constitutions. The addition was the work of the Convention of 1920 and reflected the xenophobic attitudes that were the result of World War I.

The rule with respect to discrimination among property owners is similar to those established by Article I, Section 16 and Article III, Section 18. If the creation of different classes of property owners is rationally related to a legitimate governmental end, then it is permissible. Thus a distinction made between married and unmarried property owners for the purpose of determining eligibility for homestead exemptions was a proper means for achieving the legislative policy of preservation of the family (Landon v. Pettijohn, 1989).

SECTION 26. POWERS RETAINED BY THE PEOPLE

This enumeration of rights shall not be construed to impair or deny others, retained by the people, and all powers not herein delegated, remain with the people.

This section is the same as the 1866 Constitution. As the court noted, "these provisions are characteristics of a republican form of government. If all power rests in the first instance with the people, and they delegate certain powers to certain of their representatives and retain all other powers, this distinguishes such a government from a monarchy or oligarchy" (State ex rel. Harte v. Moorhead, 1916).

The rights retained by the people have not been spelled out in specific detail, and their indistinct nature could come into conflict with the equally imprecise concept of the "police power" of the state. Such was the case in *First Trust Co. of Lincoln v. Smith* (1938). The supreme court rejected the idea that the declaration of an emergency and the exercise of the state's police power to meet the emergency could suspend the guarantees in Section 26 and other parts of the Bill of Rights. The police power, according to the court:

> is not a power mysteriously nebulous, a separate or a distinct manifestation of governmental authority. It is not superior to state Constitutions so that it may properly be said that, though an act of a governmental agency may be unconstitutional, still it may be justified under the police power, as though the same police power were a divinely mysterious governmental attribute of superior rank to the Constitution itself.

The imaginative interpretation of this section can lead to interesting results. In 1898, the supreme court determined that the citizens of Nebraska had retained their right to govern themselves in matters of purely local concern and that the municipalities did not surrender to the state their power of self-government. The legislature was powerless to take away that right of local self-government of cities and towns (State v. Moores, 1898). Within a few years, the court retreated from that extreme statement, arguing that the *Moores* decision was "unsupported by a single authority" (Redell v. Moores, 1901).

SECTION 27. ENGLISH LANGUAGE TO BE OFFICIAL

> The English language is hereby declared to be the official language of this state, and all official proceedings, records and publications shall be in such language, and the common school branches shall be taught in said language in public, private, denominational and parochial schools.

This section was a creation of the Convention of 1920 and predates more recent attempts around the country to make English the official language. The reason behind the amendment was the nativist hysteria stimulated by the World War. Its target was primarily the large number of Germans in the state. According to the publicity put out by the Convention, the purpose of the section was "to insure the youth of this state a knowledge of the language in which the spirit of our institution is expressed and to promote true Americanism."[7] Despite the section, Nebraska legislators got caught up in the latest wave of enthusiasm for English, and in 1987 a bill was introduced to make English the official language of the state. It died in committee.

This section has not been litigated.

---

[7] *Proceedings of the Constitutional Convention, 1919–20*, vol. II (Lincoln, 1920), 2480.

Article II

Distribution of Powers

SECTION 1. LEGISLATIVE; EXECUTIVE; JUDICIAL

The powers of the government of this state are divided into three distinct departments, the Legislative, Executive and Judicial, and no person or collection of persons being one of these departments, shall exercise any power properly belonging to either of the others, except as hereinafter expressly directed or permitted.

Article II has two primary purposes: it first of all prohibits one branch of government from encroaching on the duties, powers, and prerogatives of the other two and, second, it prevents one branch from improperly delegating its constitutionally assigned duties and powers to another branch (State ex rel. Meyer v. State Board of Equalization and Assessment, 1970).

The authors of the 1866 Constitution did not feel the need for an explicit statement of the doctrine of the separation of powers, leaving it, as in the U.S. Constitution, an implied factor in state government. The Convention of 1871 wanted a more specific statement and took verbatim the language of the Illinois Constitution of 1870 which, in turn, was derived from the Illinois Constitution of 1848 (see Saxby v. Sonnemann, 1925). The Convention of 1875 retained the language, and the article has never been amended.

This article is one of the shortest in the Constitution but it has always vexed state officials. There probably never was a time in history when government was so simple that its operations could be neatly segregated into closed compartments.

Certainly it is not the case today if government is to operate with any degree of effectiveness. The separation of powers, realistically, can only lead to a high degree of specialization in, and not monopolization of, governmental functions. In the nature of things, we recognize, judges will legislate, legislators will execute, and executives will adjudicate. The supreme court has the endless job of walking the dikes and levies to make sure that the separate streams of political power remain within their banks. In truth, the most it can do is try to ensure that the inevitable seepage is not excessive.

As in other jurisdictions, the Nebraska Supreme Court must try to maintain the fiction surrounding the delegation of legislative authority. The principle is firmly established that the legislature cannot delegate its constitutional powers to an administrative body (Terry Carpenter, Inc. v. Nebraska Liquor Control Comm., 1963). At the same time, a law may confer general authority upon an administrative agency and delegate the power to make rules and regulations covering the details of legislative purpose (Board of Regents v. Lancaster County, 1951). There is no delegation of legislative authority if an agency operates within clearly designated limitations and standards (State v. Cutright, 1975).

Taken literally, this doctrine would mean that the administrators within the executive branch exercise absolutely no discretion. But in the execution of the law, further law has to be made, especially if the original legislation is not much more than an invitation, because of its vagueness, to interpretation by administrators. But the separation of powers doctrine requires one to believe that delegation is not delegation, if there are adequate guidelines for the executives in the use of their discretion. If the statutes conferring discretion are "reasonably adequate, sufficient, and definite for the guidance of the agency" and if they are "sufficient to enable those affected to know their rights and obligations," the court will not find a violation of Article II (State ex rel. Douglas v. Nebraska Mortgage Finance Fund, 1979).

For example, there is nothing more basic to the legislative function than the power of the purse, the power to set the tax rates. In the Revenue Act of 1967, however, the tax rate authority was given to the State Board of Equalization, a body composed of four elected and one appointed members of the executive branch. When this was challenged, the court said it believed that the determination of the rate was a matter of applied mathematics since the statute had set out the "method and manner in which the computations shall be adjusted and determined, and the specific standards to be used in setting the rate of tax" (Anderson v. Tiemann, 1967). It was apparent then and later that in fact the legislators had willingly surrendered their power to a group which was less politically vulnerable than they. By 1983, the politics of the process had become so apparent that this experiment in avoiding responsibility was ended, and the rates are now set by the legislature.

The line between the legislature and judiciary is harder to draw. As the court stated in 1974, "We have not heretofore attempted to define precisely the line between the judicial function and power and the legislative one. Probably we cannot do so" (Lux v. Mental Health Board of Polk County, 1979). The article, however, clearly means that the "Legislature may not delegate legislative power to the courts" (Copple v. City of Lincoln, 1979).

The cases cited above plus innumerable others concern what the court has come to call the "institutional aspect" of Article II; they illuminate the "beam from which our system of checks and balances is suspended" in that they prevent "one branch of government from encroaching on the duties and prerogatives of the others or from improperly delegating its own duties and prerogatives" (State ex rel. Spire v. Conway, 1991). A more problematic and more controversial feature of Article II is the personnel or individual aspect.

The political establishment of Nebraska was shaken in 1991 by the decision in the Conway case. Mr. Conway was an assistant professor at a state college. He was elected in 1984 and re-elected in 1988 to the state legislature. A suit was brought to bar him from the Unicameral since he was a state employee. The court held that the legislature was the sole judge of its membership and so Conway could not be denied his seat. However, as a senator, he could not keep his teaching job since he was then exercising a power of the executive branch, as prohibited by Article II.

The critics of the decision argued that Conway was only a functionary in the executive branch and not the sort of policy-making official intended by the writers of the article. The court put too fine a point on its construction and the bright line it drew would make government less effective. Some feared that the logic of the case might be taken to an extreme, and the Nebraska State Education Association worried that public school teachers might be barred from election to public office. It has also been suggested that attorneys are officers of the court and thus can be prevented from running for the legislature.

Article III

Legislative

SECTION 1. LEGISLATIVE AUTHORITY; HOW VESTED

Commencing with the regular session of the Legislature to be held in January, nineteen hundred and thirty-seven, the legislative authority of the state shall be vested in a Legislature consisting of one chamber. The people reserve for themselves, however, the power to propose laws, and amendments to the constitution, and to enact or reject the same at the polls, independent of the Legislature, and also reserve power at their own option to approve or reject at the polls any act, item, section, or any part of any act passed by the Legislature. All authority vested by the constitution or laws of the state in the Senate, House of Representatives, or joint session thereof, in so far as applicable, shall be and hereby is vested in said Legislature of one chamber. All provisions in the constitution and laws of the state relating to the Legislature, the Senate, the House of Representatives, joint sessions of the Senate and House of Representatives, shall, in so far as said provisions are applicable, apply to and mean said Legislature of one chamber hereby created and the members thereof. All references to Clerk of House of Representatives or Secretary of Senate shall mean, when applicable, the Clerk of the Legislature of one chamber. All references to the Speaker of the House of Representatives or temporary president of the Senate shall mean Speaker of the Legislature. Whenever any provision of the constitution requires submission of any matter to, or action by, the House of Representatives, the Senate or joint session thereof, or the members of either body or both bodies, it shall after

January first, nineteen hundred and thirty-seven be construed to mean the Legislature herein provided.

The straightforward declaration of 1871 and 1875—"The legislative authority is vested in a senate and house of representatives"—has been greatly complicated by two major amendments. In 1912, the voters made clear that the legislature was not the sole repository of law-making power in the state. The details of the initiative and referendum are contained in Sections 2, 3, and 4 below. The amendment of 1934 created the unicameral legislature and necessitated an involved explanation of the transition from the bicameral system.

Since the first session of the Unicameral in 1937, the new system has worked well and Nebraskans have had little trouble in adjusting to it. There have been few serious proposals in the past half-century to return to two houses. The changeover has caused few constitutional problems since the court has always insisted that the words of the section are clear: the restrictions and limitations of the Constitution apply to the unicameral system as they did under bicameralism (Mekota v. State Board of Equalization and Assessment, 1945).

Most of the questions raised by this section are similar to the ones in Article II. Just what is the legislative authority of the state and what are its limits? The court has held that the Constitution is to be regarded as a restriction on legislative power (Elmen v. State Board of Equalization and Assessment, 1930). More positively, the legislature, subject only to the initiative and referendum and specific constitutional restrictions, and provided that its action is for a public purpose, has an unlimited field within which to legislate (Power Oil Co. v. Cochran, 1941).

But what is a public purpose? Courts are reluctant to enter the debate over public purposes, but they and other organs of government are occasionally forced to get engaged. In *State ex rel. Douglas v. Nebraska Mortgage Finance Fund* (1979), the supreme court had an opportunity to discuss the question as it inquired into the legality of a fund to assist low-income families in the purchase of housing. The legislature is primarily responsible for identifying a public purpose with the objective of promoting the public health, safety, morals, security, prosperity, contentment, and the general welfare of the citizens. When reasonable people can argue whether a particular expenditure is for a public purpose, the doubts must be resolved in favor of the legislature. While public benefits should be direct and not remote, the courts should not interfere in a legislative determination of public purpose "unless the act appears to be so obviously designed in all its principal parts to benefit private persons and so indirectly or remotely to affect the public interest that it constitutes the taking of property of the taxpayers for private use."

Another question is the degree to which other organs may share this power. According to the court, "the exercise of a legislatively delegated authority to make rules and regulations to carry out an expressed legislative purpose, or for the complete operation or enforcement of a law with clearly designated limitations and standards, is not an exercise of legislative power" (State ex rel. Douglas v. Nebraska Mortgage Finance Fund, 1979). The court is a little more fastidious about delegation if it concerns the definition by an administrative agency of a criminal offense (Lincoln Dairy Co. v. Finigan, 1960).

There has not been a period in Nebraska history marked by open and sustained hostility between the courts and the legislature. However, in the 1990s, the legislature has taken some very palpable hits. Senators have been told they may not serve, even in a low-level capacity, in the executive branch (State ex rel. Spire v. Conway, 1991). They were prevented from doing what many people felt was the honorable thing in giving relief to victims of a savings and loan scandal (Haman v. Marsh, 1991). They were denied the authority to define gambling in the state (State ex rel. Spire v. Strawberries, Inc., 1991). Their efforts to avoid a property tax crisis were rejected by the court (MAPCO Ammonia Pipeline v. State Board of Equalization and Assessment, 1991). They were charged with putting undue restrictions on the initiative process (State ex rel. Stenberg v. Beermann, 1992). And finally, the court lobbed a bombshell into the heart of the legislative domain by throwing out the 1991 reapportionment (Day v. Nelson, 1992). Perhaps these cases do not constitute a long-term trend, but it is clear that the current supreme court is not overawed by the claim of legislative prerogatives.

SECTION 2. FIRST POWER RESERVED: INITIATIVE

The first power reserved by the people is the initiative whereby laws may be enacted and constitutional amendments adopted by the people independently of the Legislature. This power may be invoked by petition wherein the proposed measures shall be set forth at length. If the petition be for the enactment of a law, it shall be signed by seven percent of the registered voters of the state, and if the petition be for the amendment of the Constitution, the petition therefor shall be signed by ten percent of such registered voters. In all cases the registered voters signing such petition shall be so distributed as to include five percent of the registered voters of each of two-fifths of the counties of the state and when thus signed the petition shall be filed with the Secretary of State who shall submit the measure thus proposed to the electors of the state at the first general election held not less than four months after such petition shall have been filed. The same measure, either in form or in essential substance, shall not be submitted to the people by initiative petition, either affirmatively or negatively, more often than once in three years. If conflicting measures submitted to the people at the same election be approved, the one receiving the highest number of affirmative votes shall thereby become law as to all conflicting provisions. The constitutional limitations as to the scope and subject matter of statutes enacted by the Legislature shall apply to those enacted by the initiative.

Section 2 affirms the right of the people, through a petition process, to write their own constitutional amendments and laws. This section was adopted in 1912. The Convention of 1920 recommended lessening the requirements for signatures. The number of signatories for placing an initiated statute on the ballot was changed from 5 percent of "legal voters" to 7 percent of "electors." The minimum for constitutional amendments was reduced from 15 to 10 percent. This change made the initiative route much easier. In 1988, after revelations that petition circulators were being paid by special interests, the requirements were tightened somewhat by changing "electors" (that is, people eligible to vote) to "registered voters."

Sections 2, 3, and 4 put Nebraska among the minority of states which have all the elements of "direct democracy." The power to recall elected officials is provided by statute, and it pertains only to local government.

If it were needed, the supreme court affirmed in 1986 the power of the citizens. In 1982, the voters passed an amendment prohibiting the purchase of farm or ranch property by corporations—the so-called "family farm" amendment. Even supporters agreed the same ends could have been achieved by statute, and the provision reads like a statute. In *Omaha National Bank v. Spire* (1986), the plaintiffs contended it was only a statute and labeling it as a constitutional provision did not make it so. In rejecting this line of argument, the Nebraska Supreme Court quoted approvingly the words of the trial court:

> The ultimate source of power in any democratic form of government is the people. Our Nebraska Constitution is a document belonging to the people. Subject only to the supremacy clause of the United States Constitution, the people may put in their document what they will. Even to the shock and dismay of constitutional theoreticians, the people may add provisions dealing with "non-fundamental" rights, as well as provisions bearing the most tenuous of relationships to the notion of what constitutes the basic framework of government. The people may add provisions which legal scholars may decry as legislative or statutory in nature. But the people may do it nonetheless.

SECTION 3. SECOND POWER RESERVED: REFERENDUM

The second power reserved is the referendum which may be invoked, by petition, against any act or part of an act of the Legislature, except those making appropriations for the expense of state government or a state institution existing at the time of the passage of such act. Petitions invoking the referendum shall be signed by not less than five percent of the registered voters of the state, distributed as required for initiative petitions, and filed in the office of the Secretary of State within ninety days after the Legislature at which the act sought to be referred was passed shall have adjourned sine die or for more than ninety days. Such petition shall set out the title of

> the act against which the referendum is invoked and, in addition thereto, when only a portion of the act is sought to be referred, the number of the section or sections or portion of sections of the act designating such portion. When the referendum is thus invoked, the Secretary of State shall refer the same to the electors for approval or rejection at the first general election to be held not less than thirty days after the filing of such petition.
>
> When the referendum is invoked as to any act or part of act, other than emergency acts or those for the immediate preservation of the public peace, health, or safety, by petition signed by not less than ten percent of the registered voters of the state distributed as aforesaid, it shall suspend the taking effect of such act or part of act until the same has been approved by the electors of the state.

By the referendum process, the people can circulate a petition calling for a vote on acts passed by the legislature. The Convention of 1920 lowered the requirements first adopted in 1912 from 10 percent of "legal voters" to 5 percent of "electors." The 1988 amendment changed those eligible to sign petitions to "registered voters." The referendum has not been used frequently but it has had an impact, most notably with the repeal in 1966 of the state income tax. In 1986, voters rejected a mandatory seat belt law and legislation pushing school consolidation.

The term "act of the Legislature" refers to a legislative bill which has met all the requirements, including gubernatorial action, for enactment into a law. Petitioners can begin the referendum process at that point, even though the legislature, while still in session, might later amend the targeted act (Klosterman v. Marsh, 1966).

SECTION 4. INITIATIVE OR REFERENDUM; SIGNATURES REQUIRED; VETO; ELECTION RETURNS; CONSTITUTIONAL AMENDMENTS; NON-PARTISAN BALLOT

> The whole number of votes cast for Governor at the general election next preceding the filing of an initiative or referendum petition shall be the basis on which the number of signatures to such petition shall be computed. The veto power of the Governor shall not extend to measures initiated by or referred to the people. A measure initiated shall become law or part of the Constitution, as the case may be, when a majority of the votes cast thereon, and not less than thirty-five percent of the total vote cast at the election at which the same was submitted, are cast in favor thereof, and shall take effect upon proclamation by the Governor which shall be made within ten days after the official canvass of such votes. The vote upon initiative and referendum measures shall be returned and canvassed in the manner prescribed for the canvass of votes for president. The method of submitting and adopting amendments to the Constitution provided by this section shall be supplementary to the method prescribed in the article of this Constitution, entitled "Amendments" and the latter shall in no case be construed to conflict herewith. The provisions with respect to the

initiative and referendum shall be self-executing, but legislation may be enacted to facilitate their operation. All propositions submitted in pursuance hereof shall be submitted in a non-partisan manner and without any indication or suggestion on the ballot that they have been approved or endorsed by any political party or organization. Only the title or proper descriptive words of measures shall be printed on the ballot and when two or more measures have the same title they shall be numbered consecutively in the order of filing with the Secretary of State and the number shall be followed by the name of the first petitioner on the corresponding petition.

Section 1B and 1C, adopted in 1912, described the procedures for implementing the initiative and referendum. The Convention of 1920 consolidated them into the present Section 4. The reference to non-partisanship was also added in 1920.

The section has been held to authorize legislation to prevent fraud or to make intelligible the purpose of the proposal (State v. Swanson, 1966). Legislation may be enacted to facilitate the process (Klosterman v. Marsh, 1966). However, the power of the people should be liberally construed to promote the democratic process, and the right expressed in these sections should not be circumscribed by restrictive legislation or a strict interpretation of the statutes concerning the exercise of the right (State ex rel. Morris v. Marsh, 1968).

In this connection, a law was passed saying that any person "circulating petitions . . . shall not be hired or salaried for the express purpose of circulating petitions" (Neb Rev Stat, 32-705). In 1986, after two state senators and others were indicted for violating this provision, there was much concern about the abuses in the system and demands were made for stricter safeguards. Effective reforms, however, were undermined by the U.S. Supreme Court decision in *Meyer v. Grant* (1988), which held that the payment of petition circulators was protected by the First Amendment. The Nebraska Supreme Court agreed in *State v. Radcliffe* (1988).

The question of regulating petition circulators arose again in 1992 after the legislature passed a law restricting such people to the counties within which they reside. The measure was, so the senators claimed, designed to eliminate fraud, although critics noted that the law followed on the heels of a proposed petition for legislative term limitations. The supreme court threw out the restriction, stating that the "effect of the law is to place impossible barriers to the economically less fortunate to successfully initiate legislation if they cannot afford to pay local circulators and are forbidden to solicit outside their own counties" (State ex rel. Stenberg v. Beermann, 1992).

SECTION 5. LEGISLATIVE DISTRICTS; APPORTIONMENT; REDISTRICTING; WHEN REQUIRED

At the regular session of the Legislature held in the year nineteen hundred and thirty-five the Legislature shall by law determine the number of members to be elected and divide the state into legislative districts. In the creation of such districts, any county that contains population sufficient to entitle it to two or more members of the Legislature shall be divided into separate and distinct legislative districts, as nearly equal in population as may be and composed of contiguous and compact territory. One member of the Legislature shall be elected from each such district. The basis of apportionment shall be the population excluding aliens, as shown by the next preceding federal census. The Legislature shall redistrict after each federal decennial census. In any such redistricting, county lines shall be followed whenever practicable, but other established lines may be followed at the discretion of the Legislature.

Legislative reapportionment means that districts should contain a reasonably equal number of electors. In the American context, there has also been a long standing tradition that elements other than people deserve representation. Territory, as in the counties of the state, has often been given a protected status. Covertly, the idea that certain parts of society are a little more deserving than others has crept into reapportionment debates as, for example, the argument that farmers deserve more political power than their numbers would justify. All this means that reapportionment has seldom been a purely mathematical exercise.

Even before the line of reasoning begun by the U.S. Supreme Court in *Baker v. Carr* (1962), the Nebraska Supreme Court did not feel compelled to reject inquiries into legislative reapportionment as "political questions." While admitting in 1934 that apportionment is essentially legislative, when "gross inequalities in representation are so palpable," the court must find the apportionment in violation of Section 5 (Rogers v. Morgan, 1934). Since the decisions of the federal courts establishing the principle of "one man, one vote," the Nebraska system is based solely on population, although the legislature learned in 1992 that it does not have total freedom to ignore county lines in creating districts of equal population.

Section 5 replaces Section 2 of the original Constitution, as amended in 1920. A 1934 amendment facilitated the transition to unicameralism. In 1962, voters approved an amendment permitting boundaries other than county lines to be used in apportionment; furthermore, in redistricting, "primary emphasis shall be placed on population and not less than twenty percent nor more than thirty percent weight shall be given to area." The latter provision was ruled in violation of the equal protection clause of the Fourteenth Amendment in 1964 (League of Nebraska Municipalities v. Marsh). The current language of Section 5 was approved in 1966.

Given the sometimes uneasy relationship between rural and urban areas in Nebraska, tensions arise over the issue of reapportionment. But the rules swung heavily in favor of urban interests since the 1960s and lawmakers have, however reluctantly, gone along with federal guidelines. That all reapportionment must be based on nearly equal population is firmly settled and, after the census of 1990, when Lincoln and Omaha picked up further representation, disgruntled rural voters were advised by their senators not to waste their time and money with a court challenge.

It appeared to most experts on apportionment that territorial considerations had been rendered irrelevant. However, a group of Madison County residents found some hope in the words "county lines shall be followed whenever practicable." When, after the 1991 redistricting, the county was divided between two districts, the argument was made that Madison County contained the optimum number of persons and therefore should be maintained as a single district. In a decision in July 1992, after the primary elections had been held, the supreme court agreed with the voters of Madison County and declared at least that part of the reapportionment of 1991 to be unconstitutional. The state's claim that this was a political question to be decided by the legislature was rejected because the word "shall" lessened legislative discretion (Day v. Nelson, 1992).

SECTION 6. LEGISLATURE; NUMBER OF MEMBERS; ANNUAL SESSIONS

The Legislature shall consist of not more than fifty members and not less than thirty members. The sessions of the Legislature shall be annual except as otherwise provided by this constitution or as may be otherwise provided by law.

The Constitution of 1866 set a maximum membership of the legislature at 100. The Convention of 1871 recommended 133, and that number was retained in 1875—100 representatives and 33 senators. The Convention of 1920 increased the size of the senate to a maximum of fifty. Unicameralism, in 1934, was a drastic reversal of the trend, in Nebraska and elsewhere, toward larger legislative bodies. With a maximum size of fifty, the state has the smallest legislature in the country. The proponents of unicameralism advocated a small body since they believed the large size of many legislatures confused the voters when they tried to assign responsibility.

The first session of the Unicameral had forty-three members, and this number remained in place until the 1960s when, as a way of easing the dislocations (as perceived by rural Nebraska) caused by mandatory redistricting, the size of the body was increased to forty-nine. There has been little agitation to add one more member to bring the legislature up to its constitutional limit.

A 1970 amendment changed the legislature from biennial to annual sessions. This brought Nebraska into line with most of the other states.

SECTION 7. LEGISLATORS; TERMS; EFFECT OF REDISTRICTING; ELECTIONS; SALARY; EXPENSES; MILEAGE

At the general election to be held in November 1964, one-half of the members of the Legislature, or as nearly thereto as may be practicable, shall be elected for a term

> of four years and the remainder for a term of two years, and thereafter all members shall be elected for a term of four years, with the manner of such election to be determined by the Legislature. When the Legislature is redistricted, the members elected prior to redistricting shall continue in office, and the law providing for such redistricting shall where necessary specify the newly established district which they shall represent for the balance of their term. Each member shall be nominated and elected in a nonpartisan manner and without any indication on the ballot that he or she is affiliated with or endorsed by any political party or organization. Each member of the Legislature shall receive a salary not to exceed one thousand dollars per month during the term of his or her office. In addition to his or her salary, each member shall receive an amount equal to his or her actual expenses in traveling by the most usual route once to and returning from each regular or special session of the Legislature. Members of the Legislature shall receive no pay nor perquisites other than his or her salary and expenses, and employees of the Legislature shall receive no compensation other than their salary or per diem.

This section describes the terms, method of election, and salaries for legislators. Originally Section 4, the section was amended in 1920, and since then six changes have been made by the voters. Perhaps most significant to the political life of the state is non-partisanship, an idea which unicameralists saw as critical to the success of the experiment. Today, Nebraska is the only state with a nonpartisan legislature, and that feature probably has a greater impact on its politics than does unicameralism. The critics claim that non-partisanship erodes responsibility, inhibits legislative-executive relations, and prevents effective discipline. What is more, since everyone knows the party preferences of the senators, nonpartisanship is meaningless.

The sentence concerning redistricting was added in 1966 in response to the pressures for reapportionment. The other amendments concern the oldest question in Nebraska politics: the salary of public officials. If we bracket the explanation which says that Nebraska voters are just overly frugal, the best explanation for the continuing debate is the reality of modern government versus the myth that service as a state legislator can be, should be, a part-time position. It was only in the 1970s that a serious move was made to provide all senators with an office, secretarial help, and other staff assistance. And the sternest message that legislators should not plan on doing more than coming to Lincoln for a few days, passing a few laws, and then returning to the field or factory has always been the salary and other forms of compensation.

Since 1866, Nebraskans have always insisted in spelling out in the constitution the precise dollar amount each legislator can earn. The figure has never been anything like a full-time salary. By the 1980s, the situation had become critical since the last raise in 1966—to $4,800 per year—was barely enough to cover the expenses of living in Lincoln for a few months each year. In 1984, after eight separate proposals for a direct or indirect raise had been turned down, the supreme court, in a fascinating analysis of English grammar, provided some relief to the legislators. In 1981, a law was passed which permitted a member to be reimbursed for "necessary expenses incurred while performing in the official capacity as a member of the Legislature" (Neb Rev Stat 50-202), despite constitutional language which then said that members could receive only a salary and expenses pertaining to one trip to and from a session. The Constitution went on to add, "Members of the Legislature shall receive no pay nor perquisites other than said salary and expenses." The court concluded that the word "said" modified only "salary" and that the "expenses" were not the same "actual expenses" related to the trip to and from the session (State ex rel. Douglas v. Beermann, 1984). This gave the senators maneuvering room in their efforts to avoid poverty. But as the court giveth, so may it taketh away, and in 1987 the rather handsome pension plan the senators had voted for themselves was found to violate this section (State ex rel. Spire v. Public Emp. Ret. Bd.). The plight of the solons was relieved in 1988 when, after a strenuous campaign, the voters raised the annual salary to $12,000.

SECTION 8. LEGISLATORS; QUALIFICATIONS; ONE-YEAR RESIDENCE IN DISTRICT; REMOVAL FROM DISTRICT; EFFECT

No person shall be eligible to the office of member of the legislature unless on the date of the general election at which he is elected or on the date of his appointment he is a registered voter, has attained the age of twenty-one and has resided within the district from which he is elected for the term of one year next before his election, unless he shall have been absent on the public business of the United States or of this State. And no person elected as aforesaid shall hold his office after he shall have removed from such district.

The Constitution of 1866 restricted membership in the legislature, like the right to vote, to white, male citizens. The 1875 version requires legislators to be registered voters at least twenty-one years old and residents for one year in the district from which elected. A 1972 amendment removed obsolete language pertaining to a bicameral body.

SECTION 9. LEGISLATORS; DISQUALIFICATIONS

No person holding office under the authority of the United States, or any lucrative office under the authority of this state, shall be eligible to, or have a seat in the Legislature. No person elected or appointed to the Legislature shall receive any civil appointment to state office while holding membership in the Legislature or while the Legislature is in session, and all such appointments shall be void.

The purpose of this section, in conjunction with Sections 9, 16, and 19, is "not to permit any incentive or temptation for emoluments, gains, or position, to influence members of the legislature in any of their official action" (State v. Wilkins, 1928). The holdings of the court concerning Article II reinforce this principle.

An amendment approved in 1972 removed some minor details from this section.

SECTION 10. LEGISLATIVE SESSIONS; TIME; QUORUM; RULES OF PROCEDURE; EXPULSION OF MEMBERS; DISRESPECTFUL BEHAVIOR; PENALTY

Beginning with the year 1975, regular sessions of the Legislature shall be held annually, commencing at 10 a.m. on the first Wednesday after the first Monday in January of each year. The duration of regular sessions shall not exceed ninety legislative days in odd-numbered years unless extended by a vote of four-fifths of all members elected to the Legislature, and shall not exceed sixty legislative days in even-numbered years unless extended by a vote of four-fifths of all members elected to the Legislature. Bills and resolutions under consideration by the Legislature upon adjournment of a regular session held in an odd-numbered year may be considered at the next regular session, as if there had been no such adjournment. The Lieutenant Governor shall preside, but shall vote only when the Legislature is equally divided. A majority of the members elected to the Legislature shall constitute a quorum; the Legislature shall determine the rules of its proceedings and be the judge of the election, returns, and qualifications of its members, shall choose its own officers, including a Speaker to preside when the Lieutenant Governor shall be absent, incapacitated, or shall act as Governor. No member shall be expelled except by a vote of two-thirds of all members elected to the Legislature, and no member shall be twice expelled for the same offense. The Legislature may punish by imprisonment any person not a member thereof who shall be guilty of disrespect to the Legislature by disorderly or contemptuous behavior in its presence, but no such imprisonment shall extend beyond twenty-four hours at one time, unless the person shall persist in such disorderly or contemptuous behavior.

Here are found the details of legislative sessions. This was Section 7 of the Constitution of 1875, and its language has remained basically the same with two notable exceptions: the unicameral amendment in 1934 and the amendment moving to annual sessions in 1974. Nebraskans showed their suspicions, if not their "disrespect" of the legislature by limiting the number of days in a session. This is one more sign that the state is meant to have a part-time legislature.

The other significant part of this section pertains to the legislative role of the lieutenant governor. This office was created in 1875 and, following the federal model, the person was given the position of presiding officer, first in the state senate and later in the unicameral body. Voters in 1970 approved some changes in the office in order to make it a more effective part of the executive branch but they were reluctant, for whatever reason, to remove the lieutenant governor from the legislature. The supreme court, in a 1981 decision, did much to eliminate the little legislative power the office possessed by ruling that Section 13, which requires a majority vote by "all members elected," prevents the lieutenant governor from breaking tie votes on the final reading of a piece of legislation (Center Bank v. Dept. of Banking and Finance).

The phrase "all members elected," which appears in many places in this Constitution, was clarified in Article XVII, Section 1. It includes "appointed and elected members of the Legislature."

SECTION 11. LEGISLATIVE JOURNAL; VOTE VIVA VOCE; OPEN DOORS

The Legislature shall keep a journal of its proceedings and publish them (except such parts as may require secrecy) and the yeas and nays of the members on any question, shall at the desire of any one of them be entered on the journal. All votes shall be viva voce. The doors of the Legislature and of the Committee of the Whole, shall be open, unless when the business shall be such as ought to be kept secret.

This section covers some features of the legislative process with emphasis on the need for publicity and openness in the proceedings. The language of 1875 was modified in 1934 to fit the unicameral form. Electronic roll call machines meet the requirement for a viva voce or voice vote (Day v. Walker, 1933).

SECTION 12. REPEALED, 1934.

SECTION 13. STYLE OF BILLS; MAJORITY NECESSARY TO PASSAGE; YEAS AND NAYS ENTERED ON JOURNAL

The style of all bills shall be, "Be it enacted by the people of the State of Nebraska," and no law shall be enacted except by bill. No bill shall be passed by the Legislature unless by the assent of a majority of all members elected and the yeas and nays on the question of final passage of any bill shall be entered upon the journal.

This section simply requires that bills can be passed only with a majority of the members elected and that the results of a vote shall be recorded in the legislative journal. The original language, until amended in 1912 as part of the initiative and referendum procedures, read "Be it enacted by the Legislature of the State of Nebraska." A 1920 amendment to the section concerned the question of conference committees, and it was removed in 1972 as obsolete.

The legislative journal is important to the court since it helps to ensure the true version of a bill can be found despite any clerical errors in enrolling (State ex rel. Ball v. Hall, 1935). Also, while the signatures of the presiding officer and the governor are evidence of the passage of an act, the signed legislation must agree with the wording as shown in the journal (State v. Fricke, 1924).

SECTION 14. BILLS AND RESOLUTIONS READ BY TITLE; PRINTING; BILLS TO CONTAIN ONE SUBJECT; AMENDED SECTION TO BE SET FORTH; SIGNING OF BILLS

Every bill and resolution shall be read by title when introduced, and a printed copy thereof provided for the use of each member, and the bill and all amendments thereto shall be printed and read at large before the vote is taken upon its final passage. No such vote upon the final passage of any bill shall be taken, however, until five legislative days after its introduction nor until it has been on file for final reading and passage for at least one legislative day. No bill shall contain more than one subject, and the same shall be clearly expressed in the title. And no law shall be amended unless the new act contains the section or sections as amended and the section or sections so amended shall be repealed. The Lieutenant Governor, or the Speaker if acting as presiding officer, shall sign, in the presence of the Legislature while the same is in session and capable of transacting business, all bills and resolutions passed by the Legislature.

The purpose of this section is to ensure that all bills are openly and honestly considered by the legislature. Such provisions are all the more critical in a unicameral body since there is no second house to serve as a brake on hasty or ill-considered legislation. The requirement of a final reading of the entire bill, however, does little to advance the art of legislation, and toward the end of every session visitors to the capitol are treated to amusing exercises in speed mumbling by clerks of the legislature. A proposal to eliminate this little farce, however, was turned down by the voters, in 1982.

Section 14 has been a fertile field for the production of lawsuits. Anyone opposed to a law can attempt to make the case that the threatening statute was passed unconstitutionally and is therefore void. The litigation here has not always concerned an undotted "i" or an uncrossed "t." For their part, the senators, on more than one occasion, have given cause to wonder if something funny is going on. They have gutted bills except for the title in order to add completely different material; or they have inserted non-germane amendments to pending bills. The court has generally been tolerant of all but the most egregious violation of the legislative niceties.

Section 14 applies only to final reading of a bill (Klosterman v. Marsh, 1966). Within the process leading to passage, the substitution of one bill for another by amendment is not unconstitutional as long as the changes are germane (State ex rel.

Davis v. Cox, 1920). The requirement for three readings does not apply to all amendments to the bill as originally introduced (State ex rel. Martin v. Ryan, 1912).

In a case where it was claimed that an amendment to an act was not described by the act's original title, the court stated that the provisions of Section 14 should be liberally construed and the amendment should stand as long as it was germane to the subject matter and comprehended within the object and purposes of the original legislation (Dawson County v. South Side Irrigation Co., 1945). The purpose of the title is only to describe the subject of the bill and it need not be a thorough synopsis of the legislation (Hadden v. Aitken, 1952). A bill's title serves only to notify legislators and the public of its purpose in general terms (Omaha Parking Authority v. City of Omaha, 1956).

The provision that amendatory acts contain the section amended does not apply to independent acts which are complete in themselves (Neeman v. Nebraska Natural Resources Commission, 1974). A complete and independent act may incidentally amend, modify, or have an impact upon the provisions of existing statutes but it is not an amendment within the meaning of this section (Aschenbrenner v. Nebraska Public Power District, 1980).

SECTION 15. MEMBERS PRIVILEGED FROM ARREST

Members of the Legislature in all cases except treason, felony or breach of the peace, shall be privileged from arrest during the session of the Legislature, and for fifteen days next before the commencement and after the termination thereof.

A statement similar to this appears in all three versions of the Constitution and is a common element in most other jurisdictions. This privilege is for the benefit of the people and not the legislature and is conferred on the senators so that they may discharge the trust imposed upon them by their constituents (State ex rel. Benton v. Elder, 1891).

SECTION 16. MEMBERS OF LEGISLATURE; CONFLICT OF INTEREST; STANDARDS FOR

No member of the Legislature or any state officer shall have a conflict of interest, as defined by the Legislature, directly in any contract, with the state or any county or municipality thereof, authorized by any law enacted during the term for which he shall have been elected or appointed, or within one year after the expiration of such term. The Legislature shall prescribe standards and definitions for determining the existence of such conflicts of interest in contracts, and it shall prescribe sanctions for enforcing this section.

Originally, the main thrust of this section was the prevention of a legislator from assuming any other civil appointment in state government. This idea was retained in amendments passed in 1920 and 1968. In 1972, language pertaining to office holding was removed and the prohibition against any "conflict of interest" was emphasized. This provision, it will be noted, applies to all state officers, elected and appointed.

If a legislator is found to have an interest in a contract resulting from a law passed during his or her term, the section only prevents claiming a right under such a contract but does not invalidate the law (Briggs v. Neville, 1918).

SECTION 17. IMPEACHMENT; PROCEDURE

The Legislature shall have the sole power of impeachment, but a majority of the members elected must concur therein. Proceedings may be initiated in either a regular session or a special session of the Legislature. Upon the adoption of a resolution of impeachment, which resolution shall give reasonable notice of the acts or omissions alleged to constitute impeachable offenses but need not conform to any particular style, a notice of an impeachment of any officer, other than a Judge of the Supreme Court, shall be forthwith served upon the Chief Justice, by the Clerk of the Legislature, who shall thereupon call a session of the Supreme Court to meet at the Capitol in an expeditious fashion after such notice to try the impeachment. A notice of an impeachment of the Chief Justice or any Judge of the Supreme Court shall be served by the Clerk of the Legislature, upon the clerk of the judicial district within which the Capitol is located, and he or she thereupon shall choose, at random, seven Judges of the District Court in the State to meet within thirty days at the Capitol, to sit as a Court to try such impeachment, which Court shall organize by electing one of its number to preside. The case against the impeached civil officer shall be brought in the name of the Legislature and shall be managed by two senators, appointed by the Legislature, who may make technical or procedural amendments to the articles of impeachment as they deem necessary. The trial shall be conducted in the manner of a civil proceeding and the impeached civil officer shall not be allowed to invoke a privilege against self-incrimination, except as otherwise applicable in a general civil case. No person shall be convicted without the concurrence of two-thirds of the members of the Court of impeachment that clear and convincing evidence exists indicating that such person is guilty of one or more impeachable offenses, but judgment in cases of impeachment shall not extend further than removal from office and disqualification to hold and enjoy any office or honor, profit, or trust, in this State, but the party impeached, whether convicted or acquitted, shall nevertheless be liable to prosecution and punishment according to law. No officer shall exercise his or her official duties after he or she shall have been impeached and notified thereof, until he or she shall have been acquitted.

Impeachment, or the filing of formal charges against a public official, and the conviction of the person on these charges are joint legislative and judicial functions in Nebraska. One might assume that the state's unique system for impeaching officials is a result of the unicameral legislature. After all, the federal pattern—articles of impeachment prepared by the lower house and the trial held before the upper house—is impossible when there is only a single chamber. However, the system was created in 1875 and its roots are in the political turmoil caused by the impeachment and conviction of the first governor, David Butler. The members of the 1875 Convention were quite aware of the trauma caused by a highly politicized impeachment proceeding, and they wanted to remove some of the responsibility from the legislature. Thus they brought in the supreme court and determined that conviction must be based on an extraordinary majority of the judges. The court feels that this change meant impeachment was moved from the realm of politics since the section "is to ensure a strictly judicial investigation of the charges according to judicial methods" (State v. Douglas, 1984).

A 1972 amendment only deleted obsolete references to two houses. More significant changes were added in 1986. These amendments reflected the experiences in the 1984 impeachment of Attorney General Paul Douglas. They included the words about "reasonable notice," the manner in which the case will be managed before the supreme court, the provision concerning self-incrimination, and the need for "clear and convincing evidence."

While Article IV, Section 5 says that all civil officers "shall be liable to impeachment for any misdemeanor in office," Article III, Section 17 does not contain language describing impeachable offenses, including the familiar "high crimes and misdemeanors." The supreme court has, however, used that venerable wording and has suggested that more than ordinary felonies are impeachable. Acts detrimental to the public interest may be included: "An impeachable high crime or misdemeanor is one in its nature or consequences subversive of some fundamental or essential principle of government or highly prejudicial to the public interest, and this may consist of a violation of the constitution, of law, of an official oath, or of duty by an act committed or omitted, or, without violating a positive law, by the abuse of discretionary power from improper motives or for an improper purpose" (State v. Hastings, 1893).

For a state that got off to a fast start by impeaching its first governor, Nebraska has not made extensive use of this procedure. Just four cases have come before the supreme court; the impeachment of Attorney General Douglas was the only instance of impeachment in this century. Douglas was implicated in some dealings with the officials of a failed savings and loan company and six articles of impeachment were filed against him. Four of the seven judges hearing the case voted to find him guilty on one of the counts, but he was acquitted because of the requirement for a two-thirds vote.

SECTION 18. LOCAL OR SPECIAL LAWS PROHIBITED

The Legislature shall not pass local or special laws in any of the following cases, that is to say:

For granting divorces.

Changing the names of persons or places.

Laying out, opening altering and working roads or highways.

Vacating roads, Town plats, streets, alleys, and public grounds.

Locating or changing County seats.

Regulating County and Township offices.

Regulating the practice of Courts of Justice.

Regulating the jurisdiction and duties of Justices of the Peace, Police Magistrates and Constables.

Providing for changes of venue in civil and criminal cases.

Incorporating Cities, Towns and Villages, or changing or amending the charter of any Town, City, or Village.

Providing for the election of Officers in Townships, incorporated Towns or Cities.

Summoning or empaneling Grand or Petit Juries.

Providing for the bonding of cities, towns, precincts, school districts or other municipalities.

Providing for the management of Public Schools.

The opening and conducting of any election, or designating the place of voting.

The sale or mortgage of real estate belonging to minors, or others under disability.

The protection of game or fish.

Chartering or licensing ferries, or toll bridges, remitting fines, penalties or forfeitures, creating, increasing and decreasing fees, percentages or allowances of public officers, during the term for which said officers are elected or appointed.

Changing the law of descent.

Granting to any corporation, association, or individual, the right to lay down railroad tracks, or amending existing charters for such purpose.

Granting to any corporation, association, or individual any special or exclusive privileges, immunity, or franchise whatever; provided, that notwithstanding any other provisions of this Constitution, the Legislature shall have authority to separately define and classify loans and installment sales, to establish minimum rates within classifications of loans or installment sales which it establishes, and to regulate with respect thereto. In all other cases where a general law can be made applicable, no special law shall be enacted.

Section 18 guarantees to Nebraskans equal protection of the law. This means that the law must apply equally to everyone or, if some people are penalized or benefited by the law, there must be a rational basis for the exception. Although "equal protection" emanates from Section 18, the prohibition against special legislation adds a different dimension. The "rational basis" test is sufficient in examining equal protection; all that is required is a rational relationship between a legitimate state interest and the statutory means for achieving that interest (Distinctive Printing and Packaging Co. v. Cox, 1989). The test of special legislation is more stringent in that the classifications "must be based on some *substantial* [emphasis not added] difference of situation that would naturally suggest the justice or expediency of diverse legislation with respect to the objects to be classified" (Haman v. Marsh, 1991).

The comparable section of the 1866 Constitution merely prevented the legislature from granting divorces or authorizing lotteries. By 1871, Nebraskans had become aware of excesses possible for an unrestrained legislature. Unless limited, it could pass local laws specifying, say, how the mayor of Omaha was to be elected, or special laws, perhaps changing the name of a single individual. A general ban on such legislation was not enough; a detailed listing of areas in which local or special laws were not permitted was necessary. The 1972 Constitutional Revision Commission felt the legislature could now be trusted and recommended the elimination of the list. The legislature, perhaps knowing the attitude of the citizens, did not even submit the proposal for a vote. The only amendment to this section came in 1964 and it allows the legislature to define and classify loans and installment sales.

The court has held that a law which operates uniformly and equally on all, brought within the relation and circumstance for which it provides, is a general law (Bauer v. Nebraska Game, Forestation and Parks Commission, 1940). The legislature is able to classify individuals, corporations, local governments, and property for the purpose of legislation, provided that the classification system rests upon real differences in situation and circumstances of members of the class relative to the subject of the law, and the law must operate uniformly on every member of the designated class (State ex rel. Taylor v. Hall, 1935).

The classification of municipal corporations on the basis of population, for example, does not violate this section (State v. Graham, 1884). So while the legislature may not write laws naming Omaha, it can legislate for "cities of the metropolitan class" which includes all cities in the state with a population of more than 300,000—and Omaha is the only city in the class.

To be valid, the classification may not be unreasonable, arbitrary, or unrelated to the public interest (State v. Edmunds, 1982). The court will inquire "only whether a rational relationship exists between a legitimate state interest and the statutory means selected by the legislature to accomplish that end" (State v. Michalski, 1985). A classification which is only a cover for the arbitrary treatment of certain persons or classes would be prohibited (School Dist. No. 46 of Sarpy County v. Bellevue, 1987). It is not fatal for a law to identify a class which is not all-inclusive, especially in new policy areas, since as long as the proposed action has a rational basis, the legislature should not be compelled to "choose between attacking every aspect of the problem or not attacking the problem at all . . ." (Distinctive Printing and Packaging Co. v. Cox, 1989).

The court has also ruled that Section 18 is hostile toward laws which create closed classes, that is, classes which cannot be entered by anyone in the future. A classification, therefore, which "limits the application of the law to a present condition, and leaves no opportunity for an increase in the numbers of the class by future growth or development, is special . . ." (Scottsbluff v. Tiemann, 1970).

The cumulative wisdom of the court about Section 18 was on display as it wrote an ending to one of the most wrenching chapters in the history of Nebraska politics. In 1977, legislation was passed requiring those savings and loan companies in the state that were not covered by federal deposit insurance to join a private corporation called the Nebraska Depository Institution Guaranty Corporation (NDIGC). Furthermore, the companies were required to inform their customers by signs and by statements in their advertising that deposits were protected by NDIGC to a maximum of $30,000. After the Commonwealth Savings Company in Lincoln was closed and placed in receivership in 1983, depositors were shocked to learn that there was not enough money in NDIGC to cover their losses. When the depositors, many of whom were retirees who had lost their life savings, demanded justice, the state told them it had no responsibility in this unfortunate series of events.

After seven years of intense agitation, the depositors finally convinced the legislators that the state did share some of the blame, and so a bill was passed appropriating $33.8 million; LB 272A of 1990 stated that "principles of fairness all require that the State of Nebraska fulfill the thirty-thousand-dollar guaranty of each and every deposit." A taxpayer brought suit to stop the distribution of the money, claiming that the act was special legislation. In *Haman v. Marsh* (1991), the supreme court agreed with the plaintiff on both parts of the test used to identify laws in violation of Section 18. First, LB 272A set up an unreasonable classification based on the idea that the state had a moral obligation toward the depositors. NDIGC was a private corporation and if depositors failed to read the very fine print implied in the legal arrangements, it was not the fault of the State of Nebraska. Second, the legislation created a "closed class"; that is, no other people could be permitted to join the class which was receiving a benefit from the state.

SECTION 19. COMPENSATION; INCREASE; EXTRA COMPENSATION TO PUBLIC OFFICERS AND CONTRACTORS PROHIBITED; RETIREMENT BENEFITS; ADJUSTMENT

The Legislature shall never grant any extra compensation to any public officer, agent, or servant after the services have been rendered nor to any contractor after the contract has been entered into, except that retirement benefits of retired public officers and employees may be adjusted to reflect changes in the cost of living and wage levels that have occurred subsequent to the date of retirement, nor shall the compensation of any public officer, including any officer whose compensation is fixed by the Legislature, be increased or diminished during his term of office except that, when there are members elected or appointed to the Legislature or officers elected or appointed to a court, board or commission having more than one or more members and the terms of one or more members commence and end at different times, the compensation of all members of the Legislature or of such court, board, or commission may be increased or diminished at the beginning of the full term of any member thereof. Nothing in this section shall prevent local governing bodies from reviewing and adjusting vested pension benefits periodically as prescribed by ordinance.

The surviving spouse of any retired public officer, agent, or servant, who has retired under a pension plan or system, shall be considered as having pensionable status and shall be entitled to the same benefits which may, at any time, be provided for or available for spouses of other public officers, agents, or servants who have retired in such pension plan or system at a later date, and such benefits shall not be prohibited by the restrictions of this section or of Article XIII, section 3 of the Constitution of Nebraska.

This section is intended to prevent public officials or contractors working for government from getting greater compensation than was originally agreed upon. The provision applies to the state and all its political subdivisions (Retired City Civilian Employees Club of Omaha v. City of Omaha Emp. Ret. System, 1977).

Given the awkward wording of this section, it is not surprising to learn that it has been amended five times. The original language, forbidding extra compensation or a change in compensation during a term of office, was written in 1866 and copied in 1871 and 1875. The amendment of 1920 included the material pertaining to "any officer whose compensation is fixed by the Legislature," which extended the coverage of the section to local officials. An amendment passed in 1952 added the words clarifying the salary situation of members of multi-member boards and commissions; similar language was added in 1968 to cover the legislature.

Amendments in 1972 and 1978 added the fairly complicated language pertaining to public pension plans. While pension systems were not necessarily prohibited by this section before the amendments (State ex rel. Haberlan v. Love, 1911), fairness for retirees demanded that their benefits be better protected, especially in such complex areas as cost-of-living increases and the rights of surviving spouses.

SECTION 20. SALT SPRINGS; COAL; OIL; MINERALS; ALIENATION PROHIBITED

The salt springs, coal, oil, mineral, or other natural resources on or contained in the land belonging to the state shall never be alienated; but provision may be made by law for the leasing or development of the same.

The force behind this section, first proposed in 1871, was a wild delusion. Somehow, the pioneers convinced themselves that salt deposits owned by the state would be a source of fabulous wealth; in fact, Lincoln was established in a salt basin largely for this reason. Sadly, this saline Eldorado never materialized, and the 1920 Convention made this section a little more plausible by adding "coal, oil, minerals, or other natural resources."

Since the most important lands belonging to the state are those dedicated to the support of education, most of the case law in this area is based on the several sections in Article VII, below.

SECTION 21. DONATION OF STATE LANDS PROHIBITED

Lands under control of the state shall never be donated to railroad companies, private corporations or individuals.

This section reflects the suspicions of the Convention of 1875 about the political influence of the railroads and other corporations. It prohibits the legislature from participating in any land grab by the special interests.

The supreme court has held that Nebraska's Industrial Development Act, which permits local governments to issue revenue bonds for acquiring and developing land and improvements for use by private manufacturing or industrial ventures, does not violate this section, in light of the wording of Article XV, Section 16 (now Article XIII, section 2) as approved in 1960 (State ex rel. Meyer v. Lancaster County, 1962).

SECTION 22. APPROPRIATIONS FOR STATE; DEFICIENCIES; BILLS FOR PAY OF MEMBERS AND OFFICIALS

Each Legislature shall make appropriations for the expenses of the Government. And whenever it is deemed necessary to make further appropriations for deficiencies, the same shall require a two-thirds vote of all the members elected to the Legislature. Bills making appropriations for the pay of members and officers of the Legislature, and for the salaries of the officers of the Government, shall contain no provision on any other subject.

A 1972 amendment removed the requirement that the legislature make appropriations until the expiration of the first quarter after the adjournment of the next regular session. To reinforce the "power of the purse" as described here, supplemental appropriations need an extraordinary majority. The final sentence ensures that pay increases will not sneak through as amendments to other legislation. The significance of this section is that continuing appropriations for the operation of government are prohibited; "each legislature" must review the state budget (Rein v. Johnson, 1947).

SECTION 23. REPEALED, 1972.

SECTION 24. GAMES OF CHANCE AND LOTTERIES PROHIBITED; EXCEPTIONS

> The Legislature shall not authorize any game of chance, nor any lottery, or gift enterprise when the consideration for a chance to participate involves the payment of money for the purchase of property, services, or a chance or admission ticket or requires an expenditure of substantial effort or time, except that it may authorize and regulate other lotteries, raffles, and gift enterprises which are intended solely as business promotions or the proceeds of which are to be used solely for charitable or community betterment purposes without profit to the promoter of such lotteries, raffles, or gift enterprises. Nothing in this section shall be construed to prohibit the enactment of laws providing for the licensing and regulation of wagering on the results of horseraces, wherever run, either within or outside of the state, by the parimutuel method, when such wagering is conducted by licensees within a licensed racetrack enclosure, or to prohibit the enactment of laws providing for the licensing and regulation of bingo games conducted by nonprofit associations which have been in existence for a period of five years immediately preceding the application for license, except that bingo games cannot be conducted by agents or lessees of such association on a percentage basis.

This section represents the tension between moralism and pragmatism—gambling is immoral, but it makes money. Thus, while it has generally been banned by the Constitution, the legislature and the voters have never given up in their efforts to legalize gambling.

The 1866 Constitution only prohibited lotteries. The 1871 version empowered the legislature to suppress "vice and immorality in this state" and forbade it from authorizing any form of gambling "under any pretense or any purpose whatever." The 1875 Constitution dropped the business about vice and immorality and simply prohibited the passage of laws allowing gambling. Through five amendments, the simple sentence of 1875 has grown to its present size.

In 1934, pari-mutuel betting on horse races was permitted and expanded by amendment in 1988. Bingo was legalized in 1958, while the 1962 and 1966 amendments permitted lotteries if the proceeds are used for charitable or community betterment purposes.

The 1980s saw new pressures on the legislature to expand the range of gambling in the state either through constitutional amendment or statute. Lotteries had become popular throughout the country, and novel forms of gambling such as video slot machines were seen as lucrative activities for businesses in the state. An initiative proposal for the statewide lottery was rejected by the voters in 1990, but the legislature had already made provision by statute for other forms of gambling. The legislature, in effect, took it upon itself to redefine "game of chance" to exclude video or electronic gaming devices. In a 1991 case, the court forcefully reminded the senators that they did not have the power to define gambling and that the court had always insisted that "a game of chance is one in which the result as to success or failure depends less on the skill and experience of the player than on purely fortuitous or accidental circumstances incidental to the game or the manner of playing or on the device or apparatus with which it is played" (State ex rel. Spire v. Strawberries, Inc.). The statute was in violation of Section 24.

SECTION 25. INCIDENTAL EXPENSES OF STATE OFFICERS; SPECIFIC APPROPRIATIONS ALWAYS NECESSARY; WARRANTS FOR MONEY

No allowance shall be made for the incidental expenses of any state officer except the same be made by general appropriations and upon an account specifying each item. No money shall be drawn from the treasury except in pursuance of a specific appropriation made by law, and on the presentation of a warrant issued as the Legislature may direct, and no money shall be diverted from any appropriation made for any purpose or taken from any fund whatever by resolution.

The thought behind the section is essentially the same in all three Constitutions: state officials, and especially legislators, are to be prevented from dipping into the till. A 1964 amendment removed language authorizing the state auditor to play a role in the administration of this provision.

The rule here is simple: funds in the state treasury can only be disbursed after an appropriation by the legislature (Fischer v. Marsh, 1925). It was established early on that appropriations must be specific and not implied (State v. Wallichs, 1882).

SECTION 26. PRIVILEGE OF MEMBERS

No member of the Legislature shall be liable in any civil or criminal action whatever for words spoken in debate.

This provision has remained unchanged since 1866. It is designed to ensure the legislators will be able to enjoy free and open debate. There has been no litigation here, but an attorney general's opinion held that legislators are generally immune from personal liability if acting in their official capacity where legislators traditionally have the power to act (Attorney General Opinion #24, 1979).

SECTION 27. ACTS TAKE EFFECT AFTER THREE MONTHS; EMERGENCY BILLS; SESSION LAWS

No act shall take effect until three calendar months after the adjournment of the session at which it passed, unless in the case of emergency, to be expressed in the preamble or body of the act, the Legislature shall, by a vote of two-thirds of all members elected otherwise direct. All laws shall be published in book form within sixty days after the adjournment of each session and distributed among the several counties in such manner as the Legislature may provide.

With the exception of the removal of obsolete language in 1972, this is the same section as approved in 1875. The purpose is clear: regular legislation takes effect three calendar months after the adjournment of the session that passed the law (Summerville v. North Platte Valley Weather Control District, 1960).

In declaring an emergency, the legislature does not have to state its nature (Read v. City of Scottsbluff, 1965) and when an act passes with the emergency clause, it goes into effect the day following enactment (Wilson and Company, Inc. v. Otoe County, 1941). The people still have the right to call for a referendum on emergency legislation, although the referendum cannot suspend the taking effect of an emergency act (Klosterman v. Marsh, 1966).

SECTION 28. REPEALED, 1934.

SECTION 29. LEGISLATIVE AUTHORITY IN EMERGENCIES DUE TO ENEMY ATTACK UPON THE UNITED STATES

(1) In order to insure continuity of state and local governmental operations in periods of emergency resulting from enemy attack upon the United States, or the imminent threat thereof, the Legislature shall have the power and the immediate duty, notwithstanding any other provision in this Constitution, to provide by law for:

(a) The prompt and temporary succession to the powers and duties of all public offices, of whatever nature and whether filled by election or appointment, the incumbents of which, after an attack, may be or become unavailable or unable to carry on the powers and duties of such offices;

(b) The convening of the Legislature into general or extraordinary session, upon or without call by the Governor, during or after a war or enemy caused disaster occurring in the United States; and, with respect to any such emergency session, the suspension or temporary change of the provisions of this Constitution or of general law relating to the length and purposes of any legislative session or prescribing the specific proportion or number of legislators whose presence or vote is necessary to constitute a quorum or to accomplish any legislative act or function.

(c) The selection and changing from time to time of a temporary state seat of government, of temporary county seats, and of temporary seats of government for other political subdivisions; to be used if made necessary by enemy attack or imminent threat thereof;

(d) The determination, selection, reproduction, preservation, and dispersal of public records necessary to the continuity of governmental operations in the event of enemy attack or imminent threat thereof; and

(e) Such other measures and procedures as may be necessary and proper for insuring the continuity of governmental operations in the event of enemy attack or imminent threat thereof.

(2) In the exercise of the powers hereinbefore conferred, the Legislature shall in all respects conform to the requirements of this Constitution except to the extent that, in the judgment of the Legislature, so to do would be impracticable or would admit of undue delay.

This section was approved at the height of the Cold War as a way of providing some continuity in state government in the event of an enemy attack. Its provisions have never been tested.

Article IV

Executive
(ORIGINALLY ARTICLE V)

SECTION 1. EXECUTIVE DEPARTMENTS; OFFICERS; ELECTION; TERMS; ELIGIBILITY; BOOKS TO BE KEPT AT SEAT OF GOVERNMENT; RESIDENCE OF OFFICERS; HEADS OF DEPARTMENTS; APPOINTMENTS

The executive officers of the state shall be the Governor, Lieutenant Governor, Secretary of State, Auditor of Public Accounts, Treasurer, Attorney General, and the heads of such other executive departments as set forth herein or as may be established by law. The Legislature may provide for the placing of the above named officers as heads over such departments of government as it may by law establish.

The Governor, Lieutenant Governor, Attorney General, Secretary of State, Auditor of Public Accounts and the Treasurer shall be chosen at the general election held in November, 1974, and in each alternative even-numbered year thereafter, for a term of four years and until their successors shall be elected and qualified. In the general election one vote shall be cast jointly for the candidates for Governor and Lieutenant Governor nominated by the same party. The Governor shall be ineligible to the office of Governor for four years next after the expiration of two consecutive terms for which he was elected. The records, books, and papers of all executive officers shall be kept at the seat of government, and such officers, excepting the Lieutenant Governor and members of boards and commissions when the board or commission is head of an executive department, shall reside there during their respective terms of

> office. Officers in the executive department of the state shall perform such duties as may be provided by law. The heads of all executive departments established by law, other than those to be elected as provided herein, shall be appointed by the Governor, with the consent of a majority of all members elected to the Legislature, but officers so appointed may be removed by the Governor. Subject to the provisions of this Constitution, the heads of the various executive or civil departments shall have power to appoint and remove all subordinate employees in their respective departments.

The twentieth century has been the "age of the executive" as presidents, governors, and mayors have gradually assumed greater power in relation to the legislature. Nebraska does not represent an exception to this trend, although the modernization of the executive branch has been a slow, and yet incomplete, process. The current situation cannot be described as a strong governor firmly in control of a streamlined, coherent bureaucracy.

The supreme court has implied that the executive branch is a residual category; those organs which are clearly not a part of the legislature or judiciary must be executive (State ex rel. Spire v. Conway, 1991; Swanson v. State, 1937; State ex rel. Mortensen v. Furse, 1911). Within the category, there are several distinct classes of agency. First, there are the "constitutional offices," that is, those units created by specific provisions of the Constitution. These include the six officers mentioned in Section 1—governor, lieutenant governor, secretary of state, auditor of public accounts, treasurer, and attorney general—as well as seven described in other articles: Department of Education, Board of Educational Lands and Funds, Board of Parole, Public Service Commission, Board of Trustees for the State Colleges, University of Nebraska Board of Regents, and, in 1990, Coordinating Commission for Postsecondary Education. These entities contain the executive officers of the state (Sorensen v. Swanson, 1967).

A second class is referred to as the "code agencies." The term resulted from those ferocious battles of the 1920s when Charles Bryan made an issue out of the creation of an administrative code. Today, "code agency" only means that the unit is a freestanding agency whose director serves at the pleasure of the governor. This group includes staff units such as the Department of Administrative Services and line agencies such as the Department of Agriculture, Correctional Services, Health, Motor Vehicles, Roads, and Social Services. The legislature can create agencies responsible to the governor or it can make an agency more independent of gubernatorial control (State ex rel. Howard v. Marsh, 1946).

Still another class is made up of agencies which are not fully controlled by the governor. In most cases, the directors of these agencies are selected by an independent board or commission. Among the more important are the Equal Opportunity Commission, the Game and Parks Commission, the Library Commission, and the State Historical Society. The court has held that "every commission that exercises executive duties in some capacity cannot be narrowed to the definition of being an executive department under the Governor." Agencies which are charged with the "political government" of the state are properly under the governor but certain commissions, as determined by the legislature, are "charged with the enforcement of no policy except the policy of law". Like federal regulatory agencies, these organizations are relatively free of gubernatorial control (State ex rel. Johnson v. Chase, 1946).

A final class includes a large number of statutory agencies, boards, commissions, committees, and authorities. There are also special purpose advisory committees, licensing boards affiliated with a larger agency, and quasi-governmental agencies. These units often exist in an administrative limbo, in many cases because nobody seems greatly concerned about who is actually in charge. Examples of these entities are the Boiler Safety Code Advisory Board, the Capitol Murals Commission, the Board of Hearing Aid Instrument Dispensers and Fitters, and the Wyuka Cemetery Board.

Section 1 illustrates the movement toward modernity. The language of 1875 has been amended eight times. The most significant change was made in 1920 when the prohibition against the creation of further executive offices was removed (see also Sec. 27). Heads of departments were also given the power to appoint and remove their subordinates. Amendments in 1936 and 1952 shortened the ballot by eliminating the Commissioner of Public Lands and Buildings and the Superintendent of Public Instruction as elected constitutional officers.

Making the ballot even shorter has not excited much attention since the Convention of 1920. Only occasionally have there been suggestions that there is not much sense in electing the treasurer, attorney general, auditor, and secretary of state. An amendment to make the secretary of state, attorney general, and treasurer appointive was rejected by the voters in 1938. The Constitutional Revision Commission in 1970 recommended that the auditor and treasurer be appointed officials. The legislature did not present the proposal to the voters.

Most elected officers are still required to live in Lincoln—a provision first written in 1871—but a 1958 amendment excused the members of boards and commissions. In 1962, the governor and lieutenant governor were given four-year terms and in 1964, the other elected executives had their terms extended. The governor was limited to two four-year terms in 1966; this might be seen as a weakening of the governorship since it automatically creates a "lame duck," but it has not had significant impact since only one governor—James Exon—has been elected to a second term. The final amendment to Section 1, in 1970, required a party's nominees for governor and lieutenant governor to run as a team, thus preventing the two officers from being members of different parties.

SECTION 2. GOVERNOR; LIEUTENANT GOVERNOR; ELIGIBILITY; QUALIFICATIONS; APPOINTIVE OFFICERS; INELIGIBLE FOR OTHER OFFICES

No person shall be eligible to the office of Governor, or Lieutenant Governor, who shall not have attained the age of thirty years, and who shall not have been for five years next preceding his election a resident and citizen of this state and a citizen of the United States. None of the appointive officers mentioned in this article shall be eligible to any other state office during the period for which they have been appointed.

Section 2 sets forth the qualifications for governor and lieutenant governor; the person must be at least thirty years of age, a resident of Nebraska for five years, and a citizen of the United States. The language was borrowed by the 1871 Convention from the Illinois Constitution of 1870, although the requirement for citizenship was contained in the original Nebraska Constitution. The 1871 authors were willing to go with an age of twenty-five plus a two-year residency requirement. A 1920 amendment raised the length of required residence to five years.

This section was an important factor in the messy aftermath of the election of 1890. For the first time, the Republicans lost the governorship. Democrat James Boyd emerged from a bitter contest over the counting of the ballots only to be reminded that neither he nor his father, born in Ireland, had ever become naturalized citizens until the year of the election. The Nebraska Supreme Court ruled that Boyd was ineligible and delivered against him a "judgment of ouster" (State ex rel. Thayer v. Boyd, 1891). Upon appeal to the U.S. Supreme Court, Boyd's citizenship was affirmed and he was found to be eligible for the office (Boyd v. Nebraska ex rel. Thayer, 1892).

The original language of Section 2 said that none of the executives named in Section 1 were eligible for any other state office. This meant, for example, that the lieutenant governor could not run for governor (State ex rel. McKelvie v. Wait, 1914). A 1962 amendment permitted the lieutenant governor to seek another office and in 1970, the prohibition against running for any other office was limited to appointed executive officers.

SECTION 3. TREASURER; INELIGIBILITY

The treasurer shall be ineligible to the office of treasurer for two years next after the expiration of two consecutive terms for which he was elected.

This measure, unchanged since 1875, is supposed to ensure that the person entrusted with the public fisc does not remain in office for more than eight years at a time. This section has never been litigated.

SECTION 4. ELECTION RETURNS; CANVASS BY LEGISLATURE; CONDUCT OF ELECTION CONTESTS

The returns of every election for the officers of the executive department shall be sealed up and transmitted by the returning officers to the Secretary of State, directed to the Speaker of the Legislature, who shall immediately after the organization of the Legislature, and before proceeding to any other business, open and publish the same in the presence of a majority of the members of the Legislature. The person having the highest number of votes for each of said offices shall be declared duly elected; but if two or more have an equal and the highest number of votes, the Legislature shall choose one of such persons for said office. The conduct of election contests for any of said offices shall be in such manner as may be prescribed by law.

This section contains very nearly the same language as the Constitution of 1866. A 1960 amendment authorized the legislature to prescribe by law the method for contesting elections of members of the executive branch. In 1972, obsolete material referring to a bicameral system was removed. Otherwise, the section still describes the procedures by which elections to the executive offices are to be canvassed and the procedures to be followed in case of a tie vote.

SECTION 5. IMPEACHMENT

All civil officers of this state shall be liable to impeachment for any misdemeanor in office.

The Constitution of 1866 included a provision similar to Section 5 of the article on the legislature. The Conventions of 1871 and 1875 followed the model of Illinois and made a separate statement about executive officers. This section emphasizes the point that the legislature has no other means to remove officers when the Constitution creates the office, fixes the terms, and the grounds and manner of removal (Fitzgerald v. Kuppinger, 1956). The discussion of the Nebraska method of impeachment and the grounds for impeachment is found above in Article III, Section 17.

SECTION 6. SUPREME EXECUTIVE POWER

The supreme executive power shall be vested in the Governor, who shall take care that the laws be faithfully executed and the affairs of the state efficiently and economically administered.

The phrase "and the affairs of the state efficiently and economically administered" was added in 1920, but they hardly increase the governor's power. "The supreme executive power" would seem impressive enough. However, other provisions of this Constitution which itemize the things the governor may or may not do undermine the authority of the words. In terms of the formal powers which give meaning to "executive power," comparative analyses of governors generally place Nebraska in the middle or "moderate" range. As of 1989, in comparison with other governors, the governor of Nebraska was ranked "very strong" in budget-making powers and veto power, "strong" in tenure potential and budget-changing authority, "moderate" in political control over the legislature, and "weak" in appointment powers.[8]

SECTION 7. MESSAGE BY GOVERNOR; BUDGET; CONTENTS; BUDGET BILL; PREPARATION; APPROPRIATIONS NOT TO BE IN EXCESS OF BUDGET; EXCEPTION; EXCESS SUBJECT TO VETO

The Governor may, at the commencement of each session, and at the close of his term of office and whenever the Legislature may require, give by message to the Legislature information of the condition of the state, and shall recommend such measures as he shall deem expedient. At a time fixed by law, he shall present, by message, a complete itemized budget of the financial requirements of all departments, institutions and agencies of the state and a budget bill to be introduced by the Speaker of the Legislature at the request of the Governor. Said budget bill shall be prepared with such expert assistance and under such regulations as may be required by the Governor. No appropriations shall be made in excess of the recommendations contained in such budget including any amendment the Governor may make thereto unless by three-fifths vote of the Legislature, and such excess so approved shall be subject to veto by the Governor.

The governor is empowered to communicate with the legislature and specifically to recommend legislation. The Convention of 1920 gave to the governor the power to prepare and protect a true executive budget, with the recommendations of the governor and the staff resistant to legislative change without an extraordinary majority. In 1964, "may" replaced "shall" in the first sentence and the requirement for overriding a governor's proposed budget was raised from three-fifths to two-thirds. Three-fifths was reinstated in 1972 and the reference to the speaker of the legislature was included.

This section makes it clear that the governor is the major actor in the budgetary process although, as the court has said, "the control of the purse strings of government is a legislative function; indeed, it is the supreme legislative prerogative, indispensable to the independence and integrity of the legislature, and not to be surrounded or abridged, save by the constitution itself, without disturbing the balance of the system and endangering the liberties of the people (State ex rel. Meyer v. State Board of Equalization and Assessment, 1970). But "the constitution itself" makes it clear that the legislature can only respond to the initiatives of the governor and the professional staff if it wants to exercise the power of the purse.

---

[8] Thad L. Beyle, "Governors," in Virginia Gray, Herbert Jacob, and Robert Albriton, eds., *Politics in the American States: A Comparative Analysis*, 5th ed. (Glenview, 111.: Scott Foresman, 1990), 568–73.

SECTION 8. SPECIAL SESSIONS

The Governor may, on extraordinary occasions, convene the Legislature by proclamation, stating therein the purpose for which they are convened, and the Legislature shall enter upon no business except that for which they were called together.

Since 1866, the Governor of Nebraska has possessed the authority to convene the legislature on "extraordinary occasions." The legislature, by statute (Neb Rev Stat 50–125), also claims the power to call itself into special session, with the approval of two-thirds of the membership.

Special sessions have been called with some frequency by the governors as they have tried to cope with fluctuations in the economy in face of the requirement for a balanced budget. Governors Thone and Kerrey, in the early 1980s, called lawmakers back several times to cut the state budget because of the collapse of the farm economy in the state. Several recent special sessions were the result of court decisions about the property tax.

The participants in the special session have generally been careful to stay within the parameters for action set forth in the call of the governor. The court has sometimes declared legislation unconstitutional because the items enacted were not within the governor's proclamation (Arrow Club v. Nebraska Liquor Control Commission, 1964). The governor, however, can amend the proclamation to include valid subjects for legislation while the special session is meeting (Jaksha v. State, 1986).

SECTION 9. REPEALED, 1934.

SECTION 10. GOVERNOR TO APPOINT OFFICERS; REMOVAL

The Governor shall appoint with the approval of a majority of the Legislature, all persons whose offices are established by the Constitution, or which may be created by law, and whose appointment or election is not otherwise by law or herein provided for; and no such person shall be appointed or elected by the Legislature. The Governor shall have power to remove, for cause and after a public hearing, any person whom he may appoint for a term except officers provided for in Article V of the Constitution, and he may declare his office vacant, and fill the same as herein provided as in other cases of vacancy. The Governor shall have power to remove any other person whom he appoints at any time and for any reason.

This section gives the governor the power to hire and fire subordinates within that part of the executive branch controlled by him or her. It remained unchanged from 1875 to 1972. Then the second and third sentences were added in order to clarify the power of the governor in removing state officials. The major exception concerns the offices of Article V, that is, judges. The power is also limited by the words "for cause," which means that dismissal may not necessarily be justified if it is because of a policy disagreement with the governor; it must be demonstrated that the person is being fired for "incompetency, neglect of duty, or malfeasance in office" (State ex. rel. Beck v. Obbink, 1961).

To remove an officer for cause, a hearing must be held. The charges against the person must be reasonably definite, advance notice of the hearing must be given, and the opportunity to defend one's self must be afforded (State ex rel. Meyer v. Sorrell, 1962).

SECTION 11. ELECTED STATE OFFICER; VACATION OF OFFICE; GOVERNOR FILL BY APPOINTMENT; TERM

If any elected state office created by this Constitution, except offices provided for in Article V of this Constitution, shall be vacated by death, resignation or otherwise, it shall be the duty of the Governor to fill that office by appointment, and the appointee shall hold the office until his successor shall be elected and qualified in such manner as may be provided by law.

This section simply gives the governor the authority to fill all elected state offices if they are vacated before the regular expiration of a term. Vacancies in the "offices provided for in Article V"—judges—are handled in the method described in our discussion below on judicial selection. For all other offices, appointments made while the legislature is not in session are regarded as temporary (State ex rel. Johnson v. Hagemeister, 1955).

A 1962 amendment removed obsolete references to the state senate and excluded the judges from this section. In 1972, the section was rewritten and the lieutenant governor was excepted; that exception was then removed in 1980.

SECTION 12. NONELECTIVE STATE OFFICERS; VACATION; GOVERNOR; FILL THE OFFICE BY APPOINTMENT; APPROVAL BY LEGISLATURE

If any nonelective state office, except offices provided for in Article V of this Constitution, shall be vacated by death, resignation or otherwise, it shall be the duty of the Governor to fill that office by appointment. If the Legislature is in session such appointment shall be subject to the approval of a majority of the members of the Legislature. If the Legislature is not in session, the Governor shall make a temporary appointment until the next session of the Legislature, at which time a majority of the members of the Legislature shall have the right to approve or disapprove the appointment. All appointees shall hold their office until their successor shall be appointed and qualified. No person after being rejected by the Legislature shall be again nominated for the same office at the same session, unless at request of the Legislature, or be appointed to the same office during the recess or adjournment of the Legislature.

This section merely applies the same gubernatorial power, described in Section 11 to nonelective state offices, with the same restrictions, approved in 1972, concerning judges.

SECTION 13. BOARD OF PAROLE; MEMBERS; POWERS; REPRIEVES; PROCEEDINGS; POWER TO PARDON; LIMITATIONS

The Legislature shall provide by law for the establishment of a Board of Parole and the qualifications of its members. Said board, or a majority thereof, shall have power to grant paroles after conviction and judgment, under such conditions as may be prescribed by law, for any offense committed against the criminal laws of this state except treason and cases of impeachment. The Governor, Attorney General and Secretary of State, sitting as a board, shall have power to remit fines and forfeitures and to grant respites, reprieves, pardons or commutations in all cases of conviction for offenses against the law of the state, except treason and cases of impeachment. The Board of Parole may advise the Governor, Attorney General and Secretary of State on the merits of any application for remission, respite, reprieve, pardon or commutation but such advice shall not be binding on them. The Governor shall have power to suspend the execution of the sentence imposed for treason until the case can be reported to the Legislature at its next session, when the Legislature shall either grant a pardon or commute the sentence or direct the execution, or grant a further reprieve.

Originally, the pardoning power rested solely in the hands of the governor. But in 1919, Nebraskans were shocked when it was learned that a state senator, while acting as governor, had granted a furlough to a convicted murderer. This led to the revelation that pardons, commutations, furloughs, and paroles had been granted by governors in a fashion that suggested laxity, if not venality, in the execution of the penal system. The 1920 Convention devised a Board of Pardons, consisting of the governor, attorney general, and the secretary of state. Voters in 1938 declined to approve an amendment which would have changed the makeup of the board.

The Board of Pardons was, in effect, the parole mechanism for the state's penal system, and every month the governor and his two colleagues would go to the state penitentiary to review the cases. The size of the prison population and the complexity of parole decisions demanded a better method. A 1968 amendment gave the authority to the legislature to create a separate Board of Parole; the amendment also retained the three-member board, now unnamed in the Constitution, with the power "to remit fines and forfeitures and to grant respites, reprieves, pardons or commutations." Nebraska, along with Florida and Nevada, are the only three states which do not allow the governor alone to decide the granting of some form of clemency. The board still has the sole responsibility for the power of clemency (Johnson v. Exon, 1977).

That this is an awkward arrangement was finally brought out in 1991. Harold Otey, a convicted murderer, appealed to the Board of Pardons to stay his impending execution. Attorney General Don Stenberg joined with Governor Ben Nelson to deny the appeal. The defense attorneys immediately asked for, and received, a stay of execution from the district court, basing their argument on the fact that Stenberg had campaigned on a strong pro-death penalty stand and prejudged the case since it was his staff that presented to the board the argument in favor of Otey's execution. The state responded that clemency is purely an executive function and does not have to be fair.

In *Otey v. State* (1992), the supreme court upheld the actions of the Board of Pardons. The granting of clemency is an executive function and Article II prevents judicial interference. The requirements for due process of law do not apply in such cases since the "Nebraska Board of Pardons has the unfettered discretion to grant or deny a commutation of a lawfully imposed sentence for any reason or for no reason at all." The court summarized the process in these words:

> In a death penalty case in Nebraska, it is the judicial branch of government that sentences a convicted felon to death. It is during the judicial procedure that a defendant is entitled to the full panoply of due process rights. In Nebraska, commutation of a death sentence by the State is purely a matter of grace exercised by the executive branch, and no due process rights are available to the applicant. Commutation is the giving back of an offender's life, which has been taken away by due process in the state's judicial process. In seeking clemency, the offender can expect only the right to make an application for clemency.

SECTION 14. GOVERNOR TO BE COMMANDER-IN-CHIEF OF MILITIA

> The Governor shall be commander-in-chief of the military and naval forces of the state (except when they shall be called into the service of the United States) and may call out the same to execute the laws, suppress insurrection, and repel invasion.

This section, in some form, has been in every Constitution, although all references to Nebraska's naval forces are probably superfluous. The governor appoints a commissioned officer from the Nebraska National Guard as adjutant general who is in charge of the Military Department. Members of the Guard, upon enlistment, become subject to the statutes authorized by this section (Lind v. Nebraska National Guard, 1944).

SECTION 15. BILLS TO BE PRESENTED TO GOVERNOR; APPROVAL; PROCEDURE; DISAPPROVAL OR REDUCTION OF ITEMS OF APPROPRIATION; PASSAGE DESPITE DISAPPROVAL OR REDUCTION

Every bill passed by the Legislature, before it becomes a law, shall be presented to the Governor. If he approves he shall sign it, and thereupon it shall become a law, but if he does not approve or reduce any item or items of appropriation, he shall return it with his objections to the Legislature, which shall enter the objections at large upon its journal, and proceed to reconsider the bill with the objections as a whole, or proceed to reconsider individually the items disapproved or reduced. If then three-fifths of the members elected agree to pass the bill with objections it shall become a law, or if three-fifths of the members elected agree to repass any item or items disapproved or reduced, the bill with such repassage shall become a law. In all cases the vote shall be determined by yeas and nays, to be entered upon the journal. Any bill which shall not be returned by the Governor within five days (Sundays excepted) after it shall have been presented to him, shall become a law in like manner as if he had signed it; unless the Legislature by their adjournment prevent its return; in which case it shall be filed, with his objections, in the office of the Secretary of State within five days after such adjournment, or become a law. The Governor may disapprove or reduce any item or items of appropriation contained in bills passed by the Legislature, and the item or items so disapproved shall be stricken therefrom, and the items reduced shall remain as reduced unless the Legislature has reconsidered the item or items disapproved or reduced and has repassed any such item or items over the objection of the Governor by a three-fifths approval of the members elected.

Section 15 describes the most powerful tool of the governor, the veto power, whereby that officer acts as part of the lawmaking branch (State ex rel. Crocker v. Junkin, 1907). Thirty members of the forty-nine-member Unicameral must agree to override a veto. Unlike the President of the United States, the Governor of Nebraska has the authority to "line-item" veto appropriation bills. This device allows the governor to eliminate or reduce the specific dollar amounts in appropriations. Together with the budget-making power found in Section 7, this section makes the governor the major force in budgetary politics.

The 1875 Constitution authorized the governor to strike entire items from an appropriation bill, while a 1972 amendment permitted the reduction of items. In 1974, obsolete language was removed from this section, and in 1976 the role of the legislature in overriding line-item vetoes was clarified.

The governor may not return a bill as a "clerical function" to correct minor errors; any return constitutes a veto, regardless of the nature of the governor's objections (Center Bank v. Dept. of Banking and Finance, 1981). If the governor vetoes a bill with the emergency clause attached, the override still requires only thirty votes and not the thirty-three needed for the original passage of emergency legislation (Sandberg v. State, 1972).

SECTION 16. ORDER OF SUCCESSION TO BECOME GOVERNOR; LIEUTENANT GOVERNOR; DUTIES

> In case of the conviction of the Governor on impeachment, his removal from office, his resignation or his death, the Lieutenant Governor, the Speaker of the Legislature and such other persons designated by law shall in that order be Governor for the remainder of the Governor's term. In case of the death of the Governor-elect, the Lieutenant Governor-elect, the Speaker of the Legislature and such other persons designated by law shall become Governor in that order at the commencement of the Governor-elect's term. If the Governor or the person in line of succession to serve as Governor is absent from the state, or suffering under an inability, the powers and duties of the office of Governor shall devolve in order of precedence until the absence or inability giving rise to the devolution of powers ceases as provided by law. After January 1, 1975, the Lieutenant Governor shall serve on all boards and commissions in lieu of the Governor whenever so designated by the Governor, shall perform such duties as may be delegated to him by the Governor, and shall devote his full time to the duties of his office.

The Constitution of 1866 did not provide for a lieutenant governor, and upon the impeachment of Governor Butler in 1872, Secretary of State W. H. James succeeded him. The Conventions of 1871 and 1875 created the office of lieutenant governor, but it was clear this position was not regarded as a full-time job; it is still the only officer not required to live in Lincoln. The authority to serve in lieu of the governor on various boards and commissions was provided in 1970. A 1972 amendment combined Section 16 with Section 18 which described the order of succession.

The last time a lieutenant governor succeeded to the governorship was in 1960 when the Democrat Ralph G. Brooks died and was replaced by the Republican Dwight Burney. The amendment in 1972 to Article IV, Section 1, now prevents the governor and the lieutenant governor from being members of different political parties.

The court is not well disposed toward the more exuberant visions of power by acting governors. In 1942, Lieutenant Governor William Johnson filed claim for a portion of the salary of Governor Robert Cochran for compensation for the days in which the governor was out of state on public business or vacation. The court said that common sense must govern here and Johnson was no more entitled to a governor's salary than he would be to fire the governor's appointees or to move into the governor's mansion (Johnson v. Johnson).

SECTION 17. REPEALED, 1934.

SECTION 18. REPEALED, 1972.

SECTION 19. STATE INSTITUTIONS; MANAGEMENT, CONTROL, AND GOVERNMENT; DETERMINATION BY LEGISLATURE

The general management, control and government of all state charitable, mental, reformatory, and penal institutions shall be vested as determined by the Legislature.

The 1866 Constitution was silent about the management of public institutions, but by 1871 Nebraskans were highly suspicious, and rightly so, about giving any single person control over these prized political plums. The Conventions of 1871 and 1875 provided for a board, consisting of the commissioner of public lands, the secretary of state, treasurer, and attorney general, which would supervise "all the buildings, grounds and lands of the state, the state prison, asylums, and all other institutions thereof." A detailed amendment, passed in 1912, gave the governor the power to appoint a bipartisan, three-member Board of Commissioners of State Institutions. The amendment also stripped the governor of most of the remaining power over state institutions. The Convention of 1920 simplified the language of Section 19 and renamed the board as the Board of Control.

The present language was approved in 1958. Legislation was passed returning control of most public institutions to the governor. Through the Departments of Correctional Services and Public Institutions, the governor can now be said to be in charge of a major—and expensive—function of state government. At the same time, "the Legislature has complete authority over the entities" identified in this section and has only delegated the day-to day administration of state charitable, mental, reformatory and penal institutions to the executive branch (AFSCME v. Dept. of Public Institutions, 1976).

SECTION 20. PUBLIC SERVICE COMMISSION; MEMBERSHIP TERMS; POWERS

There shall be a Public Service Commission, consisting of not less than three nor more than seven members, as the Legislature shall prescribe, whose term of office shall be six years, and whose compensation shall be fixed by the Legislature. Commissioners shall be elected by districts of substantially equal population as the

> Legislature shall provide. The powers and duties of such commission shall include the regulation of rates, service and general control of common carriers as the Legislature may provide by law. But, in the absence of specific legislation, the commission shall exercise the powers and perform the duties enumerated in this provision.

The Nebraska Public Service Commission is an elected board with the responsibility for regulating certain aspects of the transportation, communication, and warehousing industries. The powers of the PSC are plenary and self-executing in regard to the regulation of common carriers (In re Complaint of Fecht, 1984). Where the legislature has enacted specific laws to implement Section 20, the PSC is subject to and governed by those laws (Dahlsten v. Harris, 1974). It is clear that the legislature can limit the scope of the commission's power (Union Transfer Co. v. Bee Line Motor Freight, 1948), as it did in 1985 when it effectively removed the PSC from oversight of telephones in the state.

The present Public Service Commission has an interesting history. The Convention of 1871 and 1875 devoted an entire article (Art. XI) to the question of the regulation of the railroads. At the same time, the Constitution of 1875 posed a problem because it also prohibited the creation of any new executive offices, and the amending procedures were so difficult that nothing could be changed.

After voters in 1884 rejected the formation of a railroad commission, the legislature used a little subterfuge by establishing in 1885 such a body (renamed in 1887 as the Board of Transportation), ostensibly under the direction of existing state executives. The supreme court eventually terminated this constitutional farce, although the grounds for doing so were based on technical details of the way in which the law was passed (State v. Burlington and Missouri River Railroad Company, 1901).

In 1912, the voters finally approved the creation of the Railway Commission. This was to consist of three members elected on a partisan ballot at large for staggered terms of six years. A 1962 amendment permitted an increase in the number of commissioners and mandated elections by district. The name was changed to Public Service Commission in 1972, although references to the Railway Commission are found elsewhere in this Constitution.

As the state's oldest and most important regulatory agency, the PSC has been involved in a great deal of litigation. The fact that it was constitutionally created distinguishes it from executive departments or commissions resulting from legislation (State ex rel. Johnson v. Chase, 1946). Section 20 is "an independent part of the Constitution and not . . . an amendment to the executive, legislative, or judicial articles thereof" (Swanson v. Sorensen, 1967). At the same time, despite its judicial and legislative powers, the PSC is to be regarded as an administrative agency (Yellow Cab Co. v. Nebraska Railway Commission, 1963).

The power of the PSC to regulate common carriers is plenary and self-executing (Dahlsten v. Harris, 1974). However, the legislature may divest the Commission of jurisdiction over common carriers to the extent that the legislature occupies the field through the passage of specific legislation (State v. Chicago & N.W. Railway Co., 1947). The legislature cannot shift the regulation of common carriers to another state agency but must assume the responsibility itself (Railway Commission v. Ramsey, 1949). Neither may the legislature "absolutely and totally abandon or abolish constitutionally conferred regulatory control over common carriers (State ex rel. Spire v. Northwestern Bell Telephone Co., 1989). Legislation pre-empting the regulatory role of the PSC must be, in the eyes of the court, specific and not general.

SECTION 21. REPEALED, 1972.

Upon the recommendation of the Constitutional Revision Commission in 1972, Section 21 and other sections relating to the appointments, removals, and vacancy provisions were consolidated in Sections 10, 11, and 12.

SECTION 22. EXECUTIVE OFFICIALS TO KEEP ACCOUNTS; REPORTS; FALSE REPORTS; PENALTIES

The Legislature shall provide by statute for the keeping of accounts and the reporting by those agencies of the state which are required to administer cash funds not subject to appropriation by the Legislature, and an annual report thereof shall be made to the Governor under oath; and any officer who makes a false report shall be guilty of perjury and punished accordingly.

A 1964 amendment clarified the intent of this section so that it applies to the executives in charge of cash accounts. This reporting is to insure that the legislature is aware of state money not derived from the general fund. The section applies to all officers of public institutions such as the state colleges and universities or public corrections (Moore v. State, 1898).

SECTION 23. EXECUTIVE OFFICIALS AND HEADS OF INSTITUTIONS; REPORTS TO LEGISLATURE; INFORMATION FROM EXPENDING AGENCIES

All expending agencies of the state as the Legislature may provide shall at least ten days preceding each regular session of the Legislature severally report to the Governor, who shall transmit such reports to the Legislature, together with the reports of the Judges of the Supreme Court of defects in the constitution and laws, and the Governor or the Legislature may at any time require information, in writing, under oath, from the officers of all expending agencies, upon any subject relating to the condition, management and expenses of their respective offices.

The original language referred to the "officers of the executive department and of all the public institutions of the state." A 1964 amendment changed it to "all expending agencies of the state." This section merely requires annual reports on the operation of the various state agencies and courts. It is unclear how valuable this exercise is, although the supreme court did allow that at least one report on statutory defects led to needed changes (Haffke v. State, 1948).

SECTION 24. GREAT SEAL

There shall be a seal of the state, which shall be called the "Great Seal of the State of Nebraska," which shall be kept by the Secretary of State and used by him officially as directed by law.

Based on the authority of the Constitution of 1866, the legislature in 1867 approved the design of the current state seal. For some reason, the law requires a representation of the Rocky Mountains in the background, perhaps deluding careless observers into believing that Nebraska is an alpine wonderland.

The words on the Seal may be taken more seriously. In 1916, Judge Sedgwick concluded that the "principle of our Constitution of absolute equality in governmental matters is recognized in the legislation which requires the great seal of the state shall contain the words "Equality before the law" (State ex rel. Harte v. Moorhead).

SECTION 25. SALARIES OF OFFICIALS; FEES

The officers provided for in this article shall receive such salaries as may be provided by law. Such officers, or such other officers as may be provided by law, shall not receive for their own use any fees, costs, or interest upon public money in their hands. All fees that may hereafter be payable by law for services performed, or received by an officer provided for in this article, by virtue of his office shall be paid forthwith into the state treasury.

The Constitutions of 1866, 1871, and 1875 spelled out in exact dollar amounts the salaries of the elected state executives. A 1920 amendment permitted the legislature to set the salaries; another amendment in 1956 removed a statement that the salaries could not be changed more than once every eight years.

The mansion provided to the governor as an-official residence is not regarded as a form of compensation (State v. Sheldon, 1907).

SECTION 26. OFFICIALS TO GIVE BONDS

All offices of government shall give bond as may be prescribed by law.

This simple statement approved in 1964 amended the more complex wording of the original Constitution. The section provides that executives prove their capacity for a public trust by posting a money surety; the bond has been defined as a contractual obligation that the bonded official will faithfully discharge the duties of the office (Laverty v. Cochran, 1936). The last time this section posed a problem was in 1958 when the perennial candidate and part-time bartender, Richard Larsen, was elected state treasurer. He was eventually bonded after the state paid a very high premium.

SECTION 27. EXECUTIVE OFFICES; CREATION OF

No executive state office other than herein provided shall be created except by a two-thirds majority of all members elected to the Legislature.

The frugal authors of the 1875 Constitution thought they had stopped the growth of government by stating that "no other executive state office shall be continued or created." Within a few years, it was clear to most that this was an impossible denial of powers, and the 1920 Convention remedied the situation with this language, unchanged except for the removal of references to two houses in 1972. The power to create a department is also the power to discontinue the same, as the legislature may do (Swanson v. State, 1937).

SECTION 28. TAX COMMISSIONER; POWERS; COMPENSATION

A Tax Commissioner shall be appointed by the Governor with the advice and consent of the Senate. He shall have jurisdiction over the administration of the revenue laws of the state, and together with the Governor, Secretary of State, State Auditor and State Treasurer shall have power to review and equalize assessments of property for taxation within the state. He shall have such other powers and perform such other duties as the legislature may provide by law.

This section was adopted in 1920 and, as the reference to the senate indicates, has remained untouched ever since. The office of tax commissioner had existed since 1903 as the secretary of the State Board of Equalization. This board, composed of the four elected executives mentioned in this section plus the appointed tax commissioner, was also given its constitutional legitimacy by this section.

The State Board of Equalization and Assessment equalizes the valuation of property among the counties for property tax purposes. It also sets the variable motor fuel and special fuel tax rates for each fiscal year. When the state relied on the property tax, the Board was responsible for its general administration. From 1967 to 1983, the Board also had the responsibility for setting the state's sales and income tax rates. Taxpayers can appeal a decision of the Board to the Nebraska Supreme Court (DeCamp v. State Board of Equalization and Assessment, 1979).

Article V

Judicial
(ORIGINALLY ARTICLE VI)

SECTION 1. POWER VESTED IN COURTS; EXECUTIVE HEAD

The judicial power of the state shall be vested in a Supreme Court, an appellate court, district courts, county courts, in and for each county, with one or more judges for each county or with one judge for two or more counties, as the Legislature shall provide, and such other courts inferior to the Supreme Court as may be created by law. In accordance with rules established by the Supreme Court and not in conflict with other provisions of this Constitution and laws governing such matters, general administrative authority over all courts in this state shall be vested in the Supreme Court and shall be exercised by the Chief Justice. The Chief Justice shall be the executive head of the courts and may appoint an administrative director thereof.

The Nebraska judicial system now consists of a supreme court, a court of appeals, twenty-one district courts, and the county courts. Three counties have separate juvenile courts. The Worker's Compensation Court is a court of specialized jurisdiction. The details of this system are spelled out in this and other sections of Article V.

The Constitutions of 1866, 1871, and 1875 were essentially the same except the latter two introduced the county courts. The Convention of 1920 undertook a thorough revision of Article V, including Section 1 which now gave the legislature greater latitude in creating new courts. In 1970, an amendment clarified that not every county was entitled to a separate court. More significantly, it also gave administrative authority over the court system to the chief justice and authorized the appointment of a state court administrator. References to the justice of the peace courts were eliminated. The latest amendment in 1990 permitted the creation of an intermediate appeals courts between the supreme court and the district courts.

LB 732, signed by the Governor on June 6, 1991, establishes the Nebraska Court of Appeals. The court consists of six members who sit in two panels of three judges each. One member is designated as chief judge. The court of appeals hears appealed criminal and civil cases except for those involving the death penalty or those which raise constitutional questions; such cases still go before the supreme court. The supreme court may also remove a case from the lower court. Parties in a case appealed to the court of appeals may file a petition in the supreme court to bypass the lower court's review and move directly to the higher court.

The Nebraska Supreme Court has allowed the legislature considerable leeway in the creation of courts (Anderson v. Tiemann, 1967). The Worker's Compensation Court is one example of this power (Lincoln v. Nebraska Workmen's Compensation Court, 1937). Tolerance of legislative involvement in the judiciary, however, has its limits. For example, the legislature has long insisted that all supreme court decisions "must show the name of the judge writing the opinion (Neb Rev Stat 24–212)," but the court continues to issue a large number of *per curium* opinions.

The judicial power is the authority of some person or body to hear and determine a controversy and render judgments or decrees which are binding on the parties (Laverty v. Cochran, 1936). Connected with this authority is the sole power to admit persons to the practice of law in the state and to fix qualifications for admission to the state bar (State ex rel. Wright v. Barlow, 1936), as well as to define and regulate the practice of law (In re Integration of the Nebraska State Bar Assn., 1937).

According to the court, "it is the imperative duty of the judicial department to protect its jurisdictions at the boundaries of power fixed by the Constitution" (State ex rel. Wright v. Barney, 1937). The boundary is faintest where the legislature empowers the executive to make judicial decisions. Over the years, the court has decided a number of cases reaffirming the point that the "conferring upon state agencies or officers, of executive or administrative functions requiring the exercise of quasi judicial powers, does not conflict with the constitutional provisions regarding officers and bodies upon whom judicial power may be confirmed" (Anderson v. Tiemann, 1967).

The administrative supremacy of the chief justice is a fairly new development. The state court administrator serves as the executive officer in charge of the court system. The officer's responsibilities include developing coordination within the judicial branch and with other state agencies, developing plans for the improvement of the judicial system, and serving as a central source for information about the courts. The administrator also develops statistics, prepares budgets, and produces in-service training courses for judges and other court personnel.

SECTION 2. SUPREME COURT; QUORUM; DECISIONS OF UNCONSTITUTIONALITY; JURISDICTION; DISTRICT JUDGES AS ASSOCIATE JUDGES; RETIRED SUPREME COURT JUDGES; TEMPORARY DUTY; COURT DIVISIONS; ASSIGNMENTS BY CHIEF JUSTICE

The Supreme Court shall consist of seven judges, one of whom shall be the Chief Justice. A majority of the judges shall be necessary to constitute a quorum. A majority of the members sitting shall have authority to pronounce a decision except in cases involving the constitutionality of an act of the Legislature. No legislative act shall be held unconstitutional except by the concurrence of five judges. The Supreme Court shall have jurisdiction in all cases relating to the revenue, civil cases in which the state is a party, mandamus, quo warranto, habeas corpus, election contests involving state officers other than members of the Legislature, and such appellate jurisdiction as may be provided by law. The Legislature may provide that any judge of the Supreme Court or judge of the appellate court created pursuant to Article V, section 1, of this Constitution who has retired may be called upon for temporary duty by the Supreme Court. Whenever necessary to the prompt submission and determination of causes, the Supreme Court may appoint judges of the district court or the appellate court to act as associate judges of the Supreme Court, sufficient in number, with the judges of the Supreme Court, to constitute two divisions of the court of five judges in each division. Whenever judges of the district court or the appellate court are so acting, the court shall sit in two divisions, and four of the judges thereof shall be necessary to constitute a quorum. Judges of the district court or the appellate court so appointed shall serve during the pleasure of the court and shall have all the power of judges of the Supreme Court. The Chief Justice shall make assignments of judges to the divisions of the court, preside over the division of judges of which he or she is a member, and designate the presiding judge of the other division. The judges of the Supreme Court, sitting without division, shall hear and determine ail cases involving the constitutionality of a statute and all appeals involving capital cases and may review any decision rendered by a division of the court. In such cases, in event of the disability or disqualification by interest or otherwise of any of the judges of the Supreme Court, the court may appoint judges of the district court or the appellate court to sit temporarily as judges of the Supreme Court, sufficient to constitute a full court of seven judges. Judges of the district court or the appellate court shall receive no additional salary by virtue of their appointment and services as herein provided, but they shall be reimbursed their necessary traveling and hotel expenses.

The original supreme court of 1866 consisted of three members called "justices" who were also to serve as judges of the district courts. The Conventions of 1871 and 1875 retained the size but changed the name of the members to "judges," following the example of Illinois. A 1908 amendment increased the membership of the court to seven.

The Convention of 1920 undertook an extensive rewriting of Section 2. The proposal established that the presiding officer of the supreme court was to be called "chief justice." It also provided for divisions of the court through the enlistment of judges from lower courts. Perhaps the most novel idea introduced by amendment in 1920 was the requirement for an extraordinary majority to declare a statute unconstitutional. According to the Convention's publicity, "a legislative act should stand as expressing the people's will unless it is clearly in violation of some provision of the Constitution."[9] This limitation has saved several important pieces of legislation. For instance, a bill passed in 1988 called for the incorporation of Kearney State College into the University of Nebraska system. Although a four-member majority felt the law violated Article VII, Section 13, the legislation was upheld (State ex rel. Spire v. Beermann, 1991).

In a dissent to a 1970 decision, one judge was so annoyed at being in the losing majority that he suggested the requirement was itself unconstitutional. It diluted judicial power and thus "destroys the republican form of government" guaranteed by the U.S. Constitution. It also violated the requirement for due process of law (State ex rel. Belker v. Board of Educational Lands and Funds, 1970).

In the 1800s, it was the practice of the supreme court to render advisory opinions to the executive and legislature on the constitutionality of state actions. In 1893, Judge Norval dissented from this practice, arguing it was beyond the constitutional jurisdiction of the court (In re Board of Public Lands and Buildings, and Board of Purchase and Supplies). The next year, the court adopted Rule XXIII which states: "Only questions involved in matters of actual litigation before the court will be entertained or judicially determined, and no opinion will be filed in answer to any merely hypothetical question."

Declaratory judgments by the court can be obtained through the actions of the attorney general. That officer can bring suit to test the constitutionality of statutes "in the name of the State in the public interest" (State ex rel. Meyer v. Peters, 1972). "As the chief law officer of the state, he may, in the absence of some express legislative restriction to the contrary, exercise all such power and authority as the public interest may from time to time require" (State ex rel. Sorensen v. State Board of Equalization and Assessment). The rule that a person may not attack the constitutionality of a statute where his or her rights are not affected applies to private persons and not to the attorney general when acting in the public interest.

---

[9] *Proceedings, 1919–20*, II, 2845.

An amendment in 1968 extended the jurisdiction of the supreme court to certain election contests, and in 1970 retired judges of the supreme court were permitted to serve in a temporary role with the court.

"Except in the exercise of its appellate jurisdiction, the Supreme Court is one of limited and enumerated powers," and the legislature cannot, on its own initiative, expand that original jurisdiction (Sorenson v. Swanson, 1967). As it has been amended, that jurisdiction includes revenue cases, civil cases in which the state is a party, mandamus, quo warranto or a writ filed against any person unlawfully holding or exercising any public office or franchise within the state (Neb Rev Stat 25-21, 1211), habeas corpus, and certain election contests. In the matter of habeas corpus, the court will not issue a writ unless unusual circumstances are present or the matter is of statewide importance (Williams v. Olson, 1943).

The appellate jurisdiction is determined by statute (Larson v. Wegner, 1930), although Article I, Sections 23 and 24, guaranteed the right of appeal to the supreme court in almost all criminal and civil cases, until the amendment of 1990. Creation of the intermediate appeals court will relieve the higher court of an increasingly onerous caseload. The appellate jurisdiction of the court is limited to a review of judgments and final orders (Rhodes v. Houston, 1961).

SECTION 3. TERMS OF SUPREME COURT

At least two terms of the supreme court shall be held each year, at the seat of government.

This language has remained unchanged since 1875. The section has not required interpretation by the courts.

SECTION 4. SUPREME COURT JUSTICES; SELECTION; RESIDENCE

The Chief Justice and the Judges of the Supreme Court shall be selected as provided in this Article V. They shall reside at the place where the court is located but no Justice or Judge shall be deemed thereby to have lost his residence at the place from which he was selected.

Originally, the judges were to be elected at large. A 1908 amendment required them to reside "at the place where the court is holden." In 1920, a system whereby the chief justice was elected at large and the judges elected from six districts was approved. The 1920 amendment also said that judges would not lose their residence by serving in Lincoln. In 1962, direct election of the judges was ended and the method for filling supreme court vacancies (and all other judgeships), as described in Section 21, below, was approved.

The judges of the supreme court are created as a distinct class for all purposes of legislation affecting them (State ex rel. Taylor v. Hall, 1935).

SECTION 5. SUPREME COURT JUDICIAL DISTRICTS; REDISTRICTING; WHEN

The Legislature shall divide the state into six contiguous and compact districts of approximately equal population, which shall be numbered from one to six, which shall be known as the Supreme Court judicial districts. The Legislature shall redistrict the state after each federal decennial census. In any such redistricting, county lines shall be followed whenever practicable, but other established lines may be followed at the discretion of the Legislature. Whenever the Supreme Court is redistricted, the judges serving prior to the redistricting shall continue in office, and the law providing for such redistricting shall where necessary specify the newly established districts which they shall represent for the balance of their terms.

In 1875, the three supreme court judges were elected from the state at large. A 1908 amendment expanded the number to seven, and the 1920 Convention established districts from which judges were elected. The name, "Supreme Court judicial districts," was added in 1962. Redistricting of the districts was mandated by a 1970 amendment. Neither this section nor Section 7, below, is applicable to substitute judges (ConAgra, Inc. v. Cargill, Inc., 1986).

SECTION 6. CHIEF JUSTICE TO PRESIDE

The chief justice shall preside at all terms and sittings of the supreme court, and in his absence or disability the judges present shall select one of their number chief justice pro tempore.

The amendment of 1908 replaced a more complicated version of Section 6. In 1920, disability of the chief justice was added as a reason for selecting a temporary replacement. This section has never been litigated.

SECTION 7. CHIEF JUSTICE; ASSOCIATE JUSTICES; QUALIFICATIONS

No personal shall be eligible to the office of Chief Justice or Judge of the Supreme Court unless he shall be at least thirty years of age, and a citizen of the United States, and shall have resided in the state at least three years preceding his selection; nor, in the case of a Judge of the Supreme Court selected from a Supreme Court judicial district, unless he shall be a resident and elector of the district from which selected.

The basic qualifications for membership on the Nebraska Supreme Court have remained the same since 1875: at least thirty years old, a U.S. citizen, and a resident of the state for at least three years. The language was very similar to the Illinois Constitution of 1870. The 1920 amendment provided that the judges must reside in the districts from which they are selected. In keeping with the process described in Section 21, below, a 1962 amendment changed "election" to "selection."

There is no significant case law concerning this section.

SECTION 8. STAFF OF THE SUPREME COURT; BUDGET; COPYRIGHT OF STATE REPORTS

The Supreme Court shall appoint such staff as may be needed for the proper dispatch of the business of the court. The court shall prepare and recommend to each session of the Legislature a budget of the estimated expenses of the court. The copyright of the state reports shall forever remain the property of the state.

The Constitution of 1875 identified specific court officials—reporter, clerk, and librarian—and stated their salaries. A 1920 amendment permitted the hiring of other staff and dropped the salary limits. Also in 1920, the preparation of a court budget was mandated, and in 1972 the submission of the budget was required to be submitted to each session. A 1990 amendment removed the listing of specific officers with their terms and substituted it with the more permissive language now found in the section. This section has never been litigated.

SECTION 9. DISTRICT COURTS; JURISDICTION; FELONS MAY PLEAD GUILTY; SENTENCE

The district courts shall have both chancery and common law jurisdiction, and such other jurisdiction as the Legislature may provide; and the judges thereof may admit persons charged with felony to a plea of guilty and pass such sentence as may be prescribed by law.

The Nebraska district court system dates back to the Kansas-Nebraska Act of 1854. The Constitution of 1866 retained the same simple system of three districts presided over by a justice of the supreme court. The 1875 Constitution contained the present language; the section has never been amended.

The district courts are the workhorses of the Nebraska judicial system, hearing all felony and some misdemeanor cases. The larger civil cases are also brought before this court. The district courts hear some appeals from the county courts.

It is clear that the Constitution grants the district courts chancery (or equity) and common law jurisdiction, and the legislature may not infringe on that jurisdiction while at the same time it may grant other jurisdiction (State ex rel.

Wright v. Barney, 1937). The equity jurisdiction of the district courts may be exercised without statutory permission (Matteson v. Creighton University, 1920) and is beyond the power of the legislature to limit or control (Lacey v. Ziegler, 1915). The legislature cannot limit the inherent power of the district courts to punish for contempt of court (State ex rel. Beck v. Frontier Airlines, 1962). The courts have such jurisdiction in criminal cases as is provided by law (State v. Furstenau, 1958). The constitutional grant of jurisdiction is not exclusive and the county courts, by legislation, can be given the same jurisdiction (In re Estate of Steppuhn, 1985).

SECTION 10. DISTRICT COURT JUDICIAL DISTRICTS

The state shall be divided into district court judicial districts. Until otherwise provided by law, the boundaries of the judicial districts and the number of judges of the district courts shall remain as now fixed. The judges of the district courts shall be selected from the respective districts as provided in this Article V.

The Constitution of 1871 and 1875 named the counties to be included in each district. The 1920 amendment gave the legislature the power to determine the number of districts and their boundaries. The amendment of 1962 stopped the election of district judges and provided for the system described in Section 21, below.

There are now twenty-one districts, each with a judge and a court reporter. Those officers are financed by the state. Each county is also required to pay for a district court clerk. However, it has been established that the district judge is a state and not a county officer (Jones v. York County, 1928).

SECTION 11. DISTRICT COURT JUDGES; CHANGE OF NUMBER; BOUNDARIES

The Legislature may change the number of judges of the district courts and alter the boundaries of judicial districts. Such change in number or alterations in boundaries shall not vacate the office of any judge. Such districts shall be formed of compact territory bounded by county lines.

The 1875 Constitution permitted the addition of district courts through an extraordinary vote of the legislature (State v. Stevenson, 1885). A minor change was approved in 1920, and in 1972 references to a two-house legislature were removed.

SECTION 12. DISTRICT COURT JUDGES MAY HOLD COURT FOR EACH OTHER; RETIRED JUDGES; TEMPORARY DUTY

The judges of the district court may hold court for each other and shall do so when required by law or when ordered by the Supreme Court. The Legislature may provide that any judge of the district court who has retired may be called upon for temporary duty by the Supreme Court.

The transferability of district court judges were written into the Constitutions of 1871 and 1875. A 1920 amendment gave the supreme court the authority to reassign the judges. In 1970, it became permissible for retired district judges to be called back to temporary service.

The district courts are held to be courts of general jurisdiction with interchangeable judges all exercising the same jurisdiction (Garotto v. McManus, 1970). Furthermore, the power of a district court judge to hold court in a district other than his or her own does not depend upon the absence or disability of the regular judge (Iron Bear v. Jones, 1948).

SECTION 13. SUPREME COURT AND DISTRICT JUDGES; SALARIES

The chief justice, the judges of the Supreme Court and the judges of the district court shall receive such salaries as may be provided by law.

Nebraskans have been relatively more generous toward their judges than their legislators, perhaps indicating that judging the law is a full-time occupation while making the law is not. The Constitution of 1866 provided an annual salary of $2,000 for the supreme court justices; other judicial officers were to be paid by fees. The Convention of 1871 recommended $3,500 for the supreme court, but the economy-minded Convention of 1875 cut that back to $2,500. An amendment in 1908 increased the salary to $4,500. The Convention of 1920 proposed that the salary of all judges be fixed by the legislature.

SECTION 14. SUPREME COURT AND DISTRICT JUDGES NOT TO ACT AS ATTORNEYS; JUDGE NOT TO PRACTICE LAW; WHEN

No judge of the Supreme Court or district courts shall act as attorney or counselor at law in any manner whatsoever. No judge shall practice law in any court in any matter arising in or growing out of any proceedings in his own court.

The original language of 1875 also prohibited judges from receiving "any other compensation, perquisite, or benefits, for or on account of this office." The restriction was removed in 1920. The second sentence of this section was modified in 1970. The court has held that the proscription in this section also applies to county judges (State ex rel. Nebraska State Bar Assn. v. Conover, 1958).

SECTION 15. REPEALED, 1970.

SECTION 16. REPEALED, 1970.

SECTION 17. REPEALED, 1970.

SECTION 18. REPEALED, 1970.

Sections 15 through 18 were repealed in 1970 as part of a major overhaul of the lowest tier of the state's judicial system. The several hundred justice of the peace courts lost their constitutional protection and were eliminated by a law passed in 1972. County courts were reorganized into districts, and in 1974 legislation was enacted to include the county court judges within the selection process described in Section 21, below. Since 1970, the jurisdiction of the county court is determined by the legislature (In re Estate of Lay ton, 1982). That jurisdiction now includes civil cases involving less than $10,000, misdemeanor cases, and probate, estate administration, and guardianship matters.

SECTION 19. PRACTICE OF ALL COURTS TO BE UNIFORM

The organization, jurisdiction, powers, proceedings, and practice of all courts of the same class or grade, so far as regulated by law and the force and effect of the proceedings, judgments and decrees of such courts, severally, shall be uniform.

An amendment in 1920 removed the original provision that all laws relating to courts be general. The section does not require complete uniformity in all kinds of proceedings in the same court (Larutan Corp. v. Magnolia Homes Manuf. Co., 1973).

SECTION 20. JUDICIAL OFFICERS; TENURE; RESIDENCE; DUTIES; COMPENSATION

All officers provided for in this Article shall hold their offices until their successors shall be qualified and they shall respectively reside in the district or county from which they shall be selected. All officers, when not otherwise provided for in this Article, shall perform such duties and receive such compensation as may be prescribed by law.

Section 20 adds little to the provisions in this article, especially since the change in the process of selection as discussed below. The section was modified in 1920 by the removal of specific lengths for terms of judges. A 1962 amendment changed "elected" to "selected." In 1970, the word "county" was added.

SECTION 21. MERIT PLAN FOR SELECTION OF JUDGES; TERMS OF OFFICE; FILLING OF VACANCIES; PROCEDURES; VOTING FOR NOMINEE

(1) In the case of any vacancy in the Supreme Court or in any district court or in such other court or courts made subject to this provision by law, such vacancy shall be filled by the Governor from a list of at least two nominees presented to him by the appropriate judicial nominating commission. If the Governor shall fail to make an appointment from the list within sixty days from the date it is presented to him, the appointment shall be made by the Chief Justice or the acting Chief Justice of the Supreme Court from the same list.

(2) In all other cases, any vacancy shall be filled as provided by law.

(3) At the next general election following the expiration of three years from the date of appointment of any judge under the provisions of subsection (1) of this section and every six years thereafter as long as such judge retains office, each Justice or Judge of the Supreme Court or district court or such other court or courts as the Legislature shall provide shall have his right to remain in office subject to approval or rejection by the electorate in such manner as the Legislature shall provide; *Provided,* that every judge holding or elected to an office described in subsection (1) of this section on the effective date of this amendment whether by election or appointment, upon qualification shall be deemed to have been selected and to have once received the approval of the electorate as herein provided, and shall be required to submit his right to continue in office to the approval or rejection of the electorate at the general election next preceding the expiration of the term of office for which such judge was elected or appointed, and every six years thereafter. In the case of the Chief Justice of the Supreme Court, the electorate of the entire state shall vote on the question of approval or rejection. In the case of any Judge of the Supreme Court, other than the Chief Justice, and any judge of the district court or any other court made subject to subsection (1) of this section, the electorate of the district from which such judge was selected shall vote on the question of such approval or rejection.

(4) There shall be a judicial nominating commission for the Chief Justice of the Supreme Court and one for each judicial district of the Supreme Court and of the district court and one for each area or district served by any other court made subject to subsection (1) of this section by law. Each judicial nominating commission shall consist of nine members, one of whom shall be a Judge of the Supreme Court who shall be designated by the Governor and shall act as chairman, but shall not be entitled to vote. The members of the bar of the state residing in the area from which the nominees are to be selected shall designate four of their number to serve as members of said commission, and the Governor shall appoint four citizens, not admitted to practice law before the courts of the state, from among the residents of the same geographical area to serve as members of said commission. Not more than four of such voting members shall be of the same political party. The terms of office for members of each judicial nominating commission shall be staggered and shall be fixed by the Legislature. The nominees of any such commission cannot include a member of such commission or any person who has served as a member of such commission within a

period of two years immediately preceding his nomination or for such additional period as the Legislature shall provide. The names of the candidates shall be released to the public prior to a public hearing.
(5) Members of the nominating commission shall vote for the nominee of their choice by roll call. Each candidate must receive a majority of the voting members of the nominating commission to have his name submitted to the Governor.

This section describes the Missouri Plan or, as judges so chosen are pleased to call it, the "merit plan," for the selection of judges. When a vacancy occurs, a judicial nominating commission receives applications from candidates. The commission, composed of lawyers and lay people, reviews the qualifications and forwards to the governor a list of the best qualified candidates. After the judge is appointed by the governor, he or she will serve for at least three years, at which time there is an election in which the only question is whether or not the judge should be retained in office. The system contains elements of executive appointment (as in the federal government) with a degree of democratic participation, all with considerable input from the experts in the law.

Section 21 of the 1875 Constitution, as amended in 1920, originally dealt with the filling of vacancies in judgeships and the means for electing judges was described elsewhere. The amendment of 1962 established the basis of the present system, and in 1972 the membership of the nominating commissions was increased, a supreme court judge was included, and the release of the names of the candidates and the roll call vote was mandated.

The court has determined that judges are not elected to office but are appointed. The election component of this process is "only for the purpose of determining a judge's right to remain or continue in the judicial office to which he was originally appointed" (Garrotto v. McManus, 1970). Furthermore, the term of a judge so selected is peculiar to the individual; a judge's term ends with the judge's service, that is, "the term of office of such a judge can never be incomplete, no matter what event terminates his term or tenure" (Garrotto v. McManus, 1970).

Nebraska has almost thirty years of experience with the Missouri Plan for judicial selection, but there is still no conclusive evidence that the state is better or worse off for it. As in other states, the rates of retention are very high; after several hundred elections, only nine judges have been turned out of office.

A major criticism leveled at this form of judicial selection is that it gives too much weight to the legal elite and prevents diversity in the composition of the courts, especially in terms of racial and gender balance. Until 1991, when a woman was appointed to the newly created court of appeals, only men had served in Nebraska courts with statewide jurisdiction. Even then, only 6 of the state's other 131 judges were female, and all of those at the lowest level. None of the current judges are members of minority groups.

The suspicion that the system may not be as perfect as once advertised was heightened when the court determined that the requirement for a roll call vote on the candidates in Section 21, subsection (5) did not mean that the vote was to be made public. Indeed, statutory supplements to the section implied that the decisions of the commissions were to remain confidential (Marks v. Judicial Nominating Commission, 1990).

SECTION 22. STATE MAY SUE AND BE SUED

The state may sue and be sued and the Legislature shall provide by law in what manner and in what courts suits shall be brought.

This section has never been amended. According to the court, the provision "permits the state to lay its sovereignty aside and consent to be sued on such terms and conditions as the Legislature may prescribe" (Gentry v. State, 1962). The section is not self-executing and requires implementation by the legislature (Patteson v. Johnson, 1985).

SECTION 23. JURISDICTION OF JUDGES AT CHAMBERS

The several judges of the courts of record shall have such jurisdiction at chambers as may be provided by law.

This is the original language of 1875. The section permits judges to act in camera, that is, in the judge's private chamber or in a courtroom where spectators are excluded. The section does not create an inherent judicial authority, and courts "possess only such authority or jurisdiction thereat as is conferred on them by statute" (Vasa v. Vasa, 1957).

SECTION 24. STYLE OF PROCESS

All process shall run in the name of "The State of Nebraska," and all prosecutions shall be carried on in the name of "The State of Nebraska."

This section means that the title of cases will reflect the fact that legal action by the state is being conducted in the name of the state. The Constitutions of 1866 and 1871 used in the name of "The People of the State of Nebraska." Even if a municipal corporation is enforcing its own ordinance, the case must read "State of Nebraska v. . . . " This section from 1875 has never been amended.

SECTION 25. SUPREME COURT TO PROMULGATE RULES OF PRACTICE; TO MAKE RECOMMENDATIONS TO LEGISLATURE

For effectual administration of justice and the prompt disposition of judicial proceedings, the supreme court may promulgate rules of practice and procedures for all courts, uniform as to each class of courts, and not in conflict with laws governing such matters. To the same end, the court may, and when requested by the Legislature by joint resolution, shall certify to the Legislature, its conclusions as to desirable amendments or changes in the general laws governing such practice and proceedings.

The rules of practice are the orders of the court describing the practice to be followed in judicial actions and other proceedings. The Convention of 1920 proposed this section which, at the time, had no direct counterpart in any other state constitution. The supreme court has held that the section does not limit judicial power with respect to making rules about qualifications for the practice of law in the state (State ex rel. Ralston v. Turner, 1942).

SECTION 26. PROVISO AS TO EFFECT OF AMENDMENT

If the foregoing amendment shall be adopted by the electors, all existing courts which are not in the foregoing amendment specifically enumerated and concerning which no other provision is herein made, shall continue in existence and exercise their present jurisdiction, and the judges thereof shall receive their present compensation, until otherwise provided by law; and such judges or appointees to fill vacancies shall hold their offices until their successors shall be elected and qualified.

This section was adopted in 1920 to clarify the impact of the judicial amendments on the existing system. It has no present significance.

SECTION 27. JUVENILE COURTS; AUTHORIZATION

Notwithstanding the provisions of section 9 of this Article, the Legislature may establish courts to be known as juvenile courts, with such jurisdiction and powers as the Legislature may provide. The term, qualification, compensation, and method of appointment or election of the judges of such courts, and the rules governing proceedings therein, may be fixed by the Legislature. The state shall be divided into juvenile court judicial districts that correspond to district court judicial districts until otherwise provided by law. No such court shall be established or afterwards abolished in any juvenile court judicial district unless approved by a majority of those voting on the issue.

This section was adopted by the voters in 1958. A 1972 amendment changed the last phrase from "unless approved by a majority of the electors of such district." Juvenile courts have been set up in the Omaha and Lincoln metropolitan areas. These courts handle matters pertaining to neglected, dependent, and delinquent children. They share jurisdiction with district courts in all matters concerning the care, support, custody, or control of mentally retarded children under eighteen years of age. In counties without a separate juvenile court, the county court shares jurisdiction with the district court in cases involving juveniles.

In recent years, the supreme court has been critical of the operations of some juvenile courts, suggesting the courts have maintained poor records, taken too much time to resolve cases and, most of all, been insensitive to the rights of parents in cases of child abuse or neglect. The juvenile courts have been reminded on several occasions that they are courts and that their failures can result in "damage to the integrity, reputation, and fairness of the judicial process (In re Interest of D.M.B., 1992)."

SECTION 28. COMMISSION ON JUDICIAL QUALIFICATIONS; APPOINTMENT; COMPOSITION; QUALIFICATIONS

The Legislature shall provide for a Commission on Judicial Qualifications consisting of: (1) Three judges, including one district court judge, one county court judges and one judge of any other court inferior to the Supreme Court as now exists or may hereafter be created by law, all of whom shall be appointed by the Chief Justice of the Supreme Court; (2) three members of the Nebraska State Bar Association who shall have practiced law in this state for at least ten years and who shall be appointed by the Executive Council of the Nebraska State Bar Association; (3) three citizens, none of whom shall be a Justice or Judge of the Supreme Court or judge of any court, active or retired, nor a member of the Nebraska State Bar Association, and who shall be appointed by the Governor; and (4) the Chief Justice of the Supreme Court who shall serve as its chairperson.

This section, adopted in 1966, describes the membership of the Commission on Judicial Qualifications, whose duties and operation are described in Sections 29 and 30, below. A 1980 amendment increased the members in each of the three groups by one and added the chief justice as presiding officer.

SECTION 29. COMMISSION ON JUDICIAL QUALIFICATIONS; VOTE OF MAJORITY REQUIRED FOR ACTION

The commission shall act by a vote of the majority of its members and no action of the commission shall be valid unless concurred in by the majority of its members.

Section 29 was also adopted in 1966. The 1980 amendment to Section 28 changed the determination of the chair of the commission.

SECTION 30. JUDGES; DISCIPLINE; REMOVAL FROM OFFICE; GROUNDS; PROCEDURE

(1) A Justice or Judge of the Supreme Court or judge of any court of this state may be reprimanded, disciplined, censured, suspended without pay for a

definite period of time, not to exceed six months, or removed from office for (a) willful misconduct in office, (b) willful disregard of or failure to perform his or her duties, (c) habitual intemperance, (d) conviction of a crime involving moral turpitude, (e) disbarment as a member of the legal profession licensed to practice law in the State of Nebraska, or (f) conduct prejudicial to the administration of justice that brings the judicial office into disrepute, or he or she may be retired for physical or mental disability seriously interfering with the performance of his or her duties if such disability is determined to be permanent or reasonably likely to become permanent. Any citizen of the State of Nebraska may request the Commission on Judicial Qualifications to consider the qualifications of any Justice or Judge of the Supreme Court or other judge, and in such event the commission shall make such investigation as the commission deems necessary and shall, upon a finding of probable cause, reprimand such Justice or Judge of the Supreme Court or other judge or order a formal open hearing to be held before it concerning the reprimand, discipline, censure, suspension, removal, or retirement of such Justice or Judge of the Supreme Court or other judge. In the alternative or in addition, the commission may request the Supreme Court to appoint one or more special masters who shall be judges of courts of record to hold a formal hearing to take evidence in any such matter, and to report to the commission. If, after formal open hearing, or after considering the record and report of the masters, the commission finds that the charges are established by clear and convincing evidence, it shall recommend to the Supreme Court that the Justice or Judge of the Supreme Court or other judge involved shall be reprimanded, disciplined, censured, suspended without pay for a definite period of time not to exceed six months, removed, or retired as the case may be.

(2) The Supreme Court shall review the record of the proceedings and in its discretion may permit the introduction of additional evidence. The Supreme Court shall make such determination as it finds just and proper, and may order the reprimand, discipline, censure, suspension, removal, or retirement of such Justice or Judge of the Supreme Court or other judge, or may wholly reject the recommendation. Upon an order for retirement, the Justice or Judge of the Supreme Court or other judge shall thereby be retired with the same rights and privileges as if he or she had retired pursuant to statute. Upon an order for removal, the Justice or Judge of the Supreme Court or other judge shall be removed from office, his or her salary shall cease from the date of such order, and he or she shall be ineligible for judicial office. Upon an order for suspension, the Justice or Judge of the Supreme Court or other judge shall draw no salary and shall perform no judicial functions during the period of suspension. Suspension shall not create a vacancy in the office of Justice or Judge of the Supreme Court or other judge.

(3) Upon order of the Supreme Court, a Justice or Judge of the Supreme Court or other judge shall be disqualified from acting as a Justice or Judge of the Supreme Court or other judge, without loss of salary, while there is pending (a) an indictment or information charging him or her in the United States with a crime punishable as a felony under Nebraska or federal law or (b) a recommendation to the Supreme

Court by the Commission on Judicial Qualifications for his or her removal or retirement.

(4) In addition to the procedure set forth in subsections (1) and (2) of this section, on recommendation of the Commission on Judicial Qualifications or on its own motion, the Supreme Court (a) shall remove a Justice or Judge of the Supreme Court or other judge from office when in any court in the United States such justice or judge pleads guilty or no contest to a crime punishable as a felony under Nebraska or federal law, and (b) may suspend a Justice or Judge of the Supreme Court or other judge from office without salary when in any court in the United States such justice or judge is found guilty of a crime punishable as a felony under Nebraska or federal law or of any other crime that involves moral turpitude. If his or her conviction is reversed, suspension shall terminate and he or she shall be paid his or her salary for the period of suspension. If he or she is suspended and his or her conviction become final the Supreme Court shall remove him or her from office.

(5) All papers filed with and proceedings before the commission or masters appointed by the Supreme Court pursuant to this section prior to a reprimand or formal open hearing shall be confidential. The filing of papers with and the testimony given before the commission or masters of the Supreme Court shall be deemed a privileged communication.

When the Commission on Judicial Qualifications determines that disciplinary action is warranted, whether it be a reprimand or otherwise, the Commission on Judicial Qualifications shall issue one or more short announcements confirming that a complaint has been filed; stating the subject and nature of the complaint, the disciplinary action recommended or reprimand issued, or the date of the hearing; clarifying the procedural aspects; and reciting the right of a judge to a fair hearing.

When the Commission on Judicial Qualifications determines that disciplinary action is not warranted, and the existence of any investigation or complaint has become publicly known, the judge against whom a complaint has been filed or investigation commenced may waive the confidentiality of papers and proceedings under this subsection.

The Supreme Court shall by rule provide for procedure under this section before the commission, the masters, and the Supreme Court.

(6) No Justice or Judge of the Supreme Court or other judge shall participate, as a member of the commission, or as a master, or as a member of the Supreme Court, in any proceedings involving his or her own reprimand, discipline, censure, suspension, removal, or retirement.

This elaborate description of the procedures for disciplining judges was adopted in 1966, along with Sections 28, 29, and 31. Originally, judges could only be removed from office, but in 1980 the optional sanctions ranging from reprimand to retirement were permitted. Also, subsections (5) and (6) were added. The 1984 amendment expanded on the provisions of subsection (5).

Sections 28, 29, and 30 describe the Commission on Judicial Qualifications, a body composed of three judges, three lawyers and three lay persons, plus the chief justice serving as chair. Under the rules outlined here and refined by the supreme court, the commission hears complaints about the actions or qualifications of any judge. After a hearing, the Commission will make a recommendation to the supreme court about the appropriate action to be taken. The court can accept or reject the recommendation or conduct further inquiries.

The purpose of proceedings under this section is not vengeance or retribution against a particular individual but rather it is "to preserve the integrity of and the public confidence in the judiciary" (In re Complaint against Kelly, 1987). The process is to be regarded as a lesson in civics, as it informs "the public and all judges of the importance of the function performed by judges in a free society," while it also reassures citizens that "the judiciary of their state is dedicated to the principle that ours is a government of laws and not of men" (In re Complaint against Kneifl, 1984). This implies that conduct prejudicial to the administration of justice is not dependent upon the judge's motives but rather upon the impact the conduct might have upon the perception of observers (In re Complaint against Kelly, 1987).

SECTION 31. JUDGES; PROCEDURE FOR REMOVAL FROM OFFICE CUMULATIVE

These amendments are alternative to and cumulative with the methods of removal of Justices and judges provided in Article III, section 17, and Article IV, section 5, of this Constitution, and any other provision of law relating to the methods and manner of the removal of Justices, Judges, and judges of the courts of this state.

This section, adopted with Sections 28, 29, and, 30 in 1966, clarifies the relationship of the procedures described in these sections with the process for impeachment of "all civil officers" as outlined in Articles III and IV. In short, this means that the use of one procedure does not preclude the use of the other.

Article VI

Suffrage
(ORIGINALLY ARTICLE VII)

Since the confrontation over exclusion of blacks in the original suffrage article of the 1866 Constitution, Nebraska's voters have been defined to a large extent by the requirements set out in the U.S. Constitution and in federal law. The state has moved to bring its suffrage requirements in line with the several federal amendments passed since the Civil War.

The most recent response to the U.S. Constitution came in 1987. Nebraska has a closed primary which means that the voter must register before the election in a party in order to participate in that party's primary. Those registering as independents or non-partisan were prevented from voting in partisan primaries for federal and state candidates. After the 1986 U.S. Supreme Court decision in *Tashjian v. Republican Party of Connecticut,* which said that Article l, Section 2 and the Seventeenth Amendment apply to primary as well as general elections, the status of Nebraska's primary election law was questioned.

The U.S. Constitution says that electors for representative and senator are those eligible to vote for members of the "most numerous branch of the state legislature." With Nebraska's one-house, non-partisan legislature, this was interpreted by the attorney general to mean that voters who did not indicate a party preference at registration were still entitled to vote in partisan primaries for members of Congress (Attorney General Opinion #87070, 1987). The state had the option of amending the statutes to permit non-partisans to vote in congressional primaries, changing to a partisan legislature, or nominating congressional candidates by means other than a primary election. The state chose the first alternative.

SECTION 1. QUALIFICATIONS OF ELECTORS

Every citizen of the United States who has attained the age of eighteen years on or before the first Tuesday after the first Monday in November and has resided within the state and the county and voting precinct for the terms provided by law shall, except as provided in section 2 of this article, be an elector for the calendar year in which such citizen has attained the age of eighteen years and for all succeeding calendar years.

Starting in 1866 with a constitution which limited the suffrage to white males above the age of twenty-one, Nebraska has slowly extended the franchise to most of its citizens. Some changes did not come easily, and woman suffrage amendments were rejected in 1882 and 1914; the state enfranchised females only after the passage of the Nineteenth Amendment to the U.S. Constitution in 1920. The voting right was limited to U.S. citizens in 1918.

Nebraska lowered the voting age to twenty in 1970 and in 1972 came in line with federal requirements by lowering it again to eighteen. The 1988 amendment reduced the age even further by allowing teenagers who will become eighteen by the general election in November to vote in the primary election in May.

The court has always insisted that the determination of whether a person has established a residence for the purpose of voting is a judicial decision (Dilsaver v. Pollard, 1974; Berry v. Wilcox, 1895). This section does not apply to a public corporation or political subdivision operating solely in a proprietary capacity (Wittier v. Baumgartner, 1966).

SECTION 2. WHO DISQUALIFIED

No person shall be qualified to vote who is non compos mentis, or who has been convicted of treason or felony under the laws of the state or of the United States, unless restored to civil rights

The court has not defined precisely the sort of mental derangement (non compos mentis) which would disqualify one from voting.

SECTION 3. SOLDIER, SEAMAN, OR MARINE; PLACE OF VOTING

Every elector in the military or naval service of the United States or of this state may exercise the right of suffrage at such place and under such regulations as may be provided by law.

The Convention of 1875, taking into account the soldiers stationed in the forts in the state, denied voting rights to members of the regular army. After the experience with the modern mass army in World War I (see State ex rel. Simon v. Moorhead, 1918), the Convention of 1920 proposed the current language.

SECTION 4. REPEALED, 1972.

SECTION 5. ELECTORS PRIVILEGED FROM ARREST

Electors shall in all cases, except treason, felony, or breach of the peace, be privileged from arrest during their attendance at elections, and going to and returning from the same.

The original section also excused electors from military duty on election day except in time of war or public danger. This was changed in 1972. The current section simply protects voters in the exercise of the franchise and is not a license for lawlessness. There has been no court interpretation of this section.

SECTION 6. VOTES; HOW CAST

All votes shall be by ballot or by other means authorized by the Legislature whereby the vote and the secrecy of the elector's vote will be preserved.

The original wording was "All votes shall be by ballot." The Constitutional Revision Commission recommended the present language in order to avoid any confusion about the adoption of various types of voting machines.

The supreme court has ruled that the ballots of voters who intentionally sign their names to them are invalid; "secrecy of the ballot is so important a public consideration that if a clear showing of the voter's identity appears thereon the ballot should be disallowed regardless of what the voter's intent was in so identifying his ballot" (Dugan v. Vlach, 1975).

Article VII

Education
(ORIGINALLY ARTICLE VIII)

One must exercise special care in interpreting Article VII. Not only has it been amended several times as Nebraskans have worked toward the proper structure for the provision of public education, but it was also rewritten extensively by the Constitutional Revision Commission. The amendments approved in 1972 reflected the Commissions' rearrangement and redrafting of the sections in order to put the material in a more logical sequence.

SECTION 1. FREE INSTRUCTION

The Legislature shall provide for the free instruction in the common schools of this state of all persons between the ages of five and twenty-one years. The Legislature may provide for the education of other persons in educational institutions owned and controlled by the state or a political subdivision thereof.

This section combines the former Sections 6 and 12. However, the legislature did not submit to the voters the Commission's proposal for the elimination of Section 12.

The provision of free public education to the state's children is now a dearly held principle but when the question was put to the voters in 1871, after submission as a separate proposition, it was decisively defeated. Within a few years, however, the value of public education was accepted by Nebraskans and the courts endorsed the concept, stating that laws leading to free public instruction should be liberally and broadly construed (McNish v. State ex rel. Dimick, 1905).

This section, as interpreted by the courts, has been manifested in the numerous school districts in the state. The establishment and maintenance of the "common schools" is "in the hands of the people"; district officials "are charged with the obligation of carrying out the will of the people as it finds expression in the school meetings and in the legislature" (State ex rel. Thayer v. School District of Nebraska City, 1916).

SECTION 2. STATE DEPARTMENT OF EDUCATION; GENERAL SUPERVISION OF SCHOOL SYSTEM

The State Department of Education shall be comprised of a State Board of Education and a Commissioner of Education. The State Department of Education shall have general supervision and administration of the school system of the state and of such other activities as the Legislature may direct.

This general description of the administration of primary and secondary education was adopted as Section 14 in 1952 and moved to its present position in 1972. This section should be considered in conjunction with Sections 3 and 4, below.

SECTION 3. STATE BOARD OF EDUCATION; MEMBERS; ELECTION; MANNER OF ELECTION; TERM OF OFFICE

The State Board of Education shall be composed of eight members, who shall be elected from eight districts of substantially equal population as provided by the Legislature. Their term of office shall be for four years each. Their duties and powers shall be prescribed by the Legislature, and they shall receive no compensation, but shall be reimbursed their actual expense incurred in the performance of their duties. The members of the State Board of Education shall not be actively engaged in the educational profession and they shall be elected on a nonpartisan ballot.

This section, describing the governing board of the State Department of Education, was adopted as Section 15 in 1952. A 1966 amendment raised the membership from six and reduced the term of office from six years. The Department of Education and the Board of Education are authorized to exercise administrative and legislative powers, subject to implementation and limitation by the legislature as provided in this section (School Dist. No. 8 of Sherman County v. State Board of Education, 1964).

SECTION 4. COMMISSIONER OF EDUCATION; APPOINTMENT; POWERS; DUTIES

The State Board of Education shall appoint and fix the compensation of the Commissioner of Education, who shall be the executive officer of the State Board of Education and the administrative head of the State Department of Education, and who shall have such powers and duties as the Legislature may direct. The board shall appoint all employees of the State Department of Education on the recommendation of the Commissioner of Education.

Section 4, until 1972, was Section 16, as adopted in 1952. Sections 2, 3, and 4, formerly Sections 14, 15, and 16, together with the old Section 17, replaced the Superintendent of Public Instruction with the State Department of Education, headed by an appointed commissioner of education.

The Nebraska Commissioner of Education is the executive secretary of the State Board of Education and the head of the State Department of Education. This officer is responsible for the promotion and improvement of primary and secondary public education in the state.

SECTION 5. FINES, PENALTIES, AND LICENSE MONEY; ALLOCATION; USE OF FORFEITED CONVEYANCES

(1) Except as provided in subsections (2) and (3) of this section, all fines, penalties, and license money arising under the general laws of the state, except fines and penalties for violation of laws prohibiting the overloading of vehicles used upon the public roads and highways of this state, shall belong and be paid over to the counties respectively where the same may be levied or imposed, and all fines, penalties, and license money arising under the rules, bylaws, or ordinances of cities, villages, precincts, or other municipal subdivision less than a county shall belong and be paid over to the same respectively. All such fines, penalties, and license money shall be appropriated exclusively to the use and support of the common schools in the respective subdivisions where the same may accrue, except that all fines and penalties for violation of laws prohibiting the overloading of vehicles used upon the public roads and highways shall be placed as follows: Seventy-five per cent in a fund for state highways and twenty-five per cent to the county general fund where the fine or penalty is paid.

(2) Fifty per cent of all money forfeited or seized pursuant to enforcement of the drug laws shall belong and be paid over to the counties for drug enforcement purposes as the Legislature may provide.

(3) Law enforcement agencies may use conveyances forfeited pursuant to enforcement of the drug laws as the Legislature may provide. Upon the sale of such conveyances, the proceeds shall be appropriated exclusively to the use and support of the common schools as provided in subsection (1) of this section.

The idea that fines, penalties, and other miscellaneous public money should be dedicated to public education was started by the Convention of 1871 and retained in 1875. In 1956, an amendment enabled the state highway interests to get a piece of the action, and in 1984 drug enforcement agencies were given a share of the proceeds.

The court has been required to evaluate precisely the sort of revenue that is supposed to flow automatically into the school treasury. Fees from hunting and fishing licenses can be diverted elsewhere (Wilcox v. Havekost, 1944), as can fees received by the Liquor Control Commission (School District of Omaha v. Gass, 1936). An occupation tax levied to raise revenue is not covered by this section (State ex rel. Stevens v. Nickerson, 1915). Only penalties which are pecuniary punishments inflicted by laws, ordinances, or police regulations are covered by this section; court costs involved in the foregoing are not penalties (DeCamp v. City of Lincoln, 1979).

The court has determined that this provision, in conjunction with the demands of due process, prohibits the recovery by private parties of settlements in excess of actual damages incurred. A law providing for treble damages was overturned because it was punitive in its effect and thus in violation of Section 5 since it would have given to a private individual an amount of money which was more than the liquidated damages (Abel v. Conover, 1960).

SECTION 6. EDUCATIONAL LANDS; MANAGEMENT; BOARD OF EDUCATIONAL LANDS AND FUNDS; NUMBER; APPOINTMENT; SALE OF LANDS

No lands now owned or hereafter acquired by the state for educational purposes shall be sold except at public auction under such conditions as the Legislature shall provide. The general management of all lands set apart for educational purposes shall be vested, under the direction of the Legislature, in a board of five members to be known as the Board of Educational Lands and Funds. The members shall be appointed by the Governor, subject to the approval of the Legislature, with such qualifications for such terms and compensation as the Legislature may provide.

The Constitutional Revision Commission recommended the 1972 amendment which combined the former Sections 1 and 2 into the present Section 6. The old Section 1 had been amended four times as Nebraskans searched for a mechanism to protect one of its most valued assets, the land granted by Congress in 1864 for support of the common schools (13 Statutes 57).

The Constitution of 1866 sought to protect the lands in Article VII, Section 1 by enjoining the legislature to make sure that "the income arising therefrom shall be faithfully applied to the specific objects of the original grants or appropriations."

The Convention of 1875 was somewhat more uncertain about the faithfulness of the legislators and instituted a board consisting of the governor, secretary of state, treasurer, attorney general, and the commissioner of public lands and buildings to manage the lands and the funds set apart for educational purposes.

The present five-member board administers the 1.5 million acres (out of an original 2.8 million acres) with a market value of approximately $270 million. The Constitutional Revision Commission argued that the management of lands and of funds were two "different sciences" and so proposed that the language about "the general management of all lands and funds" be limited to "lands." The revenue now derived from rents and royalties are invested by the Nebraska Investment Council and the proceeds are distributed to the state's public school districts.

The court has often held that the state is a trustee of the lands under a contractual obligation incurred by the Enabling Act of 1864 and the Constitution. The state, therefore, is "required to administer the trust estate under the rules of law applicable to trustees acting in a fiduciary capacity" (State ex rel. Ebke v. Board of Educational Lands and Funds, 1954). Furthermore, "anyone dealing with the school lands must do so with knowledge of and subject to the trust obligations of the state" (State v. Cooley, 1952).

SECTION 7. PERPETUAL FUNDS ENUMERATED

The following are hereby declared to be perpetual funds for common school purposes of which the annual interest or income only can be appropriated, to wit:

First. Such percent as has been, or may hereafter be, granted by Congress on the sale of lands in this state.

Second. All money arising from the sale or leasing of sections number sixteen and thirty-six in each township in this state, and the lands selected, or that may be selected, in lieu thereof.

Third. The proceeds of all lands that have been, or may hereafter be, granted to this state, where by the terms and conditions of such grant the same are not to be otherwise appropriated.

Fourth. The net proceeds of lands and other property and effects that may come to this state, by escheat or forfeiture, or from unclaimed dividends, or distributive shares of the estates of deceased persons.

Fifth. All other property of any kind now belonging to the perpetual fund.

Until 1972, Section 7 was Section 3. This section merely reinforces the protection to be provided for the funds dedicated to the public schools. These are held to be perpetual funds and "only the annual interest or income can be appropriated for support and maintenance of schools" (State ex rel. Bottcher v. Bartling, 1948).

SECTION 8. TRUST FUNDS BELONG TO STATE FOR EDUCATIONAL PURPOSES; USE; INVESTMENT

All funds belonging to the state for educational purposes, the interest and income whereof only are to be used, shall be deemed trust funds. Such funds with the interest and income thereof are hereby solemnly pledged to the purposes for which they are granted and set apart and shall not be transferred to any other fund for other uses. The state shall supply any net aggregate losses thereof realized at the close of each calendar year that may in any manner accrue. Notwithstanding any other provisions in the Constitution, such funds shall be invested as the Legislature may by statute provide.

The original Section 9 of the 1875 Constitution was amended in 1920. In 1972, it was changed to the present Section 8 upon the recommendation of the Constitutional Revision Commission. Like Sections 7 and 9, this section reaffirms "solemnly" that the trust funds derived from educational lands will be used for the public schools (Propst v. Board of Educational Lands and Funds, 1952). The changes in 1972 included a transfer of the ultimate authority for investment of funds from the Board to the legislature.

The legislature, however, is constrained in its management by "the rules of law regulating the administration of trusts and the conduct and duties of trustees"; a breach of this trust, such as abandoning the practice of competitive bidding, "is in effect a violation of the constitutional provision and has the effect of invalidating the legislation authorizing the breach (State ex rel. Ebke v. Board of Educational Lands and Funds, 1951).

In conjunction with Section 11, below, this section prohibits the apportionment of trust funds to a school wholly or in part sectarian (State ex rel. Public School District v. Taylor, 1932).

SECTION 9. EDUCATIONAL FUNDS; TRUST FUNDS; USE

The following funds shall be exclusively used for the support and maintenance of the common schools in each school district in the state as the Legislature shall provide:

a. Income arising from the perpetual funds;

b. The income from the unsold school lands, except that costs of administration shall be deducted from the income before it is so applied;

c. All other grants, gifts and devises that have been or may hereafter be made to the state which are not otherwise appropriated by the terms of the grant, gift or devise; and

d. Such other support as the Legislature may provide.

No distribution or appropriation shall be made to any school district for the year in which school is not maintained for the minimum term required by law.

Section 9 was put together in 1972 out of material from the old Sections 4 and 7. It further guarantees the security of funds dedicated to educational purposes and indicates the type of schools eligible for state support. The funds so dedicated cannot be diverted to the general fund of the state in any fashion (State ex rel. Ledwith v. Brian, 1909).

SECTION 10. UNIVERSITY OF NEBRASKA; GOVERNMENT; BOARD OF REGENTS; ELECTION; STUDENT MEMBERSHIP; TERMS

The general government of the University of Nebraska shall, under the direction of the Legislature, be vested in a board of not less than six nor more than eight regents to be designated the Board of Regents of the University of Nebraska, who shall be elected from and by districts as herein provided and three students of the University of Nebraska who shall serve as nonvoting members. Such nonvoting student members shall consist of the student body president of the University of Nebraska at Lincoln, the student body president of the University of Nebraska at Omaha, and the student body president of the University of Nebraska Medical Center. The terms of office of elected members shall be for six years each. The terms of office of student members shall be for the period of service as student body president. Their duties and powers shall be prescribed by law; and they shall receive no compensation, but may be reimbursed their actual expenses incurred in the discharge of their duties.

The Legislature shall divide the state, along county lines, into as many compact regent districts, as there are regents provided by the Legislature, of approximately equal population, which shall be numbered consecutively.

The Legislature shall redistrict the state after each federal decennial census. Such districts shall not be changed except upon the concurrence of a majority of the members of the Legislature. In any such redistricting, county lines shall be followed whenever practicable, but other established lines may be followed at the discretion of the Legislature. Whenever the state is so redistricted the members elected prior to the redistricting shall continue in office, and the law providing for such redistricting shall where necessary specify the newly established district which they shall represent for the balance of their term.

The University of Nebraska was established in 1869, and so the Constitution of 1866 was silent about its governance. The Conventions of 1871 and 1875 proposed a board of elected regents. The original provision for six members elected at large was changed in 1920 to election by district. A 1968 amendment permitted the legislature to create up to eight regent positions, which it did, and to require redistricting. In 1974, the inclusion of the student body presidents from the three campuses as non-voting members of the board was approved, although the position of the student representative from UN-Kearney still has to be resolved.

Nebraska is one of five states that elects the members of the governing board for an institution ofhigher education. There have been proposals for an appointed board, most recently by Governor Kerrey in 1985, but the issue has never been put to the voters. That the regents are elected was a major consideration in the 1977 case, *Board of Regents v. Exon,* which said that the University of Nebraska was a largely autonomous institution within state government. As the court stated:

> The Board of Regents as now constituted consist of members chosen directly by the people. We think it is clear that the purpose of the constitutional provision was to remove the University from the plenary control of the Legislature and establish the Board of Regents as an independent body charged with the power and responsibility to operate the University as free from political influence and control as possible.

The major issue in the case concerned the power of the legislature to appropriate funds. Without a specific appropriation and at its own discretion, could the University spend the money it raised through tuition, fees, grant overhead, and gifts? The court said that the board had exclusive authority over such revenue. This decision gave the University much greater flexibility in shifting money from program to program or campus to campus.

However, the idea that the University would be free of political influence and control is naive. As the biggest item in the state budget, the University is under close scrutiny by the governor and the legislature and is highly dependent upon the appropriations recommended in the budget process. Moreover, the court has held that the University is not an independent "political subdivision" but is rather an agency of state government (Catania v. The University of Nebraska, 1979).

SECTION 11. APPROPRIATION OF PUBLIC FUNDS; HANDICAPPED CHILDREN; SECTARIAN INSTRUCTION; RELIGIOUS TEST OF TEACHER OR STUDENT

Notwithstanding any other provision in the Constitution, appropriation of public funds shall not be made to any school or institution of learning not owned or exclusively controlled by the state or a political subdivision thereof; *Provided,* that the Legislature may contract with institutions not wholly owned or controlled by the state or any political subdivision to provide for educational or other services for the benefit of children under the age of twenty-one years who are handicapped, as that term is from time to time denned by the Legislature, if such services are nonsectarian in nature.

All public schools shall be free of sectarian instruction.

The state shall not accept money or property to be used for sectarian purposes; *Provided,* that the Legislature may provide that the state may receive money from the

> federal government and distribute it in accordance with the terms of any such federal grants, but no public funds of the state, any political subdivision, or any public corporation may be added thereto.
>
> A religious test or qualification shall not be required of any teacher or student for admission or continuance in any school of institution supported in whole or in part by public funds or taxation.

The original section of 1875, forbidding the use of public funds in sectarian education, was amended in 1920 to prohibit the use of religious tests for teachers and students in the public schools. The Constitutional Revision Commission recommended that the state be allowed to receive federal grants for distribution to schools whether or not they were controlled wholly by the state; this was approved in 1972. The legislature did not forward to the voters the Commission's proposal to make it possible for the state to share the costs of educational facilities with other states. In 1976, the provision permitting the contracting with institutions for the benefit of handicapped children was approved.

Nebraskans have been able to avoid many of the agonizing debates over the details of the "establishment clause" of the First Amendment because of Section 11. As the court said:

> It is true the question under the Constitution of Nebraska and the Constitution of the United States both relate to the overall principle of separation of church and state. But, by its terms, the Constitution of Nebraska does not permit an examination of secular or sectarian purposes, a determination of primary or incidental benefit, or a balancing of the issues involved in state-church entanglement and political divisiveness. There is no ambiguity in our constitutional provision (Gaffney v. State Department of Education, 1974).

Under the authority of this section, the court in 1902 quickly settled a question that has convulsed the federal courts: reading from the Bible, singing hymns, and offering prayer, if sectarian, is prohibited in the public schools (State ex rel. Freeman v. Scheve). As the court insisted in *Gaffney,* Section 11 "says what it means and means what it says."

Or does it? In its rewriting of the section, the Constitutional Revision Commission appeared to be sure it was not changing the essence of the prohibition against state aid to non-public schools. All it did was to suggest the word "to" replace "in aid of." For the court, the change implied was dramatic. It meant that it was constitutional, in some instances, for students to ride public school buses to private schools (State ex rel. Bouc v. School Dist. of Lincoln, 1982). The state could also grant scholarship aid to students planning to enroll in private colleges (Lenstrom v. Thone, 1981). And the prohibition against lending textbooks to students in private schools, found repugnant to Section 11 in *Gaffney,* was no longer in effect (Cunningham v. Lutjeharms, 1989). In a related case, it was found acceptable for the state to contract with Creighton University, a

Catholic school, for cancer research since Section 11 "does not prohibit the state from doing business furthering a public purpose" (State ex rel. Creighton University v. Smith, 1984).

It should be noted that the third paragraph of this section, beginning with the words "The state shall not accept money or property . . . ," was put back into the Constitution in 1980 by the supreme court. The legislature failed to provide expressly for the repeal of the paragraph in submitting material to the voters in 1976. As the court has stated many times, "The adoption by the Legislature of a proposed amendment does not amend the Constitution" (Cunningham v. Exon, 1980).

SECTION 12. EDUCATION AND REFORM OF MINORS

The Legislature may provide by law for the establishment of a school or schools for the safe keeping, education, employment and reformation of all children under the age of eighteen, who, for want of proper parental care, or other cause, are growing up in mendicancy or crime.

This quaint language (today mendicants would be called homeless street people) was amended in 1920 by raising the age to eighteen years. The section permits the state to create institutions which are more educational than penal for juvenile offenders (Lingo v. Hahn, 1955).

SECTION 13. STATE COLLEGES; GOVERNMENT; BOARD; NAME; SELECTION; DUTIES; COMPENSATION

The general government of the state colleges as now existing, and such other state colleges as may be established by law, shall be vested, under the direction of the Legislature, in a board of seven members to be styled as designated by the Legislature, six of whom shall be appointed by the governor, with the advice and consent of the Legislature, two each for a term of two, four and six years, and two each biennium thereafter for a term of six years, and the Commissioner of Education shall be a member ex officio. The duties and powers of the board shall be prescribed by law, and the members thereof shall receive no compensation for the performance of their duties, but may be reimbursed their actual expenses incurred therein.

Section 13 was proposed by the Convention of 1920. At that time, it provided for a Board of Education of State Normal Schools with the State Superintendent of Public Instruction as an ex officio member. As the old teacher training schools became more general institutions of higher education, the name was changed to state college. Since the Board of Trustees is appointed and not elected, it does not enjoy the same degree of autonomy as the University Board of Regents.

In 1990, four members of the supreme court believed that the legislature's removal of Kearney State College from the Trustees and giving it to the Regents as the University of Nebraska at Kearney violated this section. They felt that Kearney State was included in the phrase "as now existing" when adopted in 1920. However, the majority could not convince the necessary fifth vote, and so Kearney joined the University system on July 1, 1991 (State ex rel. Spire v. Beermann).

SECTION 14. COORDINATING COMMISSION FOR POSTSECONDARY EDUCATION

On January 1, 1992, there shall be established the Coordinating Commission for Postsecondary Education which shall, under the direction of the Legislature, be vested with the authority for the coordination of public postsecondary educational institutions. Public postsecondary educational institutions shall include each postsecondary educational campus or institution which is governed by the Board of Regents of the University of Nebraska, the Board of Trustees of the Nebraska State Colleges, any board or boards established for the community colleges, or any other governing board for any other public postsecondary educational institution which may be established by the Legislature.

Coordination shall mean:

(1) Authority to adopt, and revise as needed, a comprehensive statewide plan for postsecondary education which shall include (a) definitions of the role and mission of each public postsecondary educational institution within any general assignments of role and mission as may be prescribed by the Legislature and (b) plans for facilities which utilize tax funds designated by the Legislature.

(2) Authority to review, monitor, and approve or disapprove each public postsecondary educational institution's programs and capital construction projects which utilize tax funds designated by the Legislature in order to provide compliance and consistency with the comprehensive plan and to prevent unnecessary duplication; and

(3) Authority to review and modify, if needed to promote compliance and consistency with the comprehensive statewide plan and prevent unnecessary duplication, the budget requests of the Board of Regents of the University of Nebraska, the Board of Trustees of the Nebraska State Colleges, any board or boards established for the community colleges, or any other governing board for any other public postsecondary educational institution which may be established by the Legislature.

The Legislature may provide the commission with additional powers and duties related to postsecondary education as long as such powers and duties do not invade the governance and management authority of the Board of Regents of the University of Nebraska and the Board of Trustees of the Nebraska State Colleges as provided in the Constitution of Nebraska, Article VII, sections 10 and 13. The Legislature may provide that coordination of the community colleges by the commission pursuant to this section may be conducted through a board or association representing all the community colleges.

Nothing in this section providing for statewide coordination shall limit or require the use of property tax revenue by and for community colleges.

The commission shall consist of eleven members, residents of the state or the districts from which appointed, who shall be appointed by the Governor with the approval of a majority of the Legislature. Six of the members shall be chosen from six districts of approximately equal population and five shall be chosen on a statewide basis.

The terms of the members of the commission shall be six years or until a successor is qualified and takes office, except that of the members initially appointed, four members shall serve for terms of two years and four members shall serve for terms of four years. The members of the commission shall receive no compensation for the performance of their duties but may be reimbursed their actual and necessary expenses.

Nebraskans, like citizens in other states, are haunted by the feeling that there must be a better way to govern an increasingly expensive and complicated system of public higher education. Section 14, adopted in 1990, is their latest effort at making sense of the situation. It replaces a statutory (and toothless) coordinating body with one with constitutionally derived powers. It describes the composition of the commission and identifies its powers for coordinating public post-secondary education.

There is sure to be litigation as the commission, the regents, and the trustees strive to mark the boundaries of their authority. In particular, the question of the subordination of an elected Board of Regents to an appointed commission demands a judicial answer.

At the same time, the section may resolve some of the lingering questions about the role of the state in the governance of the community colleges. These two-year schools evolved as junior colleges or vocational technical schools. In 1971, the legislature tried to impose some order on the schools by the passage of a law which provided for a State Board of Technical Community Colleges. Since the community colleges are funded in part by the property tax, it was charged that the statewide system violated Article VIII, Section 1A, which prohibits the state from levying a property tax for state purposes. The court held in 1974 that the statute did establish the colleges as a state function and so was unconstitutional (State ex rel. Western Nebraska Technical Com. Col. Area v. Tallon). The legislature in 1975 came back with another version of the statute, including a Coordinating Commission for Technical Community Colleges with, the court noted, "little, if any, actual authority over the technical community colleges"; in a second case two years later, the court upheld this law (State ex rel. Western Technical Com. Col. Area v. Tallon, 1976). With the constitutional status provided by this section, the new commission should not face a similar challenge to its authority over the two-year institutions.

SECTION 15. REPEALED, 1972.

SECTION 16. REPEALED, 1972.

SECTION 17. REPEALED, 1972.

These three sections, along with the original Section 14, were rewritten by the Constitutional Revision Commission and placed in a more logical sequence within the Constitution.

Article VIII

Revenue
(ORIGINALLY ARTICLE IX)

SECTION 1. REVENUE; RAISED BY TAXATION; CLASSIFICATION; UNIFORMITY

The necessary revenue of the state and its governmental subdivisions shall be raised by taxation in such a manner as the Legislature may direct. Notwithstanding Article I, section 16, Article III, section 18, or Article VIII, section 4, of this Constitution or any other provision of this Constitution to the contrary: (1) Taxes shall be levied by valuation uniformly and proportionately upon all real property and franchises as denned by the Legislature except as otherwise provided in or permitted by this Constitution; (2) tangible personal property, as defined by the Legislature, not exempted by this Constitution or by legislation, shall all be taxed at depreciated cost using the same depreciation method with reasonable class lives, as determined by the Legislature, or shall all be taxed by valuation uniformly and proportionately; (3) the Legislature may provide for a different method of taxing motor vehicles and may also establish a separate class of motor vehicles consisting of those owned and held for resale by motor vehicle dealers which shall be taxed in the manner and to the extent provided by the Legislature and may also establish a separate class for trucks, trailers, semitrailers, truck-tractors, or combinations thereof, consisting of those owned by residents and nonresidents of this state, and operating in interstate commerce, and may provide reciprocal and proportionate taxation of such vehicles; *Provided,* that such tax proceeds from motor vehicles taxed in each county shall be allocated to the counties, townships, cities, villages, school districts, and other governmental subdivisions of such county in the same proportion that the levy of each bears to the total levy of the county on taxable property; (4) the Legislature may provide that agricultural land and horticultural land, as denned by the Legislature, shall constitute a separate and distinct class of property for purposes of taxation and may provide for a different method of taxing agricultural and horticultural land which results in values that are not uniform and proportionate with all other real property and franchises but which results in values that are uniform and proportionate upon all property within the class of agricultural land and horticultural land; (5) the Legislature may enact laws to provide that the value of land actively devoted to agricultural or horticultural use shall for property tax purposes be that value which land has for agricultural or horticultural use without regard to any value which such land might have for other purposes or uses; (6) the Legislature may prescribe standards and methods for the determination of the value of real property at uniform and proportionate rates; (7) in furtherance of the purposes for which such a law of the United States has been adopted, whenever there exists a law of the United States which is intended to protect a specifically designated type, user, or owner of property or franchise from discriminatory state or local taxation, such property or franchise shall constitute a separate class of property or franchise under the laws of the State of Nebraska, and such property or franchise may not be taken into consideration in determining whether taxes are levied by valuation uniformly or proportionately upon any property or franchise, and the Legislature may enact laws which statutorily recognize such class and which tax or exempt from taxation such class of property or franchise in such manner as it determines; and (8) the Legislature may provide that livestock shall constitute a separate and distinct class of property for purposes of taxation and may further provide for reciprocal and proportionate taxation of livestock located in this state for only a part of a year. Each actual property tax rate levied for a governmental subdivision shall be the same for all classes of taxed property and franchises. Taxes uniform as to class of property or the ownership or use thereof may be levied by valuation or otherwise upon classes of intangible property as the Legislature may determine, and such intangible property held in trust or otherwise for the purpose of funding pension, profit-sharing, or other employee benefit plans as denned by the Legislature may be declared exempt from taxation. Taxes other than property taxes may be authorized by law. Existing revenue laws shall continue in effect until changed by the Legislature.

Article VIII, Section 1 has been the fault line between the principle of a just, equitable system of taxation and the realities of democratic politics. This area has always been highly unstable, but in the past few years the tremors have been so severe that observers used words like “mess,” “nightmare,” or “disaster” to describe the crises facing Nebraska’s system of public finance. Apparent relief came in May 1992 when the voters approved a major change in Article VIII. Since the amendment was in response to the supreme court’s interpretation of the article, it may be useful to review how Nebraska got to its present condition.

Despite efforts to find other reliable sources of revenue, local government in Nebraska is highly dependent upon the property tax, both real and personal. When, in a series of decisions beginning in 1988, the courts started to question whether the personal property tax and perhaps the real property tax, as determined by the legislature, violated the uniformity provisions of Section 1, policy makers faced a number of hard choices. Even if legislative action was taken, there was no guarantee that any particular solution would withstand judicial scrutiny. The 1992 amendment was intended to resolve matters.

The Development of Section 1

The essence of this section was stated simply in the Constitution of 1866: the state has the power to raise revenue through taxation in order to meet its expenses. The Conventions of 1871 and 1875 added the concept that the taxes necessary for the support of government must be proportionate; the authors in both years also began the tradition of listing groups who could be classified differently for purposes of taxation. Originally, this included "peddlers, auctioneers, brokers, hawkers, commission merchants, showmen, jugglers, inn-keepers, liquor dealers, toll bridges, ferries, insurance, telegraph and express interests or business, venders of patents."

The Convention of 1920 completely rewrote the section to permit the classification of a wider range of property and to authorize taxes other than the ones on property. The section was unchanged until 1952 when the first of nine amendments was approved. It provided for a different method of taxing motor vehicles and fixed the proportional allocation of the proceeds to local governments. Trucks and trailers were put in a separate class in 1964. In 1954, an amendment dealing with the determination of property at uniform values was approved. Provisions dealing with agricultural and horticultural land were approved in 1972, 1984, and 1990; a significant addition here was the "green space" provision allowing farmland to be taxed at its agricultural value rather than its market value for commercial or industrial uses.

Voters in 1978 approved an amendment concerning a method for appraising taxable property in political subdivisions which cross county boundaries. The state supreme court concluded that the amendment violated both the Equal Protection and the Due Process clauses of the Fourteenth Amendment because it permitted non-uniform taxation and failed to provide taxpayers with notice and an opportunity to be heard in an appeal (State ex rel. Douglas v. State Board of Equalization and Assessment, 1979).

The meaning of the phrase "necessary revenue" has not been extensively examined, but it has been established that governments can accumulate revenue in special funds in order to pay for expenses some time in the future (Banks v. Board of Education of Chase County, 1979).

The Status of the Property Tax

The primary issue in Section 1 is the property tax. In Nebraska, as elsewhere, property is either tangible or intangible. Intangible property includes representations of wealth such as stocks and bonds. In recent years, the legislature has avoided taxing intangibles because it is so easy to transfer them to non-taxing jurisdictions. Tangible property is further divided into real and personal property. Without going into specifics, real property includes land, buildings, and other permanent fixtures (Neb Rev Stat 77–103). Personal property can be defined as those tangible assets of individuals or corporations which are not real property.

The various amendments to Section 1 established that not all property was to be treated equally. The concept of a uniform and proportionate tax was further compromised by Article VIII, Section 2. Especially after the 1970 amendment permitting the legislature to "classify personal property in such manner as it sees fit, and may exempt any of such classes . . . ," the way was clear for the granting of exceptions to the idea of uniformity, as the court conceded in the 1974 case, *Stahmer v. State*.

The attitude of Nebraskans toward property taxes was also affected by the dramatic changes in the 1960s when the state government finally abandoned the tax and instituted sales and income taxes. Property taxation became less critical in the state's system of public finance and the personal property tax, in particular, seemed less attractive. Perhaps it was the result of farsighted policy making, perhaps it was the function of machinations by various interest groups, but the legislature launched a piecemeal assault on the tax by lessening its impact on specific types of property and reimbursing the local governments for a reduced tax base by revenue raised through the state sales and income taxes.

The system of property taxation thus created began to unravel in 1987 when the owners of railroad rolling stock operating in Nebraska discovered the tax advantages contained in the Railroad Revitalization and Regulatory Reform Act of 1976 (the 4-R Act). Section 306(1) forbids "any other tax which results in discriminatory treatment of a common carrier by railroad subject to this part." When the issue finally came before the U.S. Court of Appeals, it was found that three-quarters of personal property in Nebraska was exempt from taxation, meaning a disproportionate burden for the remaining taxpayers, including the railroads. The taxation of the personal property of the rail companies violated the 4-R act and the state was enjoined from collecting it (Trailer Train Co. v. Leuenberger, 1988).

Other owners of personal property seized the opportunity provided by the federal courts. They claimed now that they were being discriminated against in comparison with the railroads, and the Nebraska Supreme Court agreed with them. The owners of pipelines operating in the state were being taxed at a rate higher than that imposed on the rail companies. This violated the uniformity requirements of Section 1 as well as the Equal Protection Clause of the Fourteenth Amendment. It made no difference that the state, in exempting rail cars, was "acting involuntarily and under compulsion of federal law." The tax on certain types of income-producing personal property was unconstitutional (Northern Natural Gas Co. v. State Board of Equalization and Assessment, 1989).

The legislature tried to respond to the potential loss of an estimated 9.7 billion dollars in tax base in a special session in 1989. LB 1 redefined real property to include "pipelines, railroad track structures, electrical and telecommunication poles, towers, lines, and all items actually annexed." The act also specified the "sole test" for determining whether a fixture or improvement is real property. In short, if personal property is being questioned by the court, convert as much of it as possible, by redefinition, into real property. LB 7 declared that "a rational basis exists to classify railroad rolling stock as a separate and distinct class of property and to exempt the class from property taxation pursuant to the authority granted under Article VIII, Section 2 of the Constitution of Nebraska."

The supreme court rejected the legislature's efforts. In March 1991, it held that LB 7 did not establish a reasonable basis for distinguishing rolling stock from other types of income-producing personal property. The law was thus in violation of the uniform and proportionate clause of Section 1. It was also found to be special legislation as prohibited by Article III, Section 18 (Natural Gas Pipeline v. State Board of Equalization and Assessment, 1991). The decision, however, was not entirely unambiguous since there were five concurring opinions. The overall impact of the previously mentioned cases was that the court had incrementally developed new constitutional guidelines about the property tax. A more definitive statement of those guidelines came within a few months.

In the *MAPCO* case, the supreme court began by declaring LB 1 unconstitutional. The legislature does not have the power to redefine personal property at will; in the act, the legislature "has attempted to define and designate as a "fixture" that which is, in fact and truth, personal property and has gone beyond the bounds of its legitimate powers under our Constitution." More significantly, the Court overturned the *Stahmer* decision. Because of the ruling in *Trailer Train,* all income-producing personal property which the legislature had exempted over the years must be taxed at the same level as rolling stock in order to be in conformity with Section 1. This included agricultural machinery and business inventory, to say nothing offish, honeybees, and fur-bearing animals. The uniformity clause would seem to demand an all-or-nothing approach to property taxation (MAPCO Ammonia Pipeline v. State Board of Equalization and Assessment, 1991).

Not all observers agree with the court's dedication to uniformity. Professor William Lyons, tax specialist with the University of Nebraska College of Law, testified that "Nebraska is the only state that has a supreme court that enforces the uniformity clause with some vigor."[10] In his dissent in *MAPCO,* Judge Shanahan argued that the "logical and inevitable conclusion" of the court's line of reasoning would be the abolition of exemptions for household goods and for educational, religious and charitable organizations." In his view, the court's interpretation of the uniformity clause should admit of no exceptions. Whatever the case, the legislature at the beginning of 1992 faced the politically unpalatable alternatives of returning exempted property to the rolls or abolishing all taxes on income-producing property.

The insistence on uniformity and proportionality, however, is hardly new. The court has stressed that property taxes, and especially those on personal property must be uniform both in terms of the rate of taxation and of the valuation (Xerox Corp. v. Karnes, 1984; State ex rel. Meyer v. Peters, 1974). Even in cases where the classification of property is still permissible, the methods used to assess the value must be correlated so that valuations among classes are uniform and proportionate (Kearney Convention Center, Inc. v. Buffalo County Board of Equalization, 1984).

The 1992 amendment should take care of most of the issues raised in the court decisions. The uniform and proportionate clause is retained for real property. Tangible real property is still taxable, but the legislature has considerable discretion in making exemptions. The legislature also made an effort to reclaim its right, largely lost in *MAPCO,* to classify personal property. Specifically, personal property protected from state taxation by federal law will be in a separate class, thus apparently resolving the problem raised by the *Trailer Train* decision. Reinforcement of the legislature's discretion in personal property taxation was provided by the amendment's changes in Section 2, below.

Other Taxes

One of the great accomplishments of the 1920 Convention was the insertion of the sentence, "Taxes other than property taxes, may be authorized by law," although it took almost fifty years for the state to take full advantage of it. The section thus authorizes occupation taxes (Licking v. Hays Lumber Co., 1945). Excise taxes such as those on the sale of gasoline have also been sustained by Section 1 (Pantorium v. McLaughlin, 1927). Most of all, without further amendments, the state has the authority to levy a graduated income tax (Anderson v. Tiemann, 1967).

---

[10] *Omaha World-Herald* (July 14, 1991): 12-B.

SECTION 1A. LEVY OF PROPERTY TAX FOR STATE PURPOSES; PROHIBITION

The state shall be prohibited from levying a property tax for state purposes.

This section, as adopted in 1954, was contingent on the state's adoption of a sales or income tax. The 1966 amendment, brought about by the initiative process, compelled the state to adopt a sales and income tax system in the Revenue Act of 1967.

Problems under this section arise, first, when the state tries to impose some degree of control over previously local functions. As discussed in Article VII, Section 14, above, such was the issue in state coordination of community colleges. In the first *Tallon* case, the court determined that the state's imposition of a centralized coordinating mechanism indicated that the community colleges, financed in part by property taxes, were to be part of a statewide system. This was unconstitutional (State ex rel. Western Nebraska Technical Community College Area v. Tallon, 1974).

A second class of problems concerns local activity mandated by state government. Where state and local purposes are commingled, as in the provision of legal assistance to indigent defendants, "the crucial issue in regard to Article VIII, Section 1A, turns on determination of whether the controlling and predominant purposes are state purposes or local purposes"; since counties benefit from effective trials, they should be made to pay (Kovarik v. Banner County, 1975). Similarly, the Department of Social Services could move the equipment paid for by one county to furnish a local office in another county since the function of the department benefited all people within the region (Rock County v. Spire, 1990). The same principle holds when counties are made to pay for their citizens who are institutionalized in state facilities; the local government is ultimately the beneficiary (Craig v. Board of Equalization of Douglas County, 1969).

SECTION 1B. INCOME TAX MAY BE BASED ON LAWS OF THE UNITED STATES

When an income tax is adopted by the Legislature, the Legislature may adopt an income tax law based upon the laws of the United States.

Adopted in 1966, this section permits the legislature to base the state's income tax on the Internal Revenue Code. Such was the case between 1967 and 1985, when the individual's income tax was a percentage of his or her federal tax liability. The Nebraska Supreme Court rejected the argument that this was "an unlawful delegation of legislative power to the United States in violation of Article II, section 1, and Article III, section 1, of the Constitution of Nebraska" (Anderson v. Tiemann, 1967).

SECTION 2. EXEMPTION OF PROPERTY FROM TAXATION; CLASSIFICATION

Notwithstanding Article I, section 16, Article III, section 18, or Article VIII, section 1 or 4, of this Constitution or any other provision of this Constitution to the contrary: (1) The property of the state and its governmental subdivisions shall constitute a separate class of property and shall be exempt from taxation; (2) the Legislature by general law may classify and exempt from taxation property owned by or used exclusively for agricultural and horticultural societies and property owned and used exclusively for educational, religious, charitable, or cemetery purposes, when such property is not owned or used for financial gain or profit to either the owner or user; (3) household goods and personal effects, as defined by law, may be exempted from taxation in whole or in part, as may be provided by general law, and the Legislature may prescribe a formula for the determination of household goods and personal effects; (4) the Legislature by general law may provide that the increased value of land by reason of shade or ornamental trees planted along the highway shall not be taken into account in the assessment of such land; (5) the Legislature by general law and upon any terms, conditions and restrictions it prescribes, may provide that the increased value of real property resulting from improvements designed primarily for energy conservation may be exempt from taxation; (6) the value of a home substantially contributed by the United States Department of Veterans Affairs for a paraplegic or multiple amputee shall be exempt from taxation during the life of such veteran or until the death or remarriage of his or her surviving spouse; (7) the Legislature may exempt from an intangible property tax life insurance and life insurance annuity contracts and any payment connected therewith and any right to pension or retirement payments; (8) the Legislature may exempt inventory from taxation; (9) the Legislature may define and classify personal property in such manner as it sees fit, whether by type, use, user, or owner, and may exempt any such class or classes of property from taxation if such exemption is reasonable or may exempt all personal property from taxation; (10) no property shall be exempt from taxation except as permitted by or as provided in this Constitution; and (11) the Legislature may by general law provide that a portion of the value of any residence actually occupied as a homestead by any classification of owners as determined by the legislature shall be exempt from taxation.

This section identifies the types of property the legislature may exempt totally or partially from taxation. The exemptions are not self-executing; they require legislation and in some cases action on the part of the beneficiary (Indian Hills Community Church v. Lancaster County Board of Equalization, 1987).

The general argument in favor of the exemptions is that they promote some public good. In the 1871 and 1875 Constitutions, the favored functions included state and local governments, agricultural and horticultural societies, educational, religious, and charitable organizations, cemeteries, and, in an effort to encourage forestry, "live fences, fruit and forest trees." The 1920 Convention permitted a limited exemption for household goods. Otherwise, its changes were directed toward tightening up the section, particularly in the addition, "No property shall be exempt from taxation except as provided in this section."

Since 1954, six more changes have been added. The complete exemption of household goods and personal effects was made possible in 1954. Disabled veterans were provided a tax break in 1964. A 1966 amendment permitted the exemption of certain types of intangible property. Homestead exemptions were allowed in 1968. Exemptions for energy conservation were approved in 1980.

The most significant amendment to Section 2 came in 1970 when the legislature was given the power to "classify personal property in such manner as it sees fit" and to exempt any or all of these classes. Following *Stahmer v. State* (1974), the state legislature now had great latitude in exempting types of personal property. Eventually, the list of exemptions came to include agricultural incomeproducing machinery and equipment, business inventory, feed, fertilizer and farm inventory and grain, seed, livestock, poultry, fish, honeybees, and furbearing animals. As described above, *Stahmer* was reversed in *MAPCO* in 1991 and all the income-producing property exemptions were ruled unconstitutional (MAPCO Ammonia Pipeline v. State Board of Equalization and Assessment). As for the other exemptions, the court noted "The validity of these exemptions has not been challenged in this court and, to our knowledge, has not been challenged in the federal courts."

The court has also questioned the authority of the legislature to define certain types of property. Again, from our discussion in Section 1, the legislature does not have complete discretion in its definitions, "since (1) the Legislature cannot abrogate or contradict an express constitutional provision and (2) the legislative definition must be reasonable, and cannot be arbitrary or unfounded." Thus the court concluded that pipelines buried in the ground were moveable personal property, regardless of the action of the legislature, even though the dissenting judge claimed the decision was "undeniable hubris and a claim of unique definitional capacity which is neither warranted or countenanced under the Constitution" (MAPCO Ammonia Pipeline v. State Board of Equalization and Assessment, 1991). But the court had made such a claim before, when it prevented the legislature from defining certain types of fixtures such as furnaces and air conditioners as household goods (State ex rel. Meyer v. Peters, 1974).

The 1992 amendment to Section 2 reiterated the idea that the legislature has the power to define and classify personal property and to exempt any or all of it. With the ability to make reasonable classifications for personal property, the legislature should have the authority it lost in *MAPCO*. It remains to be seen if the supreme court agrees.

Within the currently existing classes of exemptions, the court has been required to give meaning to Section 2. It is clear that the property of government is exempt, but what is governmental? Public power districts are regarded as governmental subdivisions although Section 11, below, requires them to make payments in lieu of taxes (Nebraska Public Power District v. Hershey School District, 1980). Omaha was not required to pay taxes on a marina whose spaces were leased to private individuals (Sioux City and New Orleans Barge Lines, Inc. v. Douglas County Board of Equalization, 1971). Conventional municipal property, such as waterworks, have long been held exempt (Omaha v. Douglas County, 1914). However, governments are not exempt from paying special assessments for public improvements: "This state does not allow public lands benefitted by local improvements to obtain a free ride at the expense of other taxpayers in the improved area" (Easley v. City of Lincoln, 1983).

Educational, charitable, and religious exemptions pose special problems, especially if the institutions own income-producing property. Many of the issues were clarified in a 1991 case involving the request of the Nebraska State Bar Foundation for an exemption for its Lincoln headquarters as a charitable and educational institution. The court stated that an exemption under the federal internal revenue code "does not determine whether property is tax-exempt under state law" (Nebraska State Bar Foundation v. Lancaster County Board of Equalization, 1991). The state controls its exemptions and those exemptions are becoming harder to obtain.

In Nebraska, tax exemption provisions "are strictly construed, and their operation will not be extended by construction…" (Bethphage Community Services, Inc. v. Phelps County, 1986). The rules have become more restrictive since 1980 and, according to the court, have required a two-tier approach to evaluating the tax status of property. Judges must first look at the "particular nature, character, or status of a property owner as an organization." The second tier "is the use of the property, that is, the specific kinds and degrees of use which qualify or disqualify property concerning the charitable or educational tax exemptions . . ." (Nebraska State Bar Foundation v. Lancaster County Board of Equalization, 1991). To qualify as a charity, the exempt organization must be "operated exclusively for the purpose of the mental, social, or physical benefit of the public or an indefinite number of persons." An organization, such as the Bar Foundation, which provides services primarily to its own members, does not qualify. An educational institution is one "operated exclusively for the purpose of offering regular courses with systematic instruction in academic, vocational, or technical subjects." Again, although the Bar Foundation may underwrite courses for lawyers, it was not the organization's primary function (Nebraska State Bar Foundation v. Lancaster County Board of Equalization, 1991). Happily for the state's lawyers, the Nebraska Bar Association was able to convince the county that its building was a "governmental instrumentality" and thus tax exempt.

SECTION 2A. EXEMPTION OF PERSONAL PROPERTY IN TRANSIT IN LICENSED WAREHOUSES

The Legislature may establish bonded and licensed warehouses or storage areas for goods, wares and merchandise in transit in the state which are intended for and which are shipped to final destinations outside this state upon leaving such warehouse or storage area, and may exempt such goods, wares and merchandise from ad valorem taxation while in such storage areas.

Section 2A, adopted in 1960, enables the legislature to pass "free port" legislation, in which property in transit through the state may be stored at licensed warehouses. The law implementing this section is compatible with the requirements in Section 1 for uniform taxation (Norden Laboratories, Inc. v. Lancaster County Board of Equalization, 1973).

SECTION 3. REDEMPTION FROM SALES OF REAL ESTATE FOR TAXES

The right of redemption from all sales of real estate, for the non-payment of taxes or special assessments of any character whatever, shall exist in favor of owners and persons interested in such real estate, for a period of not less than two years from such sales thereof. Provided, that occupants shall in all cases be served with personal notice before the time of redemption occurs.

The threat of foreclosure for failure to pay taxes was much on the minds of the hard-pressed delegates to the 1871 and 1875 Conventions. The 1871 Constitution, in fact, had two sections dealing with the question. The current section, which has never been amended, gives to the former owner or other interested persons the right to reclaim the property. Specifically, the law provides "for a stay of two years from the date of the sale, during which time the owner of the fee or any person having a legal interest therein may redeem by paying, not the amount of the bid, but the full amount of taxes, interest and costs due the county" (Commercial Savings and Loan Assn. v. Pyramid Realty Company, 1931).

SECTION 4. LEGISLATURE HAS NO POWER TO REMIT TAXES; EXCEPTION; CANCELLATION OF TAXES ON LAND ACQUIRED BY THE STATE

Except as to tax and assessment charges against real property remaining delinquent and unpaid for a period of fifteen years or longer, the Legislature shall have no power to release or discharge any county, city, township, town, or district whatever, or the inhabitants thereof, or any corporation, or the property therein, from their or its proportionate share of taxes to be levied for state purposes, or due any municipal corporation, nor shall commutation for such taxes be authorized in any form whatever; *Provided*, that the Legislature may provide by law for the payment or cancellation of taxes or assessment against real estate owned or acquired by the state or its governmental subdivisions.

Just as Sections 1 and 2 try to eliminate loopholes in levying taxes, this section aims at preventing any individual or institution from enjoying a tax break once the tax has been imposed. It has retained its shape better than the other two sections, having been changed in two minor respects. The first amendment in 1958 allowed governments to cancel taxes which, after fifteen years, were apparently uncollectible. The 1966 amendment authorized the legislature to provide for the payment or cancellation of taxes against real estate owned or acquired by the state so that government could have a clear title to the property.

The power to tax is exercised when the tax is levied (Am. Prov. of Servants of Mary Real Estate Corp. v. County of Douglas, 1946). Any lessening of the impact of the tax after that point in time is beyond the power of the legislature. It is clear from this section that the legislature "cannot reduce the amount of the tax, extend the time of payment, or in any manner change the method of payment" (Steinacher v. Swanson, 1936).

Even receiving a refund is no simple matter. "The authority of public officials to refund taxes is very limited" and the "right of taxpayers to recover taxes that have been paid is also very limited" (Svoboda v. Hahn, 1976). Without any statutory permission, taxes voluntarily paid cannot be recovered. This is so even if the tax was illegal or otherwise unauthorized.

SECTION 5. COUNTY TAXES; LIMITATIONS

County authorities shall never assess taxes the aggregate of which shall exceed fifty cents per one hundred dollars of taxable value as determined by the assessment rolls, except for the payment of indebtedness existing at the adoption thereof, unless authorized by a vote of the people of the county.

Counties are constrained by this section as to the taxes they can impose on property, unless the tax ceiling is lifted by a vote of the people from that county. Earlier versions were more generous, with the 1871 Constitution permitting two dollars per hundred and the 1875 version allowing one and one-half dollars. The 1920 Convention reduced it to its present amount and a 1992 amendment changed "actual valuation" to "taxable value." The legislature can get around the limit by authorizing the creation of public corporations with the power to tax in order to carry out traditional county functions. The levy imposed by such units is not considered a county tax (Dwyer v. Omaha-Douglas Public Building Commission, 1972).

SECTION 6. LOCAL IMPROVEMENTS OF CITIES, TOWNS, AND VILLAGES

The Legislature may vest the corporate authorities of cities, towns and villages, with power to make local improvements, including facilities for providing off-street parking for vehicles, by special assessments or by special taxation of property benefitted, and to redetermine and reallocate from time to time the benefits arising from the acquisition of such off-street parking facilities, and the Legislature may vest the corporate authorities for cities and villages with power to levy special assessments for the maintenance, repair and reconstruction of such off-street parking facilities. For all other corporate purposes, all municipal corporations shall be vested with authority to assess and collect taxes, but such taxes shall be uniform in respect to persons and property within the jurisdiction of the body imposing the same, except that cities and villages may be empowered by the Legislature to assess and collect separate and additional taxes within off-street parking districts created by and within any city or village on such terms as the Legislature may prescribe.

This section grants to municipal corporations (in Nebraska, cities and villages) two distinct powers: to tax for general revenue purposes and to assess individuals and institutions for special benefits (Farnham v. Lincoln, 1906). The language of 1875 was amended in 1972 when the provision for off-street parking was approved.

SECTION 7. PRIVATE PROPERTY NOT LIABLE FOR CORPORATE DEBTS; MUNICIPALITIES AND INHABITANTS EXEMPT FOR CORPORATE PURPOSES

Private property shall not be liable to be taken or sold for the payment of the corporate debts of municipal corporations. The Legislature shall not impose taxes upon municipal corporations, or the inhabitants or property thereof, for corporate purposes.

This section protects private property from liability for the debts accrued by a municipal corporation in the conduct of its proprietary functions. It also prevents the state from forcing municipalities to levy a tax for corporate or proprietary purposes. Such purposes are regarded to be those which are in the nature of a business operation, for example, the providing of gas and water for a fee (Metropolitan Utilities Dist. v. Omaha, 1924). The prohibition in this section applies only where the levy is for proprietary purposes and which is not levied by a local authority (Obitz v. Airport Authority of the City of Red Cloud, 1967). This section has never been amended.

Municipal corporations are those which exercise governmental functions, that is, those designed for the general public benefit, although proprietary functions can be assumed by the corporations. A public power district which exercises only proprietary functions is not included within the protection of this section (Evans v. Metropolitan Utilities District, 1971). A county also does not qualify as a municipal corporation (State v. Cheyenne County, 1934).

SECTION 8. FUNDING INDEBTEDNESS; WARRANTS

The Legislature at its first session shall provide by law for the funding of all outstanding warrants, and other indebtedness of the state, at a rate of interest not exceeding eight per cent per annum.

"The sole object of this section is to provide for the payment of existing state debts, the execution of which exhausts the power conferred by this section" (State v. McBride, 1877).

SECTION 9. CLAIMS UPON TREASURY; ADJUSTMENT; APPROVAL; APPEAL

The Legislature shall provide by law that all claims upon the treasury shall be examined and adjusted as the Legislature may provide before any warrant for the amount allowed shall be drawn. Any party aggrieved by the action taken on a claim in which he has an interest may appeal to the district court.

This section gives the legislature the authority to institute a system for reviewing claims against the state treasury and gives claimants the right to appeal unfavorable decisions to the state courts. The word "claim" means those claims which the state is under legal obligation to pay (State v. Moore, 1898). Mandamus action may be taken against state officers to enforce the execution and delivery of a warrant in those cases where an appropriation has been made by the legislature (State ex rel. National Surety Corp. v. Price, 1935).

SECTION 10. TAXATION OF GRAIN AND SEEDS; ALTERNATIVE BASIS PERMITTED

Notwithstanding the other provisions of Article VIII, the Legislature is authorized to substitute a basis other than valuation for taxes upon grain and seed produced or handled in this state. Existing revenue laws not inconsistent with the Constitution shall continue in effect until changed by the Legislature.

Section 10 was adopted in 1956 and has not been litigated. It allows the legislature to use a system other than property taxation for grain and seed produced in the state.

SECTION 11. PUBLIC CORPORATIONS AND POLITICAL SUBDIVISIONS PROVIDING ELECTRICITY; PAYMENT IN LIEU OF TAXES

Every public corporation and political subdivision organized primarily to provide electricity or irrigation and electricity shall annually make the same payments in lieu of taxes as it made in 1957, which payments shall be allocated in the same proportion to the same public bodies or the successors as they were in 1957.

The legislature may require each such public corporation to pay to the treasurer of any county in which may be located any incorporated city or village, within the limits of which such public corporation sells electricity at retail, a sum equivalent to five (5) per cent of the annual gross revenue of such public corporation derived from retail sales of electricity within uch city or village, less an amount equivalent to the 1957 payments in lieu of taxes made by such public corporation with respect to property or operations in any such city or village. The payments in lieu of tax is made in 1957, together with any payments made as authorized in this section shall be in lieu of all other taxes, payments in lieu of taxes, franchise payments, occupation and excise taxes, but shall not be in lieu of motor vehicle licenses and wheel taxes, permit fees, gasoline tax and other such excise taxes or general sales taxes levied against the public generally.

So much of such five (5) per cent as is in excess of an amount equivalent to the amount paid by such public corporations in lieu of taxes in 1957 shall be distributed in each year to the city or village, the school districts located in such city or village, the county in which such city or school is located, and the State of Nebraska, in the proportion that their respective property tax mill levies in each such year bear to the total of such mill levies.

This section deals with a problem peculiar to Nebraska. Only in this state is all electrical power produced and supplied by public entities, either public corporations or special districts. A great deal of property has thus been removed from the tax rolls. Beginning in the 1930s, the legislature instituted a system whereby public power agencies were required to make payments to state (until 1966) and local governments. Fearing that this practice would be found in violation of Article VIII, Section 2, which prohibits the taxation of government, the voters adopted this section in 1958 and the legislature passed the appropriate enabling laws (Neb Rev Stat 70-651.01).

By its provisions, the public power organizations make payments to the counties within which they operate for distribution to the taxing jurisdictions within the county. The organizations are also relieved from the payment of other types of taxes, such as occupation and excise taxes. The legislature cannot circumvent this section by imposing other charges upon the public power districts for the benefit of local government (Nebraska Public Power District v. Hershey School District, 1980).

SECTION 12. CITIES OR VILLAGES; REDEVELOPMENT PROJECT; SUBSTANDARD AND BLIGHTED PROPERTY; INCUR INDEBTEDNESS; TAXES; HOW TREATED

For the purpose of rehabilitating, acquiring, or redeveloping substandard and blighted property in a redevelopment project as determined by law, any city or village of the state may, notwithstanding any other provision in the Constitution, and without regard to charter limitations and restrictions, incur indebtedness, whether by bond, loans, notes, advance of money, or otherwise. Notwithstanding any other provision in the Constitution or a local charter, such cities or villages may also pledge for and apply to the payment of the principal, interest, and any premiums on such indebtedness all taxes levied by all taxing bodies, which taxes shall be at such rate for a period not to exceed fifteen years, on the assessed valuation of the property in the project area portion of a designated blighted and substandard area that is in excess of the assessed valuation of such property for the year prior to such rehabilitation, acquisition, or redevelopment.

When such indebtedness and the interest thereon have been paid in full, such property thereafter shall be taxed as is other property in the respective taxing jurisdictions and such taxes applied as all other taxes of the respective taxing bodies.

Section 12 was adopted in 1978 and amended in 1984 and 1988. It authorizes the use of the method for urban development known as "tax increment financing." The city can issue bonds to pay for the rehabilitation of areas designated as blighted. The new owners will pay a higher property tax, but the difference between the old and new taxes will be used to retire the debt incurred during acquisition of the property. After fifteen years, the revenue from the improved property will go into the city's general fund (Neb Rev Stat 18-2147). Litigation involving this section has yet to come before the supreme court.

SECTION 13. EFFECT OF 1992 AMENDMENTS

Notwithstanding Article I, section 16, Article III, section 18, or Article VIII, section 1 or 4, of this Constitution or any other provision of this Constitution to the contrary, amendments to Article VIII of this Constitution passed in 1992 shall be effective from and after January 1, 1992, and existing revenue laws and legislative acts passed in the regular legislative session of 1992, not inconsistent with this Constitution as amended, shall be considered ratified and confirmed by such amendments without the need for legislative reenactment of such laws.

Section 13 was added as part of the amendments to Sections 1, 2, and 5 approved in May 1992. It was written to insure that the taxation measures approved by the 1992 session of the legislature in response to the personal property crisis would be valid.

Article IX

Counties
(ORIGINALLY ARTICLE X)

SECTION 1. AREA

No new county shall be formed or established by the Legislature which will reduce the county or counties, or either of them to a less area than four hundred square miles, nor shall any county be formed of a less area.

Section 1 was written by the Convention of 1871 and retained in the 1875 Constitution. It has never been amended or litigated.

The section simply limits the size of counties created after 1875. Since the last of Nebraska's ninety-three counties was created in 1913, the section has little significance today.

SECTION 2. DIVISION OF COUNTY; DECISION OF QUESTION

No county shall be divided nor any part of the territory of any county be stricken therefrom, nor shall any county or part of the territory of any county be added to an adjoining county without submitting the question to the qualified electors of each county affected thereby, nor unless approved by a majority of the qualified electors of each county voting thereon; provided, that when county boundaries divide sections, or overlap, or fail to meet, or are in doubt, the Legislature may by law provide for their adjustment, but in all cases the new boundary shall follow the nearest section line or the thread of the main channel of a boundary stream.

An election in the affected county is required before any existing county can be divided. If all or part of a county is to be added to another, voters in both counties must participate. This provision was contained in the 1871 and 1875 Constitutions. The 1920 Convention gave to the legislature the power to make minor adjustments in county boundaries.

The legislature is not prevented by this section from creating special districts whose boundaries cross county lines if necessary for the enforcement of the state's police power (State ex rel. Sheffer v. Fuller, 1909). It is permissible for the county board of one county to extend the boundaries of its special districts into the territory of another county, if otherwise allowed by state law (Syfie v. Tri-County Hospital Dist., 1971).

SECTION 3. COUNTY ADDED TO ANOTHER; PRIOR INDEBTEDNESS; COUNTY STRICKEN OFF; LIABILITIES

When a county shall be added to another, all prior indebtedness of each county shall remain a charge on the taxable property within the territory of each county as it existed prior to consolidation. When any part of a county is stricken off and attached to another county, the part stricken off shall be holden for its proportion of all then existing liabilities of the county from which it is taken, but shall not be holden for any then existing liabilities of the county to which it is attached.

Section 3 describes the treatment of indebtedness when all or part of one county is consolidated with another. The original language of 1871 and 1875 was amended in 1920. Since county consolidation in Nebraska has been discussed but never implemented, the question has not come before the supreme court.

SECTION 4. COUNTY AND TOWNSHIP OFFICERS

The Legislature shall provide by law for the election of such county and township officers as may be necessary and for the consolidation of county offices for two or more counties; *Provided,* that each of the counties affected may disapprove such consolidation by a majority vote in each of such counties.

The words after "and for the consolidation . . ." were added in 1968 to the original language of 1871 and 1875. The section gives to the legislature the power to determine the powers and responsibilities of county and township officials. It permits the consolidation of county governments after a vote of the public in the relevant counties. The number and character of county officials is at the discretion of the legislature (Dinsmore v. State, 1901).

SECTION 5. TOWNSHIP ORGANIZATION

The Legislature shall provide by general law for township organization, under which any county may organize whenever a majority of the legal voters of such county voting at any general election shall so determine; and in any county that shall have adopted a township organization the question of continuing the same may be submitted to a vote of the electors of such county at a general election in the manner that shall be provided by law.

Township government was important enough in rural Nebraska in the nineteenth century for the framers of 1871 and 1875 to include it in their Constitution. This unit of government, a subdivision of the county, has outlived its usefulness and is fading away. The few organized townships remaining show little sign of political vitality.

By statute, there are two kinds of counties in Nebraska. In the twenty-seven counties with organized townships, the governing body is the board of supervisors.The sixty-six counties without townships are governed by a board of commissioners. It is presumed that the distinction is unimportant since either type of county has the same officers and powers, but the supreme court has never been asked to rule on the question.

Article X

Public Service Corporations (ORIGINALLY A PART OF ARTICLE XI)

Article XI of the Constitution of 1875 was divided into three parts: railroad corporations, municipal corporations, and miscellaneous corporations. After the Convention of 1920, each part became a separate article.

The basic language of Article X was taken almost directly from the 1870 "Granger Constitution" of Illinois and reflected the concern of Nebraskans with the most pressing matter in the state's politics, namely, the regulation of the railroads. As the rails declined in importance and political power, so did the significance of the article. The Convention of 1920 broadened the scope to include public utilities and other common carriers in the only three amendments to this article. The Constitutional Revision Commission of 1970 recommended that all the sections be collapsed into a single paragraph which would establish the powers of an appointed Public Service Commission. The proposal was not submitted to the voters.

SECTION 1. REPORTS UNDER OATH

Every public utility corporation or common carrier organized or doing business in this state shall report, under oath, to the Railway Commission, when required by law or the order of said Commission. The reports so made shall include such matters as may be required by law or the order of said Commission.

This simply requires certified reports from certain corporations operating in the state. Applied originally to railroads, it was extended to utilities and other-common carriers in 1920. The amendment also simplified much of the detail from the section of 1875 by referring to the role of the Railway Commission (now the Public Service Commission; see Art. IV, Sec. 20). The section has not been litigated.

SECTION 2. PROPERTY LIABLE TO SALE ON EXECUTION

The rolling stock and all other movable property belonging to any railroad company or corporation in this state, shall be liable to execution and sale in the same manner as the personal property of individuals, and the Legislature shall pass no law exempting any such property from execution and sale.

Section 2 made it impossible for the legislature to exempt railroads from having their movable property seized in a court process to force payment of a legal debt. There has been no litigation in this area.

SECTION 3. CONSOLIDATION OF STOCK OR PROPERTY

No public utility corporation or common carrier shall consolidate its stock, property, franchise, or earnings in whole or in part with any other public utility corporation or common carrier owning a parallel of competing property without permission of the Railway Commission; and in no case shall any consolidation take place except upon public notice of at least sixty days to all stockholders, in such manner as may be provided by law. The Legislature may by law require all public utilities and common carriers to exchange business through physical connection, joint use, connected service, or otherwise.

In the original Section 3, railroads were flatly prohibited from consolidating with companies operating a competing or parallel line; this was designed to prevent the creation of monopolies. The 1920 amendment required the consolidation of railroads, other common carriers, and public utilities to be approved by what is now the Public Service Commission.

The 1920 amendment also contained a contradictory impulse as the last sentence authorized statutory arrangements for the consolidation of certain corporations. When Lincoln and other cities objected that the state law implementing the section would circumvent public policy against monopolies, they were warned by the court that such determinations of policy were for the legislature to make(Lincoln v. Nebraska Public Power District, 1974).

SECTION 4. RAILWAYS DECLARED PUBLIC HIGHWAYS; MAXIMUM RATES; LIABILITY NOT LIMITED

Railways heretofore constructed, or that may hereafter be constructed, in this state are hereby declared public highways, and shall be free to all persons for the transportation of their persons and property thereon, under such regulations as may be prescribed by law. And the Legislature may from time to time pass laws establishing reasonable maximum rates of charges for the transportation of passengers and freight on the different railroads in this state. The liability of railroad corporations as common carriers shall never be limited.

By declaring railways public highways, the Constitution of 1875 opened the way for regulation of this important part of the state's economy in the 1800s. By "free," it is not meant that there would be no charge but rather that individuals or corporations could not be discriminated against from using rail facilities.

As stated in the discussion of Article IV, Section 20, however, this provision did not lead to the immediate resolution of the railroad problem in Nebraska since the erection of appropriate administrative machinery was delayed until 1906. At that time, the present Public Service Commission was created to provide the sort of regulation anticipated by this section.

This section also ensured that railways could not earn immunity from liability by legislative action, although the common law liability of the corporations can be increased by the legislature (Smith v. Chicago, St. Paul and M&O Railway Co., 1916).

SECTION 5. CAPITAL STOCK; DIVIDENDS

The capital stock of public utility corporations or common carriers shall not be increased for any purpose, except after public notice for sixty days, and in such manner as may be provided by law. No dividend shall be declared or distributed except out of net earnings after paying all operating expenses including a depreciation reserve sufficient to keep the investment intact.

Section 5 was designed to stop the wild stock speculation that characterized railroad development in the nineteenth century. The original language was taken directly from the 1870 Illinois Constitution and stated that railroads could not issue stocks or bonds "except for money, labor or property actually received, and applied to the purposes for which the corporation was created." A 1920 amendment extended the provision to other types of corporations.

The section apparently served its purpose since no cases under its provisions have come before the supreme court.

SECTION 6. EMINENT DOMAIN

The exercise of the power and the right of eminent domain shall never be so construed or abridged as to prevent the taking by the legislature of the property and franchises of incorporated companies already organized, or hereafter to be organized, and subjecting them to the public necessity the same as of individuals.

While Article I, Section 21, above, refers to the taking of property from private persons, this section concerns the application of the right of eminent domain to corporations. State law has been construed to allow the use of eminent domain by railroads to acquire the right of possession and easement over property necessary for the construction and maintenance of tracks. As long as the property so acquired is used for a railroad, it cannot be taken from the company by adverse possession (Edholm v. Missouri Pacific Railroad Co., 1926).

SECTION 7. UNJUST DISCRIMINATION AND EXTORTION

The Legislature shall pass laws to correct abuses and prevent unjust discrimination and extortion in all charges of express, telegraph and railroad companies in this state and enforce such laws by adequate penalties to the extent, if necessary for that purpose, of forfeiture of their property and franchises.

The strong words here reflect the concern of the framers in the 1870s. They express the determination that the state would have to assume the responsibility for curbing what were perceived as economic depredations by the railroads. The power to enforce the section is vested by the legislature in the Public Service Commission (Myers v. Blair Telephone Company, 1975). See Article IV, Section 20, above.

SECTION 8. EMINENT DOMAIN FOR DEPOT AND OTHER USES

No railroad corporation organized under the laws of any other state, or of the United States and doing business in this state shall be entitled to exercise the right of eminent domain or have power to acquire the right of way, or real estate for depots or other uses, until it shall have become a body corporate pursuant to and in accordance with the laws of this state.

Any railroad company wishing to exercise the power of eminent domain must be organized as a corporation under the laws of the state of Nebraska. A "foreign" corporation cannot exercise such a right (Koenig v. Chicago, B&Q Railroad Co., 1889).

Article XI

Municipal Corporations

The provisions on municipal corporations remained in Article XI after the other two parts were put in separate articles. For a while, this was identified as Article XIa.

SECTION 1. SUBSCRIPTION TO STOCK PROHIBITED

No city, county, town, precinct, municipality, or other subdivision of the state shall ever become a subscriber to the capital stock, or owner of such stock, or any portion or interest therein of any railroad, or private corporation, or association.

The authors of the 1871 and 1875 Constitutions included this section in order to put an end to the reckless speculation by the frontier city-builders. In order to attract railroads and other businesses, municipal leaders would issue bonds for the support of the enterprises. Many of the projects failed, and the state's towns and villages were facing bankruptcy. And so this section clearly was "intended to prohibit any subdivision of the state from entering into private business by being associated as a stockholder, or by being a partner, or a part owner, in a private business venture or enterprise" (State ex rel. Johnson v. Consumers Public Power District, 1942).

The section continues to limit the investment possibilities by local government. In 1978, the supreme court held that cities could not deposit funds in mutual savings and loan associations (Nebraska League of Savings and Loan Associations v. Mathes). The prohibition existed even if the local government signed a waiver of membership when opening an account for deposits (Nebraska League of Savings and Loan Associations v. Johnson, 1983).

SECTION 2. CITY OF 5,000 MAY FRAME CHARTER; PROCEDURES

Any city having population of more than five thousand (5000) inhabitants may frame a charter for its own government, consistent with and subject to the constitution and laws of this state, by causing a convention of fifteen freeholders, who shall have been for at least five years qualified electors thereof, to be elected by the qualified voters of said city at any general or special election, whose duty it shall be within four months after such election, to prepare and propose a charter for such city, which charter, when completed, with a prefatory synopsis, shall be signed by the officers and members of the convention, or a majority thereof, and delivered to the clerk of said city, who shall publish the same in full, with his official certification, in the official paper of said city, if there be one, and if there be no official paper, then in at least one newspaper published and in general circulation in said city, three times, and a week apart, and within not less than thirty days after such publication it shall be submitted to the qualified electors of said city at a general or special election, and if a majority of such qualified voters, voting thereon, shall ratify the same, it shall at the end of sixty days thereafter, become the charter of said city, and supersede any existing charter and all amendments thereof. A duplicate certificate shall be made, setting forth the charter proposed and its ratification (together with the vote for and against) and duly certified by the City Clerk, and authenticated by the corporate seal of said city and one copy thereof shall be filed with the secretary of state and the other deposited among the archives of the city, and shall thereupon become and be the charter of said city, and all amendments of such charter, shall be authenticated in the same manner, and filed with the secretary of state and deposited in the archives ofthe city.

When they were adopted by the voters in 1912, Sections 2,3, and 4 represented a triumph for Progressive reformers. With "municipal home rule," the larger cities in the state would be free of excessive control by a rural-dominated legislature. Local citizens would build the features of "good government" into their charters. The charter "convention" of fifteen members was empowered to write a governing document for the city and to submit it to the voters. Significantly, or so it was thought, the 1912 amendments provided for "constitutional" home rule in that the right to develop a local charter in no way depended upon the legislature.

After seventy years, the great adventure of home rule excites few Nebraskans. Only two cities/3-Omaha and Lincoln/3-have home rule charters. Why they continue under home rule was unclear to Professor A. B. Winter in his definitive study of the subject since "the record does not reveal any advantages to this system, with the possible exception of some intangible prestige stemming from the possession of the home rule label."[11]

Home rule is meaningless in Nebraska, according to Winter, because of its interpretations by the supreme court. As he comments:

> Not only did the Nebraska Supreme Court's exercise in judicial law-making begin to erode the purposes of home rule through the injection of new rules which reduced municipal freedom of choice, but the process was further hastened when judges incorrectly employed precedents enunciating principles of state-city relationships which existed prior to the advent of home rule. This long term strategy moved the law toward restoration of the state as sovereign, with a resultant weakening of the local autonomy which home rule constitutional amendments were intended to provide.[12]

The court has stressed that home rule charters must be "consistent with and subject to the constitution and laws of this state." The cities are free to act in those areas of "strictly" or "purely" municipal concerns, but in those instances where the legislature "has enacted a law affecting municipal affairs, but which is also of state concern, the law takes precedence over any municipal action taken under the home rule charter"; furthermore, "whether or not an act of the legislature pertains to a matter of local or state-wide concern becomes a question for the courts when a conflict of authority arises" (Axberg v. City of Lincoln, 1942). "The charter powers are effective only as to matters of purely municipal concern and are ineffective as to matters of concern to others or to the state generally" (Millard v. City of Omaha, 1970).

Constitutionally, what are purely municipal concerns? Cases decided since Winter's analysis indicate that there may be no such thing. In a case which allowed the state legislature to determine the composition of the Omaha city council, the court could only say that there is "no sure test by which it is possible to distinguish between matters of strictly municipal concern and those of statewide concern, and it is therefore necessary to make such distinctions on a case-by-case analysis of the issue as it arises." Judge Clinton dissented, saying: "That examination further discloses that home rule charter provisions of the Constitution of Nebraska have, by decisions of this court, been gradually eroded until, except for the most insignificant matters, the home rule charter provisions are of no practical import except as a source of litigation" (Jacobberger v. Terry, 1982).

---

[11] A. B. Winter, "Nebraska Home Rule: The Record and Some Recommendations," *Nebraska Law Review* 59 (1980): 614.

[12] Ibid., 615.

SECTION 3. REJECTION OF CHARTER; EFFECT; PROCEDURE TO FRAME NEW CHARTER

But if said charter be rejected, then within six months thereafter, the mayor and council or governing authorities of said city may call a special election at which fifteen members of a new charter convention shall be elected to be called and held as above in such city, and they shall proceed as above to frame a charter which shall in like manner and to the like end be published and submitted to a vote of said voters for their approval or rejection. If again rejected, the procedure herein designated may be repeated until a charter is finally approved by a majority of those voting thereon, and certified (together with the vote for and against) to the secretary of state as aforesaid, and a copy thereof deposited in the archives of the city, whereupon it shall become the charter of said city. Members of each of said charter conventions shall be elected at large, and they shall complete their labors within sixty days after their respective election. The charter shall make proper provision for continuing, amending or repealing the ordinances of the city.

If the provisions of Section 2 fail to result in a charter, Section 3 is applicable. A city can repeat the procedures every six months until an acceptable charter is approved by the voters.

SECTION 4. CHARTER; AMENDMENT; CHARTER CONVENTION

Such charter so ratified and adopted may be amended, or a charter convention called, by a proposal therefor made by the law-making body of such city or by the qualified electors in number not less than five per cent of the next preceding gubernatorial vote in such city, by petition filed with the council or governing authorities. The council or governing authorities shall submit the same to a vote of the qualified electors at the next general or special election not held within thirty days after such petition is filed. In submitting any such charter or charter amendments, any alternative article or section may be presented for the choice of the voters and may be voted on separately without prejudice to the others. Whenever the question of a charter convention is carried by a majority of those voting thereon, a charter convention shall be called through a special election ordinance, and the same shall be constituted and held and the proposed charter submitted to a vote of the qualified electors, approved or rejected, as provided in Section 2 hereof. The city clerk of said city shall publish with his official certification, for three times, a week apart in the official paper of said city, if there be one, and if there be no official paper, then in at least one newspaper, published and in general circulation in said city, the full text of any charter or charter amendment to be voted on at any general or special election.

No charter or charter amendment adopted under the provisions of this amendment shall be amended or repealed except by electoral vote. And no such charter or

> charter amendment shall diminish the tax rate for state purposes fixed by act of the Legislature, or interfere in any way with the collection of state taxes.

An amendment to a home rule charter, according to Section 4, can be proposed to the voters in three ways. The city council can submit a proposal, eligible voters can circulate and sign a petition, or the voters may approve the creation of a charter convention which can recommend a new charter or a revision of the existing one. However made, the proposed amendments cannot impede the collection of taxes by the state.

The requirement that provisions in the home rule charter can be amended or repealed only by the voters does not stand up against the superior power of the state legislature. State action in areas of statewide concern can make charter provisions inoperative without action by the city's voters (Millard v. City of Omaha, 1970).

SECTION 5. CHARTERS OF CITY OF 100,000; HOME RULE CHARTER AUTHORIZED

> The charter of any city having a population of more than one hundred thousand inhabitants may be adopted as the home rule charter of such city by a majority vote of the qualified electors of such city voting upon the question, and when so adopted may thereafter be changed or amended as provided in Section 4 of this article, subject to the constitution and the laws of the state.

This section was added by the Convention of 1920, and at that time it applied only to Omaha. All it did was allow Omaha to adopt its existing charter as a home rule charter rather than go through the procedures described in Section 2. It neither adds to nor subtracts from Omaha's legal status as a home rule city as discussed under Section 2, above.

Article XII

Miscellaneous Corporations (ORIGINALLY A PART OF ARTICLE XI)

The Constitution of 1875 included the material on "General Corporations" within Article XI which was later put into a separate Article XIb. As recommended by the Constitutional Revision Commission, the voters in 1972 approved the consolidation of all the material then in the article into a one-paragraph section.

SECTION 1. LEGISLATURE TO PROVIDE FOR ORGANIZATION, REGULATION, AND SUPERVISION OF CORPORATIONS AND ASSOCIATIONS; LIMITATION; ELECTION FOR DIRECTORS OR MANAGERS; VOTING RIGHTS OF STOCKHOLDERS

The Legislature shall provide by general law for the organization, regulation, supervision and general control of all corporations, and for the organization, supervision and general control of mutual and cooperative companies and associations, and by such legislation shall insure the mutuality and co-operative features and functions thereof. Foreign corporations transacting or seeking to transact business in this state shall be subject, under general law, to regulation, supervision, and general control, and shall not be given greater rights or privileges than are given domestic corporations of a similar character. No corporations shall be created by special law, nor their charters be extended, changed or amended, except those corporations organized for charitable, educational, penal or reformatory purposes, which are to be and remain under the control of the state. The Legislature shall provide by law that in all elections for directors or managers of incorporated companies every stockholder owning voting stock shall have the right to vote in person or proxy for the number of shares owned by him, for as many persons as there are directors or managers to be elected or to cumulate such shares and give one candidate as many votes as the number of directors multiplied by the number of his shares shall equal, or to distribute them upon the same principal among as many candidates as he shall think fit, and such directors or managers shall not be elected in any other manner; *Provided*, that any mutual or cooperative company or association may, in its articles of incorporation, limit the number of shares of stock any stockholder may own, the transfer of such stock, and the right of each stockholder or member to one vote only in the meetings of such company or association. All general laws passed pursuant to this section may be altered from time to time, or repealed.

The most important result of this section is that it gives to the legislature constitutional authorization to regulate certain sectors of the economy, as for example, the insurance industry (Clark v. Lincoln Liberty Life Ins. Co., 1941). It also reinforces the prohibition against special legislation found in Article III, Section 18, and so corporations can receive their charters only under general law (Lincoln Street Railway Co. v. City of Lincoln, 1901). Interestingly, this restriction applies to public corporations except for those specifically exempted in the section (Wittier v. Baumgartner, 1966).

A foreign corporation is generally regarded as one not organized under and subject to the laws of Nebraska (Omaha National Bank v. Jensen, 1953). The provision that such corporations shall have no greater rights than domestic ones refers to the granting of franchises and corporate privileges rather than to taxation (State ex rel. Beatrice Creamery Co. v. Marsh, 1929).

The provision concerning cumulative voting, originally contained in Section 5, was augmented in 1920 by the creation of a special category for mutual or cooperative companies. The legislature can determine the specifics of voting rights of stockholders (State ex rel. Kemper v. Dorchester Farmer's Co-op, 1918).

SECTIONS 2–6. REPEALED, 1972.

SECTION 7. REPEALED, 1938.

SECTION 8. CORPORATION ACQUIRING AN INTEREST IN REAL ESTATE USED FOR FARMING OR RANCHING OR ENGAGING IN FARMING OR RANCHING; SECRETARY OF STATE, ATTORNEY GENERAL; DUTIES; LEGISLATURE; POWERS

That Article XII of the Constitution of the State of Nebraska be amended by adding a new section numbered 8 and subsections as numbered, notwithstanding any other provisions of this Constitution.

(1) No corporation or syndicate shall acquire, or otherwise obtain an interest, whether legal, beneficial, or otherwise, in any title to real estate used for farming or ranching in this state, or engage in farming or ranching.

Corporation shall mean any corporation organized under the laws of any state of the United States or any country or any partnership of which such corporation is a partner.

Farming or ranching shall mean (i) the cultivation of land for the production of agricultural crops, fruit, or other horticultural products, or (ii) the ownership, keeping or feeding of animals for the production of livestock or livestock products.

Syndicate shall mean any limited partnership organized under the laws of any state of the United States or any country, other than limited partnerships in which the partners are members of a family, or a trust created for the benefit of a member of that family, related to one another within the fourth degree of kindred according to the rules of civil law, or their spouses, at least one of whom is a person residing on or actively engaged in the day to day labor and management of the farm or ranch, and none of whom are nonresident aliens. This shall not include general partnerships.

These restrictions shall not apply to:

(A) A family farm or ranch corporation. Family farm or ranch corporation shall mean a corporation engaged in farming or ranching or the ownership of agricultural land, in which the majority of the voting stock is held by members of a family, or a trust created for the benefit of a member of that family, related to one another within the fourth degree of kindred according to the rules of civil law, or their spouses, at least one of whom is a person residing on or actively engaged in the day to day labor and management of the farm or ranch and none of whose stockholders are non-resident aliens and none of whose stockholders are corporations or partnerships, unless all of the stockholders or partners of such entities are persons related within the fourth degree of kindred to the majority of stockholders in the family farm corporation. These restrictions shall not apply to:

(B) Non-profit corporations.

These restrictions shall not apply to:

(C) Nebraska Indian tribal corporations.

These restrictions shall not apply to:

(D) Agricultural land, which, as of the effective date of this Act, is being fanned or ranched, or which is owned or leased, or in which there is a legal or beneficial interest in the title directly or indirectly owned, acquired, or obtained by a corporation or syndicate, so long as such land or other interest in title shall be held in continuous ownership or under continuous lease by the same such corporation or syndicate, and including such additional ownership or leasehold as is reasonably necessary to meet the requirements of pollution control regulations. For the purposes of this exemption, land purchased on a contract signed as of the effective date of this amendment, shall be considered as owned on the effective date of this amendment.

These restrictions shall not apply to:

(E) A farm or ranch operated for research or experimental purposes, if any commercial sales from such farm or ranch are only incidental to the research or experimental objectives of the corporation or syndicate.

These restrictions shall not apply to:

(F) Agricultural land operated by a corporation for the purpose of raising poultry.

These restrictions shall not apply to:

(G) Land leased by alfalfa processors for the production of alfalfa.

These restrictions shall not apply to:

(H) Agricultural land operated for the purpose of growing seed, nursery plants, or sod.

These restrictions shall not apply to:

(I) Mineral rights on agricultural land.

These restrictions shall not apply to:

(J) Agricultural land acquired or leased by a corporation or syndicate for immediate or potential use for nonfarming or nonranching purposes. A corporation or syndicate may hold such agricultural land in such acreage as may be necessary to its nonfarm or nonranch business operation, but pending the development of such agricultural lands for nonfarm or nonranch purposes, not to exceed a period of five years, such land may not be used for farming or ranching except under lease to a family farm or ranch corporation or a non-syndicate or non-corporate farm or ranch.

These restrictions shall not apply to:

(K) Agricultural lands or livestock acquired by a corporation or syndicate by process of law in the collection of debts, or by any procedures for the enforcement of a lien, encumbrance, or claim thereon, whether created by mortgage or otherwise. Any lands so acquired shall be disposed of within a period of five years and shall not be used for farming or ranching prior to being disposed of, except under a lease to a family farm or ranch corporation or a non-syndicate and non-corporate farm or ranch.

These restrictions shall not apply to:

(L) Bona fide encumbrances taken for purposes of security.

These restrictions shall not apply to:

(M) Custom spraying, fertilizing, or harvesting.

These restrictions shall not apply to:

(N) Livestock futures contracts, livestock purchased for slaughter, or livestock purchased and resold within two weeks.

If a family farm corporation, which has qualified under all the requirements of a family farm or ranch corporation, ceases to meet the defined criteria, it shall have fifty years, if the ownership of the majority of the stock of such corporation continues to be held by persons related to one another within the fourth degree of kindred or their spouses, and their landholdings are not increased, to either re-qualify as a family farm corporation or dissolve and return to personal ownership.

The Secretary of State shall monitor corporate and syndicate agricultural land purchases and corporate and syndicate farming and ranching operations, and notify the Attorney General of any possible violations. If the Attorney General has reason to believe that a corporation or syndicate is violating this amendment, he or she shall commence an action in district court to enjoin any pending illegal land purchase, or livestock operation, or force divestiture of land held in violation of this amendment. The court shall order any land held in violation of this amendment to be divested within two years. If land so ordered by the court has not been divested within two years, the court shall declare the land escheated to the State of Nebraska.

If the Secretary of State or Attorney General fails to perform his or her duties as directed by this amendment, Nebraska citizens and entities shall have standing in district court to seek enforcement.

The Nebraska Legislature may enact, by general law, further restrictions prohibiting certain agricultural operations that the legislature deems contrary to the intent of this section.

In their campaign for the initiative which put this section on the ballot, the proponents called it the "family farm amendment." The title sums up what the amendment was intended to do. Nebraskans were concerned with the concentration of agricultural land in the hands of large corporations, including banks and insurance companies; the rush toward agribusiness appeared to threaten the traditional system of agriculture as typified by the family owned and operated farm or ranch. In an effort that recalled to some the old-time Populist spirit, the proponents won a convincing victory in the election of 1982.

The wordy amendment is less complicated than it seems. The ownership and operation of farms and ranches by corporations are prohibited. It is possible, however, for families which are organized as limited corporations to continue as a family farm or ranch. Subsections (A) through (N) identify the types of corporate activity which are still permissible.

Many observers, including advocates of the amendment, say that the question of the family farm could have been handled just as well by ordinary legislation, that the amendment in fact is legislation posing as a constitutional principle. The Nebraska Supreme Court addressed that argument, writing that "a proposed amendment to our Constitution does not have to deal with fundamental rights or the organization of government, but may deal with any subject." In the same case, the court also ruled that the section did not violate federal statutes or the due process and equal protection clauses of the Fourteenth Amendment to the U.S. Constitution (Omaha National Bank v. Spire, 1986).

The legal struggle then shifted to the federal courts, and in 1991 the issue was resolved. The Eighth U.S. Circuit Court of Appeals rejected the argument that the section violated the equal protection clause of the Fourteenth Amendment. The preservation of the family farm, the court held, was a reasonable objective of public policy and the method described in the amendment was not irrational. "It is up to the people of the State of Nebraska, not the courts, to weigh the evidence and decide on the wisdom and utility of measures adopted through the initiative and referendum process" (MSM Farms, Inc. v. Spire).The U.S. Supreme Court refused to hear an appeal of the decision.

In August 1991, the attorney general enforced the amendment for the first time by requiring a Kentucky-based corporation to divest itself of its Nebraska farm property.

Article XIII

State, County, and Municipal Indebtedness (ORIGINALLY ARTICLE XII)

SECTION 1. STATE MAY CONTRACT DEBT; LIMITATIONS; EXCEPTIONS

The state may, to meet casual deficits, or failures in the revenue, contract debts never to exceed in the aggregate one hundred thousand dollars, and no greater indebtedness shall be incurred except for the purpose of repelling invasion, suppressing insurrection, or defending the state in war, and provision shall be made for the payment of the interest annually, as it shall accrue, by a tax levied for the purpose, or from other sources of revenue, which law providing for the payment of such interest by such tax shall be irrepealable until such debt is paid; *Provided,* that if the Legislature determines by a three-fifths vote of the members elected thereto that (1) the need for construction of highways in this state requires such action, it may authorize the issuance of bonds for such construction, and for the payment of the interest and the retirement of such bonds it may pledge any tolls to be received from such highways or it may irrevocably pledge for the term of the bonds all or part of any state revenue closely related to the use of such highways, such as motor vehicle fuel taxes or motor vehicle license fees and (2) the construction of water retention and impoundment structures for the purposes of water conservation and management will promote the general welfare of the state, it may authorize the issuance of revenue bonds for such construction, and for the payment of the interest and the retirement of such bonds it may pledge all or any part of any state revenue derived from the use of such structures; and *provided further,* that the Board of Regents of the University of Nebraska, the

Board of Trustees of the Nebraska State Colleges, and the State Board of Education may issue revenue bonds to construct, purchase, or otherwise acquire, extend, add to, remodel, repair, furnish, and equip dormitories, residence halls, single or multiple dwelling units, or other facilities for the housing and boarding of students, single or married, and faculty or other employees, buildings and structures for athletic purposes, student unions or centers, and for the medical care and physical development and activities of students, and buildings or other facilities for parking, which bonds shall be payable solely out of revenue, fees, and other payments derived from the use of the buildings and facilities constructed or acquired, including buildings and facilities heretofore or hereafter constructed or acquired, and paid for out of the proceeds of other issues of revenue bonds, and the revenue, fees, and payments so pledged need not be appropriated by the Legislature, and any such revenue bonds heretofore issued by either of such boards are hereby authorized, ratified, and validated. Bonds for new construction shall first be approved as the Legislature shall provide.

The clear purpose of the original language was to limit the indebtedness of state government, except for extraordinary contingencies, to $100,000 (State v. Stuefer, 1902). Nebraska was steadfast in its adherence to the principle of "pay-as-you-go" until the 1960s. At that time, the problems of financing large capital projects from current revenues became evident and the section was amended to exempt three types of state debt.

In 1968, the state was allowed to issue bonds for the construction of highways with the debt to be retired through motor fuel taxes and license fees. Colleges and universities, in 1972, were given the permission to issue revenue bonds for the construction of dormitories, student unions and other money-making facilities. Finally, a 1982 amendment authorized revenue bonds for water retention and impoundment projects.

In areas outside the three specific areas, there is little opportunity for the state to incur debt. In declaring unconstitutional a law to promote the construction of gasohol plants, the court found a secondary or contingent obligation of the state to redeem municipal bonds (State ex rel. Douglas v. Thone, 1979). The section serves "to prevent the anticipation of revenue by the creation of obligations to be paid from revenue to be received in future fiscal periods"; thus, those obligations "which are to be paid from revenue subject to appropriation by future Legislatures are subject to the state debt limitation provision" (State ex rel. Meyer v. Steen, 1968). But the court did uphold the acquisition of a state office building in Omaha, to be built by the city and financed in part through a lease by the city to the state. The court held that the lease was cancelable by future legislatures and that the state had no obligation beyond the current year's rent (Ruge v. State, 1978).

SECTION 2. INDUSTRIAL DEVELOPMENT; POWERS OF COUNTIES AND MUNICIPALITIES

Notwithstanding any other provision in the Constitution, the Legislature may authorize any county or incorporated city or village, including cities operating under home rule charters, to acquire, own, develop, and lease real and personal property suitable for use by manufacturing or industrial enterprises and to issue revenue bonds for the purpose of defraying the cost of acquiring and developing such property by construction, purchase, or otherwise. The Legislature may also authorize such county, city, or village to acquire, own, develop, and lease real and personal property suitable for use by enterprises determined by law if such property is located in blighted areas as determined by law and to issue revenue bonds for the purpose of defraying the costs of acquiring and developing or financing such property by construction, purchase, or otherwise. Such bonds shall not become general obligation bonds of the governmental subdivision by which such bonds are issued. Any real or personal property acquired, owned, developed, or used by any such county, city, or village pursuant to this section shall be subject to taxation to the same extent as private property during the time it is leased to or held by private interests, notwithstanding the provisions of Article VIII, section 2, of the Constitution. The acquiring, owning, developing, and leasing of such property shall be deemed for a public purpose, but the governmental subdivision shall not have the right to acquire such property by condemnation. The principal of and interest on any bonds issued may be secured by a pledge of the lease and the revenue therefrom and by mortgage upon such property. No such governmental subdivision shall have the power to operate any such property as a business or in any manner except as the lessor thereof.

Notwithstanding any other provision in the Constitution, the Legislature may also authorize any incorporated city or village, including cities operating under home rule charters, to appropriate from local sources of revenue such funds as may be deemed necessary for an economic or industrial development project or program subject to approval by a vote of the majority of the registered voters of such city or village voting upon the question. For purposes of this provision, funds from local sources of revenue shall mean funds raised from general taxes levied by the city or village and shall not include any funds received by the city or village which are derived from state or federal sources.

This section permits local governments to acquire property through the proceeds of revenue bonds for the purpose of industrial and business development. The property acquired by government can then be leased to private economic interests; the tax exemption granted to governments in Article VIII, Section 2 is waived and so the property is retained on the tax rolls. The local governments are not permitted to use the power of eminent domain in this process, although there are other ways in which cities can acquire sites for manufacturing by condemnation (Monarch Chemical Works, Inc. v. City of Omaha, 1979).

The original Section 2 dealt with internal improvement bonds. The Constitutional Revision Commission suggested that the language be stricken, since such bonds are no longer issued, and in its place, Section 16, approved in 1960, should be moved from Article XV. The switch was approved in 1972. The new Section 2 was amended in 1982 to include blighted property. The second parsgraph agraph of the section was added in 1990. It allows cities and villages to use local sources of revenue, with voter approval, for economic and industrial development.

SECTION 3. CREDIT OF THE STATE; EXCEPTION

The credit of the state shall never be given or loaned in aid of any individual, association, or corporation, except that the state may guarantee or make long-term, low-interest loans to Nebraska residents seeking adult or post high school education at any public or private institution in this state. Qualifications for and the repayment of such loans shall be prescribed by the Legislature.

The original intent of the 1875 framers remains the same. Nebraska governments cannot extend their credit to private individuals or institutions. In concluding that the strictures apply to local governments as well, the supreme court said the provision means that public money shall not be used for private purposes and the state and its subdivisions are protected against "reckless financial involvement in private enterprises supposed to serve the public good but which are in fact dominated by private interest" (State ex rel. Beck v. City of York, 1957).

The legislature, however, can appropriate funds for private institutions if a public purpose is served; if there is a public purpose, "it does not matter whether the agency through which it is dispensed is public or not since the appropriation is not made for the agency but for the object which it serves. The test is in the result, not in the means" (United Community Services v. Omaha National Bank, 1956). A public purpose is for the legislature to define, insofar as a government program "has for its objective the promotion of the public health, safety, morals, security, prosperity, contentment, and the general welfare of all the inhabitants" (State ex rel. Douglas v. Thone, 1979).

In 1972, the section was amended to permit the granting of loans to students enrolling in public and private higher education in the state. The act implementing this provision served a public purpose and did not violate this section (Lenstrom v. Thone, 1981).

Article XV, Section 17, specifies an exception to this section in that it permits state and local governments to invest pension and retirement funds.

Article XIV

Militia
(ORIGINALLY ARTICLE XIII)

SECTION 1. PERSONNEL; ORGANIZATION; DISCIPLINE

The Legislature may provide for the personnel, organization, and discipline of the militia of the state.

The original language pertaining to the membership, personnel, and discipline of the state militia can be traced to the Constitution of 1866. The Constitutional Revision Commission recommended the current phrasing for the sake of brevity and clarity. The change was approved in 1972.

In the only case arising from this article, the supreme court rejected a claim from a national guard member for worker's compensation by making a distinction between service in the militia and state employment:

> This provision does not create but recognizes the existence of the militia and authorizes the legislative provision for its components. It would appear therefore that a militia was constitutionally considered an attribute of sovereignty and that any legislative provision for call of personnel to the militia would be a call to sovereign service rather than to employment by the state or an agency of the state. (Lind v. Nebraska National Guard, 1944)

Article XV

Miscellaneous Provisions (ORIGINALLY ARTICLE XIV)

SECTION 1. OFFICIAL OATH; REFUSAL; DISQUALIFICATIONS

Executive and judicial officers and members of the legislature, before they enter upon their official duties shall take and subscribe the following oath, or affirmation: "I do solemnly swear (or affirm) that I support the constitution of the United States, and the constitution of the State of Nebraska, and will faithfully discharge the duties. . . . . .of according to the best of my ability, and that at the election at which I was chosen to fill said office, I have not improperly influenced in any way the vote of any elector, and have not accepted, nor will I accept or receive, directly or indirectly, any money or other valuable thing from any corporation, company or person, or any promise of office, for any official act or influence (for any vote I may give or withhold on any bill, resolution, or appropriation.") Any such officer or member of the Legislature who shall refuse to take the oath herein prescribed, shall forfeit his office, and any person who shall be convicted of having sworn falsely to, or of violating his said oath shall forfeit his office, and thereafter be disqualified from holding any office of profit or trust in this state unless he shall have been restored to civil rights.

This section describes the oath of office to be taken by elected executive, legislative, and judicial officers. It was written in 1875 and has never been amended. The oath must be taken in this exact form (State ex rel. Johnson v. Chase, 1946). Judges still take this oath even though, technically, their selection under the "merit plan" is not an election. The violation of the oath by a judge aggravates the offense of disregarding the oath taken as a lawyer (State ex rel. Nebraska State Bar Assn. v. Conover, 1958).

SECTION 2. OFFICIAL IN DEFAULT AS COLLECTOR AND CUSTODIAN OF PUBLIC MONEY OR PROPERTY; DISQUALIFICATION; FELON DISQUALIFIED

No person who is in default as collector and custodian of public money or property shall be eligible to any office of trust or profit under the constitution or laws of this state. No person convicted of a felony shall be eligible to any such office unless he shall have been, restored to civil rights.

Section 2 dates from 1875 with only minor amendments made in 1972. It prevents convicted felons from holding public office and poses a penalty for those officers who are in default with public assets. "Default," the court has ruled, involves more than mere civil liability. Instead, there must be a willful omission to account for and pay over public funds with corrupt intent or with "such a flagrant disregard of duty as to fairly justify the inference that the conduct complained of was willful and corrupt" (State ex rel. Brazda v. Marsh, 1942).

SECTION 3. REPEALED, 1986.

SECTION 4. WATER A PUBLIC NECESSITY

The necessity of water for domestic use and for irrigation purposes in the State of Nebraska is hereby declared to be a natural want.

SECTION 5. USE OF WATER DEDICATED TO THE PEOPLE

The use of the water of every natural stream within the State of Nebraska is hereby dedicated to the people of the state for beneficial purposes, subject to the provisions of the following section.

SECTION 6. RIGHT TO DIVERT UNAPPROPRIATED WATERS

The right to divert unappropriated waters of every natural stream for beneficial use shall never be denied except when such denial is demanded by the public interest.

Priority of appropriation shall give the better right as between those using the water for the same purpose, but when the waters of any natural stream are not sufficient for the use of all those desiring to use the same, those using the water for domestic purposes shall have preference over those claiming it for any other purpose, and those using the water for agricultural purposes shall have the preference over those using the same for manufacturing purposes. Provided, no inferior right to the use of the waters of this state shall be acquired by a superior right without just compensation therefor to the inferior user.

SECTION 7. USE OF WATER FOR POWER PURPOSES

The use of the waters of the state for power purposes shall be deemed a public use and shall never be alienated, but may be leased or otherwise developed as by law prescribed.

These four sections—and especially the first three—are often considered in cases before the supreme court as a group whose general purpose is to establish the power of the state to regulate Nebraska's most precious natural resource. The sections represent a package recommended by the Convention of 1920; they have never been amended.

With or without the amendments, the Nebraska courts would probably be major players in the state's water policy. The legislature has been reluctant to develop a comprehensive plan for the management of water and, by default, issues come before the courts. At present, the dynamics of water policy are with the courts and state and local administrative units.[13]

Judicial policy making is not without its drawbacks. The courts decide in a piecemeal fashion and only after the fact. The aggregation of several small bits may not add up to a coherent policy. Moreover, in a policy area such as water, a high degree of technical expertise is necessary and the courts may make pronouncements that violate the laws of physics and geology. Finally, water is an increasingly scarce resource and ever more interests are anxious to stake claims for their share; courts are usually poor instruments for the resolution of such political confrontations. With those limitations in mind, we can turn to a review of several of the major issues raised, if not completely resolved, by these water-related provisions.

Natural Want and Beneficial Use

The supreme court's reading of a combination of Sections 4, 5, and 6 has established the idea that the water of the state is dedicated to meet the needs of the

[13] See Robert D. Miewald and Peter J. Longo, "Institutions in Water Policy: The Case of Nebraska," *Natural Resources Journal* 29 (1989): 751–62.

people but that individuals can claim the use of that water if the purpose is "beneficial." A natural want is a natural need, and Nebraskans have met this need, first of all, through the creation of an extensive irrigation system (Spurrier v. Mitchell Irrigation District, 1930). But how is the state to identify the needs beyond agriculture? The supreme court avoids listing specific uses and instead concentrates on the quality of the use or purpose, with special emphasis on careful management of water. If the resource is being put to good use, "it shall not exceed the least amount of water that experience indicates is necessary in the exercise of good husbandry for the production of crops" (Enterprise Irrigation District v. Willis, 1939). Through statute and judicial decisions, the state has the right, as a function of the Constitution and of its police powers, "to regulate the natural rivers and streams so that waste is eliminated" (In re Water Appropriations Nos. 442A, 461, 462 and 485, 1981).

The interpretation that Section 6 is an admonition against waste allowed the supreme court to extricate itself from a bind of its own making. The issue involved inter-basin transfer of water from one river system to another within the state. Statutes provided that the unused portion of water taken for irrigation should be returned to the original stream or to the Missouri River. In a 1936 case, the court interpreted the law in the narrowest possible way, thus making the movement of water from one basin to another almost impossible (Osterman v. Central Nebraska Public Power and Irrigation District). The court eventually responded to criticism of the *Osterman* decision in 1980. It argued that the Constitution demanded that every stream be dedicated to the good of the whole state and nothing in the Constitution requires that water to be confined to a single watershed basin.*Osterman*was overruled and the Director of the Department of Water Resources was allowed to approve water transfers which were found to be in the public interest (Little Blue NRD v. Lower Platte North NRD).

The Doctrine of Prior Appropriation

Over a long period of time, stretching back to English common law, doctrines for determining the right of individuals to use water have developed. Riparian rights permit property owners on the banks of streams or other adjoining bodies of water to claim the use of the water, generally for use only on their riparian property. Prior appropriation doctrine establishes a registration system in which users, whether or not they own adjoining property, can make a claim on water not yet appropriated. Depending upon the date of registration, senior appropriators have priority, in times of shortage, over juniors. The principle is, "first in time, first in right." Like the settlers in the other Western states, Nebraskans soon learned that riparianism is workable only in humid areas and cannot solve the problems of allocation in arid or semi-arid conditions.

In 1895, the legislature established the doctrine of prior appropriation for the state. It was no longer possible to claim riparian rights to water. The concept then was expressed by Section 6 in 1920. Individuals, governments, or corporations may claim the use of unappropriated water, and their priority will be determined by the date on which the claim is filed with the Department of Water Resources. However, riparian rights were not abolished by the statute or by the amendment (Wassenburgerv. Coffee, 1966). Those holding riparian rights before 1895 retain them and do not lose them through non-use. This complicates the administration of a system of prior appropriation since it is unclear how much water is encumbered by riparian rights.

Prior appropriation establishes a clear method for determining who, within a particular category of use, has the right to a limited supply of water. The priority assigned to various uses is less clear, although the several sections imply that the ordering is domestic use, including municipal water facilities, agriculture, manufacturing, and electric power production. How such a system of priorities would work is not altogether clear from the case law, although it does appear that domestic users, whether or not they have established either riparian or appropriative rights, have the highest priority (Brummond v. Vogel, 1969).

The most significant issue, at present, is whether uses not mentioned in the Constitution can assume a place among the identified categories. Specifically, is there any way to accommodate in-stream use? Or, conversely, can domestic, agricultural, and industrial users drain a stream dry so that it is impossible to realize other possible uses? Among such uses which have become important in wake of the environmental movement are recreation, wildlife protection, and pure aesthetics.

In 1990, the supreme court considered an appeal of the first in-stream flow appropriation granted by the Department of Water Resources. First, although the Constitution uses the word "divert," water does not have to be physically removed from a stream by an appropriator. Second, and most important, Section 6 does provide for a "public interest" exception to the right to divert. That is, the state can determine that it is in the public interest to retain water in a stream for, in this case, the stocking of game fish. As the court stated, "Nebraska's constitutional right to appropriate can and must be limited by the demands of the public interest" (In Re Application A-16642, 1990).

Groundwater

When the Convention of 1920 developed the sections on water, irrigation from wells accounted for a small percentage of use; well water was confined to domestic or livestock watering purposes. It is not remarkable, then, that the sections refer only to surface water or "natural streams." In the years since, Nebraskans have become highly conscious of the fact that the state sits atop a vast store of underground water, most of which is located in the Ogalalla Aquifer. After the development of center-pivot irrigation systems in the 1950s, thousands of wells were dug, and by the 1970s it was clear that some areas of the state were suffering from a significant lowering of the water table. The rate of replacement was often so slow that groundwater "mining" was taking place.

Groundwater had become as important as surface water for municipal, agricultural, and industrial purposes, but the statutes and the case law lagged behind. Even today, to the dismay of hydrologists, ground and surface water are regarded as two largely distinct subjects. They are covered by different statutes, different administrative institutions, and different bodies of case law, thus making it difficult to manage what is, in physical terms, a single resource.

In its first significant statement on groundwater in 1933, the supreme court did not rely on the Constitution but, in the dicta of the case of *Olson v. City of Wahoo*, did establish a basic principle helpful in later cases. Essentially, Nebraska rejected the English Rule and accepted a modified American Rule. The English Rule says that property owners also own everything under the ground down to the center of the planet. With the American Rule, as suggested in *Olson*, the owner of the overlying property has the right to the beneficial use of captured groundwater, but that right is not the same as absolute ownership. Moreover, the California modification of the American Rule says that, in times of shortage, each person drawing from a groundwater supply will suffer proportionately.

In 1966, the court ruled that groundwater in fact is covered by Section 4 in that waters underground "are part of the waters referred to in the Constitution as a natural want. . . . Without any declaration of public policy as to the use of underground waters other than the constitutional declaration that they are a natural want, we adhere to the rule that such waters must be reasonably used for a beneficial purpose without waste" (Metropolitan Utilities District of Omaha v. Merritt Beach Co.). This 1966 decision reinforced the American Rule as stated in Olson and led to the forceful statement of the right of government to regulate groundwater promulgated in the *Sporhase* cases.

Joy Sporhase, a farmer on the western edge of the state, owned property across the state line in Colorado. He drilled a well on his Nebraska land and used the water to irrigate his Colorado crops without getting from the Department of Water Resources the permit required for the interstate transportation of groundwater. The supreme court approved the injunction to stop Sporhase by noting that groundwater is a special commodity that cannot be classified as "commerce." Groundwater in Nebraska has never been a private possession or an item freely exchangeable for value.

Further, since water is the only natural resource absolutely essential to human survival, the application of rules designed to facilitate commerce in less vital resources to the transfer of water must be done, if at all, with extreme caution: "It is this caution which prevents us from holding that Nebraska ground water is an article of commerce" (State ex rel. Douglas v. Sporhase, 1981).

The United States Supreme Court, in 1982, corrected the Nebraska court by finding that groundwater in fact is an article of commerce. Although Congress has not acted to regulate its movement across state lines, the Nebraska statute requiring reciprocity before interstate transport could be approved imposed an impermissible burden on interstate commerce (Sporhase v. Nebraska ex rel. Douglas).

Despite the setback in the *Sporhase* case, the Nebraska Supreme Court has not modified its position regarding the ownership of groundwater. In an important 1987 case, concerning the storage of water underground by an irrigation district, the court reaffirmed that the "protected right of landowners is the right to the use of the ground water, and does not reach the ownership of the water itself. Nebraska's ground water is itself publicly owned" (In Re Application U-2). Even the right to use can be modified by legislation so that the storage of groundwater can be protected.

The larger question, still unanswered, about groundwater is its relation to surface water. While the two types of water cannot be separated hydrologically, they do form two distinct bodies of Nebraska law and the statutes and case law do not provide easy answers about their interrelatedness. For example, pumping groundwater can lower the flow of streams, but the priority system for surface water is set by the Constitution while groundwater priorities are determined by statute. Would a high statutory priority have to defer to a lower constitutional one? This is the sort of question one might expect the legislature to answer, but given past experience, it will probably be for the courts to provide a definitive solution.

SECTION 8. EMPLOYMENT OF WOMEN AND CHILDREN; MINIMUM WAGE

Laws may be enacted regulating the hours and conditions of employment of women and children, and securing to such employees a proper minimum wage.

Section 8 was part of the Progressive agenda adopted by the Convention of 1920. It granted to the legislature a power that body already had. There has been no litigation of this provision.

SECTION 9. CONTROVERSIES BETWEEN EMPLOYERS AND EMPLOYEES; INDUSTRIAL COMMISSION; APPEAL TO SUPREME COURT

Laws may be enacted providing for the investigation, submission, and determination of controversies between employers and employees in any business or vocation affected with a public interest and for the prevention of unfair business practices and unconscionable gains in any business or vocation affecting the public welfare. An Industrial Commission may be created for the purpose of administering such laws, and appeal shall be as provided by law.

This is another product of the Progressive era. The section authorizes the legislature to enter the field of labor-management relations in order to, in the words of the 1920 Convention, "reach the profiteer and unfair business practices and protect the public against rapacious greed."[14] As with Section 8, this amendment did not add to the existing power of the legislature.

The legislature created in 1947 a Court (now Commission) of Industrial Relations, a body whose existence is derived from Article III, Section 1 and not this section, according to the supreme court (Orleans Education Assn. v. School District of Orleans, 1975). The commission's jurisdiction is limited to labormanagement relations in the public sector. The five judges consider such issues as the appropriate bargaining units for government employees, comparable pay for government units, and impasse resolution in public labor disputes. After a 1990 amendment, appeals from the Commission no longer go automatically to the Nebraska Supreme Court.

SECTION 10. REPEALED, 1934.

SECTION 11. REPEALED, 1972.

SECTION 12. REMOVAL OF STATE CAPITAL

The seat of government of the state shall not be removed or relocated without the assent of a majority of the electors of the state voting thereupon, at a general election or elections, under such rules and regulations as to the number of elections and manner of voting and places to be voted for, as may be prescribed by law. Provided the question of removal may be submitted at such other general elections as may be provided by law.

In 1875, the status of Lincoln was not completely resolved and so the delegates submitted this section to the voters as a separate proposition. The issue is now dead and no cases have been brought under Section 12.

SECTION 13. LABOR ORGANIZATIONS; NO DENIAL OF EMPLOYMENT; CLOSED SHOP NOT PERMITTED

No person shall be denied employment because of membership in or affiliation with, or resignation or expulsion from a labor organization or because of refusal to join or affiliate with a labor organization; nor shall any individual or corporation or association

[14] *Proceedings, 1919–20*, II, 2581.

of any kind enter into any contract, written or oral, to exclude persons from employment because of membership in or nonmembership in a labor organization.

Adopted in 1946, Nebraska's version of a "right-to-work" law requires that employment be on the basis of the "open shop," in which employees may decide on their own to join or not join a union. This is in contrast to the "closed" or "union" shop in which workers must either be a union member to get the job or join a union after being hired. The section applies to public as well as to private employment (AFSCME v. Woodward, 406 F2d 137, 1969).

The agency shop question has not been decided by the court. Such an arrangement requires that employees who are not union members must, as a condition of further employment, contribute to the union an amount equal to the fees and dues paid by union members in the organization. The attorney general concluded that such a contract between employer and the union would violate this section (Attorney General Opinion #55, 1979).

While the section probably reflects a generally anti-union attitude among Nebraskans and while the "open shop" does impose a burden on unions, the supreme court has often used the amendments to provide protection for union members. An employer, by action or non-action, may not terminate an employee if the motive is to discourage union membership or activity (Mid-Plains Education Association v. Mid-Plains Nebraska Technical College, 1972). Furthermore, "public employees may not be discriminated against or punished because they have sought collective bargaining and have reached an impasse with the public employer" (AFSCME, Local 2088 v. Douglas County, 1980). Section 13 also works to support the free speech rights of employees who might otherwise be fired at will (Wood v. Tesch, 1986).

SECTION 14. LABOR ORGANIZATION; DEFINITION

The term "labor organization" means any organization of any kind, or any agency or employee representation committee or plan, which exists for the purpose, in whole or in part, of dealing with employers concerning grievances, labor disputes, wages, rates of pay, hours of employment, or conditions of work.

This section was adopted in 1946 and should be read in conjunction with the "right-to-work" section described above.

SECTION 15. LABOR ORGANIZATIONS; AMENDMENT SELF-EXECUTING; LAWS TO FACILITATE OPERATION PERMITTED

This article is self-executing and shall supersede all provisions in conflict therewith; legislation may be enacted to facilitate its operation but no law shall limit or restrict the provisions thereof.

Section 15 is also part of the "right-to-work" package approved by the voters in 1946. It limits the power of the legislature to modify the intent of the amendments.

SECTION 16. REPEALED, 1972.

SECTION 17. RETIREMENT AND PENSION FUNDS; INVESTMENT

Notwithstanding section 3 of Article XIII or any other provision in the Constitution:

(1) The Legislature may provide for the investment of any state funds, including retirement or pension funds of state employees and Nebraska school employees in such manner and in such investments as it may by statute provide; and

(2) The Legislature may authorize the investment of retirement or pension funds of cities, villages, school districts, public power districts, and other governmental or political subdivisions in such manner and in such investments as the governing body of such city, village, school district, public power district and other governmental or political subdivision may determine but subject to such limitations as the Legislature may by statute provide.

Section 17, adopted in 1966, empowers the legislature to approve methods of investing pension or retirement funds of state (sub-section 1) or local (subsection 2) governments despite the provision in Article XIII, Section 3 that "the credit of the state shall never be given or loaned." The section also provides an exception to the restrictions in Article XI, Section 1 which prohibit local government from subscribing to the stock of any private organization (Nebraska League of Savings and Loan Assns. v. Mathes, 1978).

SECTION 18. GOVERNMENTAL POWERS AND FUNCTIONS; INTERGOVERNMENTAL COOPERATION; LEGISLATURE MAY LIMIT

The state or any local government may exercise any of its powers or perform any of its functions, including financing the same, jointly or in cooperation with any other governmental entity or entities, either within or without the state, except as the Legislature shall provide otherwise by law.

This language was adopted in 1972 at the recommendation of the Constitutional Revision Commission in order to remove any doubts about questions of intergovernment.al cooperation. The section permits various governmental Units to sign agreements with each other for the joint performance of functions. There has not been much litigation in this area, but apparently the supreme court has little problem with contracts between, say, the state auditor and county governments (York County v. Johnson, 1988).

Article XVI

Amendments
(ORIGINALLY ARTICLE XV)

SECTION 1. HOW PROPOSED

The Legislature may propose amendments to this Constitution. If the same be agreed to by three-fifths of the members elected to the Legislature, such proposed amendments shall be entered on the journal, with yeas and nays, and published once each week for three consecutive weeks, in at least one newspaper in each county, where a newspaper is published, immediately preceding the next election of members of the Legislature or a special election called by the vote of four fifths of the members elected to the Legislature for the purpose of submitting such proposed amendments to the electors. At such election said amendments shall be submitted to the electors for approval or rejection upon a ballot separate from that upon which the names of candidates appear. If a majority of the electors voting on any such amendment adopt the same, it shall become a part of this Constitution, provided the votes cast in favor of such amendment shall not be less than thirty-five per cent of the total votes cast at such election. When two or more amendments are submitted at the same election, they shall be so submitted as to enable the electors to vote on each amendment separately.

This section describes the manner in which the legislature may propose constitutional amendments and how those amendments must be publicized and approved. Until 1920, it contained language requiring approval of "a majority of the electors voting at such election." This majority, according to the supreme court, had to be based on the total number of voters in a general election and not those who indicated a decision about any single amendment (Techumseh National Bank v. Saunders, 1897). While the party-circle law allowed some possibility for amendment, the Convention of 1920 recommended the present language pertaining to a majority voting on the amendment. The requirement for at least 35 percent of the total vote cast was to insure a minimal level of support for a change.

The 1920 Convention also reduced the time period for publicizing the amendments from three months to four weeks, which was lowered further in 1952 to three weeks. A 1968 amendment allows the legislature to call a special session for the purpose of proposing amendments.

Article XVI, Section I is supplemented by Article III, Sections 2 and 4 which describe the initiative process. This means that some of the provisions about the initiative give added meaning to the language of this section. For example, amendments approved under Article XVI become effective as of the date set out in Article III, namely, after the official canvass and proclamation by the governor (Swanson v. State, 1937).

A proposition to amend the constitution approved by the legislature is not a law but rather a "mere proposal" and "possesses no validity until ratified by a majority of all the votes cast at the election" (Swanson v. State, 1937). In restoring a part of Article VII, Section 11 to the Constitution, the supreme court reminded the legislature that there must be explicit language in a proposal concerning the deletion of any part of the document (Cunningham v. Exon, 1980).

The supreme court decides ultimately what can or cannot be admitted as a constitutional change. The basic rule is that the formal procedures should not be construed to thwart unreasonably the will of the people. If, as happened in 1906, the amendment was not published according to the schedule in one small county, the people's vote will not be voided (State ex rel. Thompson v. Winnett, 1907). "Substantial compliance" with the niceties of amending seems to satisfy the court (Swanson v. State, 1937). However, in 1929, an amendment approved by the voters was rejected by the court because adequate notification and publicity was not provided before the election (State ex rel. Hall v. Cline, 1929).

However proposed, once it is approved, an amendment assumes an equal status with all other provisions in the Constitution. "A constitutional amendment becomes an integral part of the instrument and must be so construed. It must be harmonized, if possible, with all other provisions, and effect must be given to every section and clause as well as the whole instrument" (Luikart v. Higgins, 1936).

SECTION 2. CONVENTION

When three-fifths of the members elected to the Legislature deem it necessary to call a convention to revise, amend, or change this constitution, they shall recommend to

> the electors to vote at the next election of members of the Legislature, for or against a convention, and if a majority of the electors voting on the proposition, vote for a convention, the Legislature shall, at its next session provide by law for calling the same; *Provided*, the votes cast in favor of calling a convention shall not be less than thirty-five per cent of the total votes cast at such election. The convention shall consist of no more than one hundred members, the exact number to be determined by the Legislature, and to be nominated and elected from districts in the manner to be prescribed by the Legislature. Such members shall meet within three months after their election, for the purpose aforesaid. No amendment or change of this constitution, agreed upon by such convention, shall take effect until the same has been submitted to the electors of the state, and adopted by a majority of those voting for and against the same.

Amendments or a new constitution can be recommended by a constitutional convention. Such a process requires three trips to the polls by voters. First, they must approve the calling of a convention, then elect members, and finally vote on any recommendations. The language of 1875 was amended in 1952 to clarify some of the provisions. In particular, the size of the convention and the election by district of the members were spelled out.

No convention has been called since 1920, and so the 1952 changes have not been tested in the legislature or before the courts.

Article XVII

Schedule
(ORIGINALLY ARTICLE XVI)

This article bears little resemblance to the long and complicated "schedule" written by the 1875 Convention. Its twenty-two sections were reduced to nine by the Convention of 1920. One section was added in 1940, but the Constitutional Revision Commission recommended to the voters in 1972 that five sections be repealed. After so many modifications, the article does not look like the "schedule" found in most constitutions.

SECTION 1. TERMS; REFERENCE TO MEMBERS OF THE LEGISLATURE TO INCLUDE APPOINTED AND ELECTED MEMBERS

Whenever they shall appear in this Constitution, the terms members of the Legislature, elected members of the Legislature, or similar terms referring to the members of the Legislature, shall include appointed and elected members of the Legislature.

This section makes clear that legislators appointed by the governor have the same status as those elected to their position. This language replaced completely the section as written by the Convention of 1920 which, in turn, had replaced the words written in 1875. There has been no litigation on this section.

SECTION 2. REPEALED, 1972.

SECTION 3. REPEALED, 1972.

SECTION 4. GENERAL ELECTION OF STATE

The general election of this state shall be held on the Tuesday succeeding the first Monday of November in the year 1914 and every two years thereafter. All state, district, county, precinct, township and other officers, by the constitution or laws made elective by the people, except school district officers, and municipal officers in cities, villages and towns, shall be elected at a general election to be held as aforesaid. An incumbent of any office shall hold over until his successor is duly elected and qualified.

Article XVI, Section 13 of the Constitution called for annual elections, but an amendment in 1912 changed to biennial general elections. A 1972 amendment removed obsolete language pertaining to judicial elections. The provisions here do not apply to municipal or school district elections. Neither are they applicable to judicial selection under the merit plan (Garrotto v. McManus, 1970) or to the election for members to a constitutional convention (Baker v. Moorhead, 1919).

SECTION 5. TERMS OF OFFICE OF ALL ELECTED OFFICERS

Unless otherwise provided by this Constitution or by law the terms of all elected officers shall begin on the first Thursday after the first Tuesday in January next succeeding their election.

This section simply states when the term of office begins for those officials elected to a fixed term. A newly created office becomes vacant upon the act of creation and the vacancy can be filled by appointment, as authorized by the legislature, prior to the election for a fixed term (State ex rel. Redmond v. Smith, 1980). An amendment in 1972 removed obsolete language from this section.

SECTION 6. LEGISLATURE TO PASS NECESSARY LAWS

The Legislature shall pass all laws necessary to carry into effect the provisions of this constitution.

It does not appear that the supreme court believes this section gives to the legislature any more power than it has by virtue of Article II, Section 1 and Article III, Section 1. Conversely, it strengthens the principle that only the legislature has the power to make laws (Terry Carpenter, Inc. v. Nebraska Liquor Control Commission, 1963; School District No. 39 of Washington County v. Decker, 1955).

SECTION 7. REPEALED, 1972.

SECTION 8. REPEALED, 1972.

SECTION 9. CONSTITUTION TO BE ENROLLED

This constitution shall be enrolled and deposited in the office of the Secretary of State, and printed copies thereof shall be prefixed to the books containing the laws of this state, and all future editions thereof.

The secretary of state is made responsible for the printing and distribution of the current Constitution.

(Amendment proposed by Legislative Bill No. 30, Fifty-fifth Session of the Nebraska Legislature, to be known as Section 10, failed of adoption at election held on November 5, 1940.)

SECTION 11. REPEALED, 1972.

Authentication Clauses

The Constitution of 1875 was authenticated and attested by the following members of that convention:

[Here follows a list of the names of the members of the Convention of 1875.]

The Constitution of 1920 was authenticated and attested by the following members of that convention:

[Here follows a list of the names of the members of the Convention of 1920.]

■ BIBLIOGRAPHY

The following bibliography is divided into three parts: an essay on material covering the development of the Nebraska Constitution from territorial days to the present; a listing of general works on Nebraska government and politics; and a listing of material pertaining to the interpretation of specific provisions of the Constitution. A very useful introduction to legal materials pertaining to Nebraska is found in Sally H. Wise and Patricia A Cervenka, "Legal Research Tools for the Nebraska Practitioner: An Annotated Bibliography," *Nebraska Law Review* 70 (1991): 519–54.

I. CONSTITUTIONAL DEVELOPMENT

A copy of the Nebraska Constitution, in pamphlet form, can be obtained from the Office of the Secretary of State. Another version, annotated briefly with the relevant case law, is found in Volume 2 of the *Nebraska Revised Statutes*. The latest reissue was 1988 and thus does not contain the 1990 and 1992 amendments.

A number of official documents provide details of constitutional development in Nebraska. These include: *Official Report of the Debates and Proceedings in the Nebraska Constitutional Convention*, 3 vols. Volumes 11, 12, and 13. Nebraska State Historical Society, 1906, 1907, 1913. Volumes I and II were edited by Addison Sheldon. Volume III was edited by Albert Watkins and includes, according to the subtitle, "The Journal of the Convention of 1875; A History of the Attempt to Form a State Organization in 1860, of the Abortive Constitutional Convention of 1866, and of the Origins of the Conventions of 1871 and 1875."

The minutes of the 1871 Convention were prepared from a shorthand transcription of the debates. The 1875 minutes were compiled from newspaper accounts and contain only the barest description of the proceedings. The minutes of the 1920 Convention are contained in *Journal of the Nebraska Constitutional Convention, 1919–20, 2* vols., compiled by Clyde Barnard and published in 1920.

A useful companion to the official *Proceedings* of the 1920 Convention is A. E. Sheldon, *Nebraska Constitutions of 1866, 1871 and 1875 and Proposed Amendments Submitted to the People September 21, 1920,* Bulletin No. 15, Nebraska History and Political Science Series (Lincoln: Nebraska Legislative Reference Bureau, 1920). This pamphlet provides a section-by-section comparison of the three constitutions together with the amendments of 1920.

The recommendations of the 1970 Constitutional Revision Commission are contained in *Report of the Nebraska Constitutional Revision Commission* (Lincoln, 1970). Three volumes of the minutes of the Commission are also available.

The Nebraska Blue Book published biennially by the Clerk of the Legislature, contains statistics on the votes on all constitutional amendments since 1882. Versions of the *Bluebook* before 1988–89 also had a useful summary of constitutional history since statehood.

The background of constitutional developments is found in the standard histories of Nebraska. Two older works are J. Sterling Morton, *ilustrated History of Nebraska*, 3 vols. (Lincoln: J. North, 1905–13) and Addison E. Sheldon, *Nebraska: The Land and the People*, 3 vols. (Chicago: Lewis Publishing, 1931). Morton and Sheldon were participants in the politics of their day, and their accounts of events are sometimes opinionated. But the sheer mass of material they present gives valuable insight into the early history of the state. A more conventional history of Nebraska is provided in James Olson, *History of Nebraska*, 2nd ed. (Lincoln: University of Nebraska Press, 1966).

There is no book-length treatment of the constitutional history of Nebraska. Two articles by Professor A. B. Winter provide overviews: "Constitutional Revision in Nebraska: A Brief History and Commentary," *Nebraska Law Review* 40 (1961): 580–95, and "The State Constitution," in Robert D. Miewald, ed., *Nebraska Government and Politics* (Lincoln: University of Nebraska Press, 1984). Douglas Bakken, "Chronology of Nebraska Statehood," Nebraska History 48 (1967): 81–89, is a helpful guide to the several steps in the transition from territory to state. Victor Rosewater, "A Curious Chapter in Constitution-Changing," *Political Science Quarterly* 36 (1921): 409–19, describes the difficulty of amending the Constitution before 1920.

The Convention of 1920 is described in John P. Senning, "The Nebraska Constitutional Convention," *National Municipal Review* 9 (1920): 421–26, and Addison E. Sheldon, "The Nebraska Constitutional Convention, 1919–20," *American Political Science Review* 15 (1921): 391–97. A doctoral dissertation by John G. W. Lewis, *The Nebraska Constitutional Convention of 1919–1920* (Urbana: University of Illinois, 1924), is available at the Nebraska Historical Society at Lincoln. Bruce Raymond, *Nebraska's Constitutions: An Historical Analysis*, an M.A. thesis (Department of History, University of Nebraska, 1937), contains interesting material on the campaign for delegates to the 1920 Convention.

A symposium in the *Nebraska Law Review* in 1961 touched on the need for constitutional revision. The articles include: Ray Simmons, "A Constitutional Convention Is Neither Needed nor Desirable," *Nebraska Law Review 40* (1961): 604–20; and Charles Thone, "A Constitutional Convention: The Best Step for Nebraska," *Nebraska Law Review* 40 (1961): 580–95. The work of the Constitutional Revision Commission is the topic of Stanley Talcott, "Amending the Nebraska Constitution in the 1971 Legislature," *Nebraska Law Review* 50 (1971): 676–91.

II. NEBRASKA GOVERNMENT AND POLITICS

The following books and articles discuss past and present developments in the politics and government of the state:

Cherny, Robert. *Populism, Progressivism, and the Transformation of Nebraska Politics, 1885–1915*. Lincoln: University of Nebraska Press, 1981.

Creigh, Dorothy W. *Nebraska: A Bicentennial History*. New York: W. W. Norton, 1977.

Miewald, Robert D., ed.*Nebraska Government and Politics*. Lincoln: University of Nebraska Press, 1984.

Peirce, Neal. "Nebraska." In Peirce, *The Great Plains States of America: People, Politics and Power in the Nine Great Plains States*. New York: W. W. Norton, 1973.

Peirce, Neal, and Jerry Hagstrom. "Nebraska: Periodically Populist." In Peirce and Hagstrom, *The Book of America: Inside 50 States Today*. New York: W. W. Norton, 1983.

Reichley, James. "Nebraska: Sons of the Pioneers." In Reichley, *States in Crisis: Politics in Ten American States*. Chapel Hill: University of North Carolina Press, 1964.

University of Nebraska, Department of Journalism. *Prairie Paradox: Nebraska, Its Politics*. Lincoln: University of Nebraska, 1966.

III. CONSTITUTIONAL INTERPRETATION

These books and articles deal with issues relating to specific provisions of the Nebraska Constitution. The appropriate article in the Constitution is indicated in brackets.

Aiken, David. "Nebraska Ground Water and Administration." *Nebraska Law Review* 59 (1980): 917–1000. [Art. XV]

Axelrod, Allan. "Home Rule." *Nebraska Law Review* 30 (1951): 224–38. [Art. XI]

Aylsworth, Leon. "Nebraska's Nonpartisan, Unicameral Legislature." *National Municipal Review* 26 (1937): 77–81. [Art. III]

Breckenridge, Adam C. "The Mockery of Classification." *National Municipal Review* 36 (1947): 571–73. [Art. III]

Breckenridge, Adam C. "Nebraska County Government: 100 Years." *County Officer* 19 (1954): 80–88. [Art. IX]

Breckenridge, Adam C. "Nebraska as a Pioneer in the Initiative and Referendum." *Nebraska History* 34 (1954): 215–23. [Art. III]

Breckenridge, Adam C. *One House for Two: Nebraska's Unicameral Legislature*. Washington, D.C.: Public Affairs Press, 1957. [Art. III]

Buller, Katy Ann. "Revenue Bonds: Constitutional Law." *Creighton Law Review* 14 (1980): 223–33. [Art. XIII]

Cahill, Fred V. *The Separation of Powers in Nebraska*. M. A. Thesis. Lincoln: University of Nebraska, Department of Political Science, 1938. [Art. II]

Comer, John C, and James Johnson, eds. *Nonpartisanship in the Legislative Process: Essays on the Nebraska Legislature*. Washington, D.C.: University Press of America, 1978. [Art. III]

Crane, Jolene. "*Sporhase v. Nebraska ex rel. Douglas*: A Call for Ground Water Legislation." *Denver Law Journal* 60 (1983): 631–43. [Art. XV]

Crosby, Robert. "Why I Want to Get Rid of My Job." *State Government* 20 (1947): 193–94. [Art. IV]

Crowder, Farnsworth. "Tattle-Tale Gray on America's White Spot." *Survey Graphic* 27 (1938): 495–501, 521, 523–25. [Art. VIII]

Gradwohl, John M. "Labor-Management Relations and Nebraska Constitutional Revision." *Nebraska Law Review* 40 (1961): 648–96. [Art. XV]

Gradwohl, John M. "Arbitrability in Nebraska." *Nebraska Law Review* 70 (1991): 381–411 [Art. I]

Hagart, Virgil. "The Case for the Nebraska Merit Plan." *Nebraska Law Review* 41 (1962): 723–45. [Art. V]

Harnsberger, Richard S., and Norman W. Thorson. *Nebraska Water Law and Administration.* St. Paul: Butterworth Legal Publishers, 1984. [Art. XV]

Icenogle, T. Edward. "The Impact of Defining "Beneficial Use" upon Nebraska Water Appropriation Law." *Nebraska Law Review* 57 (1978): 199–209. [Art. XV]

Jaksha, Edward A. *Of the People: Democracy and the Petition Process.* Omaha: Simmons Boardman Books, 1988. [Art. III]

Janney, Richard. "Home Rule Charters in Nebraska." *Creighton Law Review* 5 (1971): 98–116. [Art. XI]

Johnson, Forrest. "The Nebraska Constitution and Taxation." *Nebraska Law Review* 40 (1961): 733–39. [Art. VIII]

Klein, Mike. "Groundwater Management in Nebraska without a Legislative Solution: Is There an Alternative?" *Nebraska Law Review* 57 (1978): 78–90. [Art. XV]

Longo, Peter J. "The Constitutionalism and Water Policy of Sporhase Revisited: A West German Alternative." *Environmental Law* 20 (1990): 917–28. [Art. XV]

Miewald, Robert D., and Peter J. Longo. "Institutions in Water Policy: The Case of Nebraska." *Natural Resources Journal*29 (1989): 751–62. [Art. XV]

Morrison, Frank, and Richard Shugrue. "Streamlining the Executive in Nebraska." *Nebraska Law Review* 40 (1961): 634–47. [Art. IV]

Norris, George W. "The One-House Legislature." *Annals of the American Academy of Political and Social Science* 181 (1935): 50–58. [Art. III]

Oeltjen, Jarret, Richard Harnsberger, and Ralph Fischer. "Interbasin Transfer: Nebraska Law and Legend." *Nebraska Law Review* 51 (1971): 87–146. [Art. XV]

Peterson, Betty. "Procedure for Amending the Nebraska Constitution." *Nebraska Law Review* 22 (1943): 39–44. [Art. XVI]

Powers, Mary T. "The Right to Privacy in Nebraska." *Creighton Law Review* 13 (1980): 935–53. [Art. I]

Riley, William. "Nonpartisan Unicameral-Benefits, Defects, Re-examined." *Nebraska Law Review* 52 (1973): 377–403. [Art. III]

Ross, William G. "A Judicial Janus: Meyer v. Nebraska in Historical Perspective." *University of Cincinnati Law Review* 57 (1988): 125–204. [Art. I]

Senning, John P. "Constitutional Essentials for a Unicameral Legislature." *University of Kansas City Law Review* 11 (1942): 10–15. [Art. III]

Shugrue, Richard E. "An Approach to Mutual Respect: The Christian Schools Controversy." *Creighton Law Review* 18 (1984–85): 219–57. [Art. I]

Sittig, Robert. "Legislative Apportionment in Nebraska." In Leroy Hardy, Alan Heslop, and Stuart Anderson, eds., *Reapportionment Politics: The History of Redistricting in the 50 States.* Beverly Hills, Calif.: Sage, 1981. [Art. III]

Sittig, Robert. *The Nebraska Unicameral after Fifty Years.* Lincoln: University of Nebraska, Department of Political Science, Governmental Research Institute, 1986. [Art. III]

Smith, Loran B. *Advisory Opinions and the Nebraska Attorney General.* Ph.D. dissertation (Lincoln: University of Nebraska, Department of Political Science, 1980). [Art. IV]

Turner, George. "History and Commentary on the Judicial Article." *Nebraska Law Review* 40 (1961): 621–25. [Art. V]

Uhling, Terry T. "Ground Water Preferences in Nebraska." *Nebraska Law Review* 59 (1980): 831–57. [Art. XV]

Wilhite, Ann. "Sixty-Five Years till Victory: A History of Woman Suffrage in Nebraska." *Nebraska History* 49 (1968): 149–63. [Art. VI]

Willborn, Steven L. "Off the Mark: The Nebraska Supreme Court and Judicial Nominating Commissions." *Nebraska Law Review* 70 (1991): 277–305. [Art. V]

Winter, A. B. "Nebraska Home Rule: The Record and Some Recommendations." *Nebraska Law Review* 59 (1980): 601–30. [Art. XI]

■ TABLE OF CASES

A

B

C

L

M

N

O

P

R

S

T

U

V

W

X

Y

■ INDEX

About the Authors

ROBERT D. MIEWALD, Professor of Political Science, University of Nebraska at Lincoln, is a specialist in constitutional law and Nebraska state government. He is the editor of Nebraska Government and Politics (1984) and the author of *Public Administration: A Critical Perspective* (1978).

PETER J. LONGO, Assistant Professor of Political Science, University of Nebraska at Kearney, writes on Nebraska law and public policy matters and on current constitutional issues.

www.ingramcontent.com/pod-product-compliance
Ingram Content Group UK Ltd.
Pitfield, Milton Keynes, MK11 3LW, UK
UKHW051948190926
475595UK00038B/42

9 780199 779314